LITERARY WASHINGTON

LITERARY WASHINGTON

*A Complete Guide to the
Literary Life in the
Nation's Capital*

DAVID CUTLER

Special Printing For

WIW
Washington Independent Writers

MADISON BOOKS
Lanham • New York • London

Copyright © 1989 by

David Cutler

Madison Books

4720 Boston Way
Lanham, MD 20706

3 Henrietta Street
London WC2E 8LU England

Library of Congress Cataloging-in-Publication Data

Cutler, David.
–Literary Washington.
1. Literary landmarks—Washington (D.C.)—Guide-
books. 2. American literature—Washington
(D.C.)—Bio-bibliography. 3. Authors, American—
Homes and haunts—Washington (D.C.)—Guide-
books. 4. Washington (D.C.)—
Description—1981—Guide-books. 5. Washington
(D.C.)—Intellectual life. 6. Washington (D.C.) in
literature.
I. Title.
PS144. W18C8   1989   917.5304'4   89-8228
ISBN 0-8191-7299-5

Contents

Preface

This book, nearly two years in the making, is the result of an obsession gone berserk. If I could have known then what I know now, *Literary Washington* might never have come about. On the other hand, I believe every worthwhile book finds its own way of happening. And so I'm glad to have included so much and sorry that some inevitably got left out.

As fate would have it, the mere fact this book drew my family, friends, colleagues, editor, publisher and dozens of sources into the vortex of my obsession should not in any way, I hope, diminish your pleasure in reading and using it. I have an entirely new respect for the hard work of writing, and plan to take a break from it for awhile.

As far as I know, what you hold in your hands is unique. In attempting to chronicle the literary life of Washington, D.C. and nearby environs, one sees how completely a city's character is both reflected and shaped by its writers and readers. The book really doesn't create anything new—it just brings together information from many sources into a single volume.

And yet, perhaps there is a way in which this book (and all books) create something after all. You, alert reader, may be moved to discover yet more about your city's literary present and past. Perhaps you will get involved in helping others learn to read, or purchase stacks of books from a bookstore you never knew existed, or join a writer's organization or take a local writing course. What you read may prompt action, thereby further enriching the literary life around us.

Should this happen, please let me know by writing: c/o Madison Books, 4720 Boston Way, Lanham, MD 20706. I guess it's going to be harder to shake this obsession than I thought.

—DAVID CUTLER

Acknowledgements

I am indebted to my patient, loving family and to many friends and colleagues for their help in making this book possible.

It all began with a map and article I wrote for Allene Symons of *Publisher's Weekly* in mid-1987. Allene, who has since left *PW* to sell lots of books in California, deserves special thanks for suggesting that the map idea be turned into a book.

Without the generous financial support of Washington Independent Writers, and the particular advice and encouragement of Isolde Chapin, Bill Adler, Jr. and two successive WIW Boards of Directors, I never could have made it. An unabashed fan of WIW, as well as an officer for several years, I'm more impressed than ever with this dynamic organization and how it continues to improve our city's literary life.

For reviewing portions of *Literary Washington* before publication, I would like to thank each member of my Editorial Board, namely:

John Y. Cole, Director, The Center For The Book, Library of Congress
Doris Grumbach, Author & Book Critic (National Public Radio)
Rudy Maxa, Senior Writer, *Washingtonian* Magazine
Diane Rehm, Host, The Diane Rehm Show (WAMU-FM Radio)
Colin Walters, Book Editor, *The Washington Times*

The Board's generous help in deciding questions of what the book needed (or perhaps didn't need) was invaluable. Many other people reviewed sections of the book at my request, including Gail Ross, Tim Wells, John Greenya, Mark Perry, Marguerite Kelly, Isolde Chapin, Bill Adler and others. Thanks to all.

This book would have been vastly poorer without the talents and enthusiasm of two extraordinary people. Zak Mettger was relentless in her pursuit of facts, figures and other details for this book, tracking down sources on the weekends and in remote places for the most current information available. Ed Terrien stayed over off-and-on for a month or so, co-writing and helping to shape much of what we found and making it sing. This book, in many ways, is more theirs than mine, and I am everlastingly grateful for their patience, perception and stamina.

And, speaking of patience, many thanks go to my superb editor, Chuck Lean, for his support and guidance throughout. Jed Lyons, Gisele Byrd, Vivien Hoke and others at Madison Books get high marks for maintaining grace under pressure as my deadlines proved ever more elusive to meet.

Regarding the book's maps, my thanks to the staff of Travel Graphics International (TGI) for preparing the downtown map art reprinted in this book on such short notice. TGI publishes full-color pocket maps of the metro area (including the downtown detail map reprinted herein), available either directly from the publisher or on sale from local bookstores and gift shops. Thanks also to Randy Bartow of Regardie's Magazine for allowing us to reprint the regional map herein.

On the computer front, Mark Hulbert is still the reigning wizard for retrieving an entire file we thought was lost. He is a good friend. Special thanks also go to my friends Kathy Shane McCarty and Iris Rothman for the loan of their laptops, and their help and advice. To all "the friends of the book"—my partner Jeri Held, Mary Levering, Amy Pastan, Maxine Atwater, Orin Heend, David Schulman, Ron and Jan Balderson, John Hanley, dozens of helpful research librarians, and so many others—a heartfelt thank you. And to my parents, Tina and Bruce, I thank you for giving John and Ann and I the love for reading and writing that animates this book.

Finally, to my wife Laurie and my daughter Leah—this closing note is to inform you that your husband/father is finished with his book and is available for viewing and social interaction again. I love you both very much, and dedicate this book to you.

Introduction

"Words are all we have."

—SAMUEL BECKETT

Words are so strong, so palpably real, that they can propel us into danger and then miraculously snatch us from destruction. They can sooth, they can woo, they can hurt, they can sing, they can paint pictures or tell stories or be whispered quietly into the night.

This book is about the power of words and the people who write them. It is about a metropolitan area bursting with literary life, where, not surprisingly, a significant number of well-known authors live and work. It is about the publishers, agents, book producers, organization directors, readings coordinators, teachers, editors, book fair promoters, librarians, bookstore owners and even certain saloon owners (and their bartenders) who help make this place one of the most exciting literary cities in the United States.

As you read and use this book, I believe you'll agree with my premise. Washington, D.C. is experiencing a literary and publishing renaissance, albeit perhaps a quiet one.

Such comments as "the city has more writers than lawyers" or "this area reputedly has the nation's most writers per population" or "it's a literary boom town" have appeared in the local press off-and-on for the past five years, but the writers of those comments couldn't get enough space to prove what they knew. The cumulative effect of *Literary Washington*—the sheer number and diversity of its contents—will hopefully bring more of the city's literary people and places to light.

Here's a specific example of what I mean. Earlier this year, I received a promotional brochure from Book-of-the-Month Club. After I took advantage of their "exceptional offer" and signed up, I sat down to peruse the 97 top books they wanted me to choose from. And guess what? Eleven of those books were by Washington authors—William Greider, Stanley Karnow, Jane Mayer & Doyle McManus, Pete Earley, Hendrick Smith, Richard Restak, David Brinkley, Daniel Boorstin, Neil Shee-han, David Wise and I.F. Stone. Aside from New York and possibly Boston and Los Angeles, I doubt that any other American city could make a similar claim.

Why do some cities have a discernible literary life and others don't? This question is often asked, and yet it may be the wrong question. For the most part, Americans have been notoriously bad about chronicling and preserving this country's literary heritage. Many of the fascinating biographical stories about the historic authors in this book were quite hard to find, and virtually all of the places where these authors once lived have been sadly destroyed. *Every* city has a literary life, if we will take the trouble to find and preserve it.

Since 1801, when the first book was published in George Washington's "new Federal City," literary endeavor has thrived here. Like life itself, every day a new book is born among us, a new reading series is begun, a freshly printed business card announces the launching of an ambitious new publishing venture, a new bookstore opens its doors.

This is as it should be. For, if we are to believe the demographers, Washington is far and away the most affluent and educated metropolitan area in the United States. Reading and buying books is a local passion, part of the daily fabric of Washington life. Researching and writing books falls to the city's many authors, who are becoming ever more prolific and diverse. Bringing books to life falls to the many local publishers, agents, editors, teachers, critics and other lovers of literature who have devoted their lives to the cause. And Washington is now fortunate to have, in Barbara Bush, a First Lady who is committed to improving literacy, here in town and across the nation.

Charlton Ogburn, Jr. once described the history of Washington as "divid [-ing] itself into three periods. The first, tapering off through the 1830's, was a time in which the American people were very much aware of the world abroad and looked to Washinton for leadership: there were strong Presidents and the capital was a exciting place. The same may be said, for the most part of 20th Century Washington, the third period. The middle period was one of national self-absorption when, with the towering exception of the Civil War years, Washington followed rather than led the country."

The reader of *Literary Washington* will see what Ogburn describes reflected in these pages. And now I think we are poised on the verge of even greater things to come. There abounds more literary life here, past and present, than any single writer could hope to chronicle—and far more than this volume could hope to hold. What books have wrought animates this bureaucratic and sometimes fickle city by the Potomac, revealing its humanity.

—DAVID CUTLER
March, 1989

Historic Authors

"Literature is, primarily, a chain of connections from the past to the present. It is not reinvented every morning, as some bad writers like to believe."

—GORE VIDAL

We who live in the nation's capital, steeped as we are in tradition and surrounded by monuments to the past, live with a curious contradiction. As close observers of news in the making, we tend to focus on the "now" rather than the "then." Legions of enterprising citizens are drawn here in hopes of affecting the daily making of history. In this sense, our history is the future. Our stake in what's ahead lies in the shifting tides of what's-happening-here-and-now.

The price of neglecting the past is on permanent display in the halls of Congress. But Washington has suffered equal, quieter losses in the neglect of its own rich literary heritage. Other American cities have embraced and preserved the reputations of their famous authors. Yet here, fixated upon what we believe are momentary issues of life-and-death importance (sometimes they are, usually not), we have unfortunately lost from memory too much of our literary past. And that is a shame, because comparing many of today's literary personalities to many 19th-century authors is like comparing—to borrow from Twain—the lightning bug to lightning.

Imagine Anne Royall today sitting upon the President's clothes while he swims in the Potomac, refusing to move until she is granted an interview. Imagine a modern-day President being verbally assaulted by the likes of Walt Whitman, who wrote: "The President eats dirt and excrement for his daily meals, likes it and tries to force it on the States." Picture poet Joaquin Miller roaming Pennsylvania Avenue bedecked in high-heeled boots, tasseled sombrero, bright bandana and a fur coat with gold-nugget buttons as he recites from his *Songs of the Sierras*. Or spellbinding Daniel Webster holding any crowd he chooses in the palm of his oratorical hand.

Some of these historic authors were wildly successful

in their time, yet are strangers to us today. Like novelist Emma Southworth, who wrote in the last fifty years of the 19th century some 73 novels, many of which sold over a million copies each—an astonishing figure for any time. Today, Southworth is virtually unread. Conversely, the acclaim attending the lasting reputation of Walt Whitman was absent from much of his modest career as a poet during the late 1800s.

Washington was, and to some extent still is, a transient city. Famous authors, now dead, who lived and worked here at least a year have received mention below. Only two U.S. Presidents—Theodore Roosevelt and Woodrow Wilson—have been included because both men wrote a prodigious amount of "pure literature" in addition to the usual quota of state papers, articles, memoirs, personal correspondence, diaries and political tracts one expects Presidents to write. It is certainly true that other Presidents (notably Jefferson, Madison, Lincoln and John F. Kennedy) wrote brilliantly, but none wrote so much for the popular audience or cultivated the literary life as completely as Roosevelt and Wilson did. It should also be noted that many of the now-deceased poets who served as Consultants in Poetry to the Library of Congress have been omitted from the following list. Among these distinguished poets are the likes of Robert Frost, Robert Lowell, Randall Jarell, Allen Tate and Stephen Spender.

Whenever known, mention is made of where a writer lived. Sadly, nearly all of these buildings are now gone. The demands of "development" have consumed them, destroying our tangible links to the past and obliterating any reminders of literature's human dimension. This is driven home dramatically in James M. Goode's historic picture book, *Capital Losses: A Cultural History of Washington's Destroyed Buildings*, an invaluable resource for the drafting of this section.

What follows are brief sketches of many of the historic authors who lived and worked in Washington. It is not entirely complete—that job remains to be done in a longer book. What follows instead is a collection of gems gathered by an enthusiastic generalist. If it had color, if it surprised, if it was interesting—it got included.

Henry Adams   Author, historian, novelist, educator (1838–1918).

The popular fictional genre we now call the "Washington novel" was invented by Adams in 1880, with the publication of his brilliant *Democracy.* The novel examines the financial and political scandals of the Grant administration, and skillfully captures the political affairs of Washington in the decade following the Civil War.

In his time, no man better knew the ins and outs of political and literary Washington than Henry Adams. The grandson of President John Quincy Adams, he served as private secretary to his father, a Massachusetts Congressman, worked the city as a newspaper correspondent and circulated about town with a keen eye out for current developments. His vantage point for observation was ideal: he built his home across from the White House, on the present site of the **Hay-Adams Hotel (at 16th & H Streets, NW)**.

Perhaps no finer literary salon has ever existed in our nation than the home of Adams. He and his wife Marian served up breakfasts that became a local institution in the late 1880s. They were a witty, urbane pair, and she once described him as a man "who chews more than he bites off." In time, they came to be regarded as Washington's foremost private citizens.

Even with his consuming social activities and prodigious correspondence, Adams was able to sustain a considerable literary output. Four years following his first novel, he brought out a second, *Esther,* which was less successful with the public but was thought by Adams to be a better work. An accomplished historian, Adams also wrote the nine-volume *History of the United States During the Administration of Jefferson and Madison.* He followed with biographies of Albert Gallatin and John Randolph, two more novels, a study of medievalism and his superb autobiography *The Education of Henry Adams,* which was actually published after his death. It received the Pulitzer Prize in 1919.

The home of Adams was built as an attached dwelling to the home of his friend (and Secretary of State) John Hay by architect Henry Hobson Richardson, who designed a common facade for both structures. Here, as Adams recalls in his autobiography:

"Hay and Adams had the advantage of looking out of their windows on the antiquities of Lafayette Square, with the sense of having all that any one had; all that the world had to offer; all that they wanted in life. . . . Their chief title to consideration was their right to look out of their windows on great men, alive or dead, in Lafayette

Square, a privilege which had nothing to do with their writings."

Although the adjoining houses were among the most important private residences ever built in Washington, they were razed in 1927 by builder Harry Wardman to make way for the Hay-Adams Hotel. However, the ground-floor arches were rescued and reinstalled as main and garage entrances to a Tudor house being built at 2618 31st Street, NW.

Adams is buried in **Rock Creek Cemetery,** off North Capitol Street at **Rock Creek Church Road** & **Webster Street, NW,** in a setting designed by architect Stanford White. The grave of his wife, who committed suicide after her father's death in 1885, is in the same cemetery, and is graced by a famous sculpture by Augustus Saint-Gaudens, the leading American sculptor of the nine-teenth century. When he saw it, Mark Twain was moved to call it "Grief," a name that has remained affixed to its haunting form. A replica stands in the courtyard of the National Museum of American Art.

Louisa May Alcott   Novelist, memoirist (1832–1888).

Disdaining what she called the "trap" of marriage, Alcott set her sights on a career that might give her family financial support (which indeed came about with the huge success of her 1869 novel, *Little Women*).

Embarking on the writing life, she wrote several unproduced plays and dozens of sketches, stories, and poems, some of which appeared in *The Atlantic Monthly*. In 1854, she published a first book, *Flower Fables*, but her career was interrupted by service as a Civil War nurse in Washington.

Reporting to what was then **the Union Hotel,** at **30th and M Streets, NW (northeast corner),** Alcott found the establishment converted into a hospital for treatment of contagious diseases. Here she worked as a volunteer nurse, but exposure to so much pain and death was too much for her and she suffered a nervous breakdown.

Her vivid letters, describing medical conditions of the time, would later be collected in her book *Hospital Sketches*. Today a gas station sits on the site of the former hotel where Alcott nursed hundreds of Union troops.

Stephen Vincent Benet   Poet, novelist, short-story writer (1898–1943).

Although this Washington-born writer is most remembered for his famous short story *The Devil and Daniel Webster* (1937), Benet's true strength was as a folk balladist. Even his folk tale about Webster is really prose in name only.

History and tradition served to inform all of Benet's published works. He poured exhaustive period detail into his emotional epic poem *John Brown's Body,* for which he received the Pulitzer Prize for Poetry in 1929. Benet was awarded a second Pulitzer for his epic poem *Western Star* in 1943.

As a young boy, in 1901, Benet lived with his family just down the block from James Thurber and his family, near **20th and I Streets, NW** (now all office buildings). Thurber also recalled in a private letter when he and Benet worked together during World War I in Washington:

"In 1918, when I was a code clerk in the State Department, Steve Benet was also one, until he went to Ordnance. He sat across the table from me, both of us fresh out of college, Yale and Ohio State respectively, he sporting his Wolf's Head pin, and my vest bespangled with the pins of Phi Psi, Sigma Delta Chi, and Sphinx, Senior Honorary at Ohio State (I was taken into that the same time as Elliot Nugent and Chic Hartley). I lost track of those pins darn near forty years ago."

Ambrose Bierce   Short-story writer, essayist, journalist (1842–1914).

Having done his part for William Randolph Hearst's campaign to defeat the notorious "refunding bill" of 1896, witty, vitriolic Bierce returned to Washington two years later to set up shop as feature writer for the Hearst chain. "Bitter Bierce" seemed well suited for the job, keeping hypocritical politicians on their toes with his mordant approach to Capitol Hill doings. Bierce performed for Hearst for the next decade, with occasional time off for travel.

The next phase of Bierce's life found him pursuing an independent writing career, building on the successes of his published books: *Can Such Things Be?* (1893), *The Devil's Dictionary* (1906) and *In the Midst of Life.* Life seemed to be going well for Bierce as he prepared with a Washington publisher for the publication of his *Collected Works.* He seemed to enjoy hobnobbing among his cronies along **"Newspaper Row,"** serving as cook and host in his living quarters in **the Olympia Apartments** for brilliant Sunday breakfasts.

But Bierce was not a happy man. One autumn day in 1913, he set out for Mexico on a mysterious journey, seeking "the good, kind darkness." It is thought he found it there amid the turmoil of the Mexican Revolution, for he vanished utterly, never to return to his home in the nation's capital.

Sterling Brown Poet, essayist, critic, lecturer, educator (1901–1989).

It is saddening to realize that Brown is so recently gone from Washington's literary scene. His devotion to his Howard University students, past and present, was legendary, and he willingly sacrificed some time from writing to invest in the future of promising young talent.

Discussing his role as professor, Brown once told a newspaper reporter: "We give extra. I have given extra. That's the reason I am not a writer of more books, because I gave my creative energy to the classroom, and to the conferences and to people coming to this house and sitting down."

His home in the Brookland section of upper Northeast Washington, D.C. was a veritable salon of creative activity. Said *Washington Post* columnist William Raspberry: "The most incredible assortment of people would show up. The group could include a stiff professor or two, people from SNCC [the Student Nonviolent Coordinating Committee], white English teachers from the suburbs, usually a reporter or two. It was just fun. He would talk about other writers, kick their butts sometime or say how great they were. He would give value to the thoughts of the people around him in the room. It made you feel included in this grand salon, not simply to show up, but to be treated like what you thought had merit."

Brown's *Southern Road* was published in 1932. Critics and public alike were impressed with his ear for music in language and his capacity for humor. Brown was one of the first intellectual writers to seriously appropriate folk material for purposes of crafting serious-minded poetry. On the heels of *Southern Road,* Brown brought out several important works of literary criticism. Other of his works include *The Last Ride of Wild Bill* and *Eleven Narrative Poems.* His *Collected Poems* was issued in 1980.

Born in Washington and educated at Dunbar High School, Brown went on to earn a master's degree from Harvard in 1923. In 1929 he joined the faculty at Howard University and taught there full-time into the mid–1970s, and then on and off after that. Howard University vice president Michael Winston said: "He was one of the great professors of his time—of this country."

Frances Hodgson Burnett   Novelist, famous hostess (1849–1924).

The world knew Burnett as the author of the famous *Little Lord Fauntleroy*, but, in Washington, Burnett was equally well known for her performances as a frequent, gracious hostess. Her first court of social functions was at **1219 I Street, NW** (the house in which she wrote *Fauntleroy*, now gone).

Here, one afternoon reception was graced with the memorable entrance of Oscar Wilde, who was on the road performing his American lecture tour of 1882. There he stood, arrayed in "black silk clawhammer coat, fancily flowered dark waistcoat, knee breeches, silk stockings and patent leather pumps with broad buckles," and all of Washington gasped at the outrageous genius in his eccentric attire.

From 1886 to 1890, Burnett moved her court to **1730 K Street, NW** (now an office building). Then, drawing from the tremendous success of *Fauntleroy's* success as both book and play, she commissioned the construction of a grand new home at **1770 Massachusetts Avenue, NW**. Here she eventually wrote more than 50 books until her death in 1924.

Rachel Carson   Zoologist, author (1907–1964).

A sensitive interpreter of science for the general public, Carson published her first book in 1941, *Under the Sea Wind*. Ten years later she followed with *The Sea Around Us*, then *The Edge of the Sea*. But it was her famous book *Silent Spring* (1963) that shook up a nation and catapulted her into the national spotlight. In this work, she was the first to alert the public to the dangers of widely-used insecticides.

Carson lived at **204 Williamsburg Drive** in **Silver Spring, MD** from 1949 to 1957. The following year, she built her final home at **11701 Berwick Road,** also in **Silver Spring.** She had the house constructed on a one-acre lot, preserving half the land in its natural state to serve as a habitat for small animals.

Bruce Catton   Author, journalist, historian (1899–1978).

Having originally moved to Washington to work as a

newspaperman, Catton went to work for the government, becoming Director of Information for the War Production Board in 1942. Later, he would move on to the departments of Commerce and Interior. Drawing on his experience at the War Production Board, Catton published *The War Lords of Washington* in 1948. For a number of years he wrote a Washington column and book reviews for *The Nation*.

It was while living here that Catton developed a deep interest in the Civil War, culminating in several books, most significantly his trilogy on the Army of the Potomac: *Mr. Lincoln's Army* (1951), *Glory Road* (1952) and *A Stillness at Appomattox* (1953). The third extraordinary book in this series earned him a Pulitzer Prize for History in 1954.

For many years, after winning the Pulitzer, Catton served as editor of *American Heritage* magazine. Scholar David K. Adams commented that Catton's "view of history as a crusade of ideas (rather than as a matter of economic factors and power conflicts) . . . represents popular history at a very high level of achievement."

Elmer Davis Novelist, short-story writer, essayist, newspaperman, broadcaster (1890–1958).

Davis achieved fame during the early years of World War II for his news analysis on CBS Radio (1939–42). Prior to his radio experience, Davis worked as a political commentator for *The New York Times* (1914–24).

Davis interrupted his broadcasting career to head the Office of War Information until the war's close in 1945, when he resumed radio work, this time with ABC. A man with a sense of duty and a moral conscience, Davis increasingly devoted attention to serious writing. In 1954, his book *But We Were Born Free*, an attack on political witch-hunters, became a bestseller. This was followed by *Two Minutes Till Midnight*, which addressed nuclear weapons and peace.

James Thurber was a good friend of Davis, recalling in a 1958 private letter that "Washington was also the home of my favorite American of this century, the late Elmer Davis, to whom I dedicated my last book of fables." And Thurber's fellow *New Yorker* writer E. B. White said of Davis that he "got up in the morning to work in defense of freedom as methodically as most of us get up and brush our teeth."

Frederick Douglass Author, editor, diplomat, orator (1817–1895).

Born the son of a slaveowner and a mother who was a slave, Douglass was able to escape his owners on a Maryland plantation by masquerading as a sailor. In time, he found acceptance in Washington as a free man, enjoying respect for his writing and oratorial skills. In 1877, he said of Washington, D.C.: "Wherever the American citizen may be a stranger, he is at home here."

After his escape in 1838, Douglass first fled to New England, where he made anti-slavery speeches and soon found himself in great demand as a speaker for abolition. Douglass was so effective and articulate before crowds that people began expressing doubt that he'd ever been born a slave and had struggled to educate himself. These suspicions led Douglass to write his first book, *Narrative of the Life of Frederick Douglass, An American Slave* (1845), now recognized as an important American work.

The book proved so popular that Douglass, fearing he might suffer recapture by his legal masters, fled to England. There he enjoyed wide acclaim, and was able to earn and raise enough money to purchase his freedom.

Returning to the United States, Douglass founded an influential anti-slavery weekly, "The North Star" in New York (later renamed "Frederick Douglass's Paper"). In 1855, he came out with his best-known work, *My Bondage & My Freedom*. After the Civil War, Douglass then held a number of government positions, including marshal of the District of Columbia, recorder of deeds for the District and minister and counsel general to Haiti. In 1881, he wrote a second autobiography, *The Life & Times of Frederick Douglass*, which is a classic of American literature.

During his years in Washington, Douglass first lived with his family in a large Victorian house near the U.S. Capitol, at **318 A Street, NE.** For years after Douglass' death, it was known as the Frederick Douglass Town House and then became the first site of the Smithsonian's Museum of African Art. Today it houses private offices.

In 1877, Douglass purchased **Cedar Hill,** a 14–room house on fifteen acres high above the Anacostia River in southeast Washington. Now open to the public as a historic home, Cedar Hill (located at **1411 W Street, SE**) is an elegant white house that is full of Douglass' original furnishings and memorabilia. Of special note is the library, which contains Douglass' original desk, walking canes and other effects.

Cedar Hill is open to the public (daily 9 am to 5 pm), is served by Tourmobile buses and has a Visitor's Center with copies of Douglass' books for sale along with gifts and other items.

Paul Laurence Dunbar   Poet, novelist (1872–1906).

This prominent poet of the "Harlem Renaissance" movement, born of former slaves in Ohio, was ranked among the leading poets of his day.

Lyrics of a Lowly Life in 1896 established Dunbar as the first African-American poet of national reputation since Phillis Wheatley. And, like her, he was ravaged by tuberculosis in his tragically short life.

In the year following his publishing triumph, Dunbar came to Washington and left his mark on the city's cultural life for the next fifteen months while working at the **Library of Congress.** He might have remained in Washington, had not tuberculosis forced him to quit his job and leave. Much later, he published perhaps his best known novel, *The Sport of the Gods* (1902).

F. Scott Fitzgerald   Novelist, short-story writer, screenwriter (1896–1940).

Fitzgerald's mother was immensely proud of marrying into a Maryland family that could claim lineage to a distinguished American, and named her son Francis Scott, boasting that her husband's great-great grandfather had been the brother of Francis Scott Key's grandfather.

At the time of Fitzgerald's death, no one could accuse him of being a practicing Catholic. Certainly not the church, who refused to honor his wish to be buried in the family plot at **St. Mary's Cemetery** in suburban Rockville, Maryland. He was originally interred in Rockville Cemetery instead. When Fitzgerald's wife Zelda died by fire in a local nursing home disaster in 1948, she was buried next to her husband.

But daughter Scottie did not want to let her father's wish go unfulfilled. In 1975, she succeeded in getting her parents' remains disinterred and belatedly buried in St. Mary's small church graveyard (located at **600 Viers Mill Road** in Rockville). On the headstone marking their grave is the last, haunting line of *The Great Gatsby*,

"So we beat on, boats against the current, borne back ceaselessly into the past."

Edward Everett Hale Novelist, short-story writer, critic, memoirist, Senate Chaplain (1822–1909).

Hale, an ordained chaplain, was the first critic who gave warm approval to Walt Whitman's *Leaves of Grass*. His most famous story, "The Man Without a Country," was first published in 1863 in *The Atlantic Monthly* and was later collected with other of his pieces in *If, Yes and Perhaps* (1868). *Franklin in France* represents the best of Hale's scholarly works.

In a pair of memoirs, *A New England Boyhood* and *Memories of a Hundred Years,* Hale recorded his remarkable career as clergyman, philanthropist, popular writer and government servant. For years, he lived at **1741 N Street, NW** in downtown Washington, near Dupont Circle. A portion of his house is now part of today's Tabard Inn.

While serving as chaplain of the U.S. Senate (1903–9), Hale was asked: "Dr. Hale, do you pray for the Senate?" "No," Hale replied, "I look at the Senators and pray for the people."

Edith Hamilton Translator, classical scholar, essayist, educator (1867–1963).

Founder and headmistress of Bryn Mawr School in Baltimore, MD, Hamilton's greatest literary achievements were her engaging interpretations of classical civilizations.

It seems unlikely any graduate of a liberal arts college or university would fail to recognize her influential books: *The Greek Way* (1930), *The Roman Way* (1932), *Mythology* (1940) and *The Echo of Greece* (1957). These works simultaneously drew praise from scholars for Hamilton's depth of understanding and were embraced by general readers for the way Hamilton could bring ancient ideals alive.

She chose to spend the last twenty years of her life at **2448 Massachusetts Avenue, NW,** in a house backing onto Rock Creek Park in the heart of Washington, DC.

Dashiell Hammett Novelist, short-story writer, screenwriter (1894–1961).

Hammett wrote a number of famous detective novels, including *The Adventures of Sam Spade* and *The Maltese Falcon* (both popularized as successful Hollywood films). Hammett himself wrote for the screen, including *The Glass Key, The Thin Man* and *Watch On The Rhine.*

As a writer of hard-boiled fiction, Hammett saw his books banned from many library shelves during the 1950s. Yet, despite his radical politics, he asked before his death to have his remains buried with those of other men who had fought or died for the United States. Having served as a sergeant in the U.S. Army's Motor Ambulance Corps in World War I, Hammett also saw action in World War II with the U.S. Army Signal Corps from 1942 through 1945.

Today, you can seek out and visit Hammett's simple gravestone in **Arlington National Cemetery,** which commemorates the famous writer's volunteer service during both World Wars: "Samuel D. Hammett, Maryland, Tec5 HO CO, Alaskan Department, World War I & II, May 27, 1894 - January 10, 1961."

Bret Harte Short-story writer, poet, novelist, playwright, critic, journalist (1836–1902).

Harte's popular short stories of life on the American frontier were instrumental in shaping the mythology of the West, which in turn fed Hollywood's insatiable appetite for western melodrama.

With the publication of *The Luck of Roaring Camp and Other Sketches* in 1870, worldwide fame and fortune descended upon the struggling young writer. Harte immediately resigned from a teaching position in California to travel East, where he wrote for *The Atlantic Monthly.* However, his subsequent stories never achieved the quality and success of his early work.

Seven years later, Harte jumped at an offer by Ohio poet John James Piatt to place Harte's name on the masthead of a new literary periodical, *The Capital.* Lured by the promise of a $5,000 yearly salary to serve as the magazine's editor, Harte moved to Washington and spent several anxious months living at the old Riggs House at **1617 I Street, NW** (now an office building) while waiting for Piatt to pull together the magazine's financing.

When Piatt's plans finally collapsed and forced him into bankruptcy, Harte found himself stranded in the nation's capital. But Harte's political friends came to the rescue, securing for him the job of U.S. consul to Germany and later Scotland. Harte spent the remaining years of his life in London, never venturing back to the United States.

Francis Scott Key   Poet, lawyer (1779–1843).

A successful lawyer throughout his life, Key served as the United States Attorney for the District of Columbia from 1833 to 1841. A devout Episcopalian, he started out with his political allegiance given over to the Federalists, but in time became a Democrat as well as a friend to President Andrew Jackson.

However, it is for Key's inspiration one cataclysmic night in 1814 in Baltimore Harbor that he is chiefly remembered. Rocking in a sloop and watching first with horror as Fort McHenry was bombarded, then with jubilation as twilight revealed the still-waving American banner, Key was inspired to record his feelings in the lines of a poem.

Soon the poem was being sung to the British drinking song, "Anacreon in Heaven." But Key never lived to see his poem immortalized as America's national anthem— that happened by presidential proclamation in 1931, nearly a century after he died. And, like many other poets, Key's other poems weren't collected and published in book form until fourteen years after his death, under the title *Poems of the Late Francis S. Key, Esq.*

For twenty years during his early career, Key lived in a house located at **3518 M Street, NW** (the structure was torn down in 1948 to accommodate construction of Key Bridge). A year after Key wrote "The Star-Spangled Banner," he purchased **The Maples**, at **630 South Carolina Avenue, SE.** He lived there only briefly. Today it is **The Friendship House**, with its entrance at **619 D Street, SE.**

Margaret Leech   Novelist, biographer, historian (1893–1974).

Leech's most accomplished and widely read book, *Reveille in Washington*, received the Pulitzer Prize for History in 1942. Steeping herself in Washington's innumerable historical records and conducting extensive outside research, Leech managed to write the book in a lively style while faithfully relating what happened in the nation's capital during The Civil War.

Historian David McCullough, writing in the May, 1986 issue of *American Heritage* magazine, says, "If asked to name my favorite book about the city, I would have to pick Margaret Leech's Pulitzer Prize history, *Reveille in Washington*, first published in 1941, one of my all-time favorite books of any kind, which I have read and reread and pushed on friends for years."

Walter Lippmann   Journalist, author, editor, teacher, public official (1889–1974).

As an assistant to Woodrow Wilson, Lippmann is believed to have wielded influence on Wilson's thinking in his preparations for peace and formulation of policy on world issues.

After he left government, Lippmann took editorial positions with *The New Republic* and *The New York World* before joining *The New York Herald Tribune* as a columnist in 1931. Several times a week, when Lippmann spoke in "Today & Tomorrow," the world listened. He eventually won two Pulitzer Prizes—one in 1962 for international reporting and the other as a special citation in 1958 "for wisdom, perception and high sense of responsibility" in writing about national and international affairs.

His influential books include *A Preface To Politics* (1913), *The Stakes of Diplomacy* (1915), *The New Imperative* (1935), *The Good Society* (1937) and *The Communist World and Ours*.

It seems Lippmann was always among the powerful in the nation's capital, right from the start. His first home following marriage was the former bachelor quarters of Supreme Court Justice Felix Frankfurter, located at **1727 19th Street, NW.** He then moved in 1938, purchasing a house at **3434 Volta Place, NW,** in which Alexander Graham Bell's parents once lived. His final move came in 1964, when he took up digs at the former quarters of the dean of The Washington Cathedral, at **3525 Woodley Road, NW.**

Henry Cabot Lodge   Biographer, essayist, historian, editor, elected official (1850–1924).

A close friend of Henry Adams, under whom Lodge studied political science at Harvard, this perennial senator from Massachusetts lived on the avenue bearing the name of his native state, at **1765 Massachusetts Avenue, NW.** Lodge's home served as a social, political and literary salon during most of the two decades preceeding the Coolidge era.

Lodge's published works include: *A Short History of the English Colonies in America* (1881), *Alexander Hamilton* (1882), *Daniel Webster* (1883) and a two-volume study in 1888 titled *George Washington*. Lodge turned to a public examination of his own life in 1913 with the publication of *Early Memories*.

Clare Boothe Luce   Playwright, author, novelist, diplomat (1903–1987).

Principally a playwright of biting, sarcastic wit, Luce penned *The Women* in 1936, which satirized wealthy U.S. women, *Kiss the Boys Goodbye* in 1938, which ridiculed Hollywood's star system and warned of approaching fascism, and *Margin for Error* in 1940, a mystery melodrama portraying a Nazi consul's murder. Her 1940 book *Europe in the Spring* gave a report of her travels through volatile Europe and urged an American crusade for democracy the world over.

Luce entered public service when she was elected as a U.S. Congresswoman from Connecticut in 1943, and was appointed to serve as U.S. ambassador to Italy from 1953 to 1956.

Her will made provision for millions of dollars to be donated to a number of educational and charitable interests, including the Clare Boothe Luce Fund to help provide financial support to women students and teachers.

Archibald MacLeish   Poet, playwright, essayist, critic, memoirist, public official (1892–1982).

A man of letters who enjoyed a diverse career, MacLeish's literary reputation was firmly established with the publication of his long narrative poem *Conquistador* in 1932. The description of Mexico's conquest, it won the Pulitzer Prize for Poetry the following year. As cultural advisor to President Roosevelt, MacLeish was appointed Librarian of Congress in 1939, a post he held until 1944.

Concurrently with this post, MacLeish organized and served as the head of a new government agency called the U.S. Office of Facts and Figures (1941–42). He was the Assistant Director of the Office of War Information (1942–43), and served as Assistant Secretary of State from 1944–45.

No stranger to the machinations of power, MacLeish knew how to lyrically protect the administration he served, as in this passage from "A Poet Speaks From The Visitor's Gallery":

> History's not written in the kind of ink
> The richest man of most ambitious mind
> Who hates a president enough to print
> A daily paper can afford or find.
>
> Gentlemen have power now and know it,

But even the greatest and most famous kings
Feared and with reason to offend the poets

Whose songs are marble and whose marble sings.

After the war, MacLeish represented the United States in the organization of UNESCO. In 1952, his *Collected Poems* brought him a second Pulitzer, and his 1958 verse drama, *JB*, based on the life of the biblical prophet Job, earned yet another Pulitzer.

First and foremost a poet, MacLeish was drawn to writing drama for radio, describing the airwaves as the theater of "the word-excited imagination." The Orson Welles production of the poet's *The Fall of the City* was well received. In commenting upon his enthusiasm for the medium, MacLeish said: "Only the ear is engaged and the ear is already half-poet. It believes at once: creates and believes."

Joaquin Miller   Poet (1841–1913).

Called "the poet of the Sierras," Miller for a time lived in a log cabin located at **16th Street and Crescent Place, NW** on **Meridian Hill** (now Meridian Hill Park). In 1912, the cabin was moved to **Rock Creek Park** (at Beach and Military Drives), where today a summer poetry reading series is held each year.

A westerner who wandered through a myriad of jobs and off-beat experiences, Miller migrated to Washington during Chester Arthur's administration to seek political office. He didn't land a job, but considering his appearance this is hardly surprising. After moving into his log cabin, Miller went about the conservative capital clad in a frock coat and corduroy trousers tucked into high-heeled boots, a huge tasseled sombrero jauntily clamped above his long blonde hair and bushy mustachios bristling above his lip. These oddities of appearance, coupled with his rustic abode, didn't propel him to the top of the social register.

Accustomed as he was to adversity, Miller plied his natural trade about town—the writing and reading of poetry. Unfazed by lukewarm public reaction, Miller at last sailed for staid England decked out in jack boots, his trusty sombrero, flashy bandana and a fur coat with gold-nugget buttons. As he boastingly explained: "It helps sell the poems, boys, and tickles the duchesses!"

The gold-nugget buttons were perhaps unnecessary, for the English embraced his volume *Songs of the Sierras* for its sonorous verse and brilliant imagery. Returning to the west coast, the aging bohemian, ever ahead of his time, retired to the hills overlooking Oakland, California to practice and preach the simple life and advocate free love. It's interesting to contemplate what influence he might have wielded upon conservative Washington had he only stayed.

Edward R. Murrow   Broadcaster, author, government servant (1908–1965).

Head of the CBS Radio's European bureau during World War II, Murrow captivated America with his riveting dispatches describing the Battle of Britain. His scripts were collected to form his first book, *This is London* (1941). Other books were to come out of subsequent radio and television programs, including *See It Now, Hear It Now, This I Believe* and *Person to Person.*

Among the many programs Murrow wrote, produced, edited or directed from 1947 to 1960 was an expose of the destructive Senator Joe McCarthy. Murrow left his lucrative work in television in 1961 to become director of the U.S. Information Agency until 1963. While here in Washington, he lived at **5171 Manning Place, NW.**

John Howard Payne   Playwright, actor, journalist, diplomat (1791–1852).

Payne's life sadly epitomizes the classic struggle of serious artists. Acclaimed as a prodigy, Payne at 14 published the "Thespian Mirror," a theatrical review which attracted the attention of New York literary and theatrical circles. Thus thoroughly seduced by the promise of the theater, Payne authored and saw produced his first drama, *Julia, or The Wanderer,* at age 15. At 18, he won acclaim for his acting in a New York production of John Home's popular drama, *Douglas.*

But in a matter of brief years, a curious backlash set in against Payne's acting and writing. People reacted against the early acclaim and praise he enjoyed as a youth. Friends of his father collected funds and sent young Payne off to Europe, where he was expected to reclaim his reputation and earn a fortune. He settled in Europe in 1813, for several years barely eluding bankruptcy as he continued to act and write plays. In 1821, Payne tried producing his own melodramas, but they proved so unsuccessful that he landed in debtor's prison. To buy his way out, he wrote *Therese, Orphan of*

Geneva, which brought in just enough money for his freedom.

Payne thought he had finally hit upon financial success with the operatic production of his play, *Clari, The Maid of Milan*—for it contained the immensely popular song, "Home, Sweet Home," for which he had written the lyrics. But there was one catch: he discovered he had sold the play outright and could collect no royalties.

He continued to write and adapt other plays, remaining always poor. In England, he met and fell in love with Mary Shelley, widow of poet Percy Bysshe Shelley, and courted her fervently. Again, there was one catch: she wanted nothing to do with him.

Returning to America in a state of destitution, Payne came to see his friends in Washington, who arranged benefit performances in one of the city's theaters. This brought Payne a sizeable windfall. Could his luck finally be turning? His friend Daniel Webster and others lobbied to get Payne a consul post in far off Tunis. Payne went there and died.

The four Sisters of Charity who nursed Payne on his deathbed reported that in his delirium he sang "Home, Sweet Home," and was the sweetest man they ever buried in the Tunisian graveyard.

But mere burial didn't end Payne's meandering journey on earth. Thirty-one years following his death, Payne's body was ordered exhumed by wealthy local arts patron William W. Corcoran and brought back to Washington in a lead coffin. Having never forgotten the time as a boy when he witnessed Payne act on stage, Corcoran was determined to honor the author of one of the most popular songs of the 19th century.

Then, as now, money talked. Invitations to the reburial were printed with a Matthew Brady daguerreotype of Payne. A portrait of a youthful Payne was presented to Corcoran, who draped it with flowers and hung it in the Corcoran Gallery (where it remains today). Corcoran also commissioned a bust of Payne and had a hearse made to order, to be drawn by four white horses, while the coffin lay in state in the Corcoran Art Gallery.

The procession up to Georgetown's Oak Hill Cemtery (owned by Corcoran) was led by President Chester Arthur, his entire cabinet, the Supreme Court, members of the House and Senate and other capital notables. The red-uniformed Marine Band, led by John Phillip Sousa, played "Home, Sweet Home," and all those present joined in singing the last verse and chorus.

Today, the bust of Payne rests on a tall pedestal on the grounds of **Oak Hill Cemetery.** Seen from the corner of **30th and R Streets, NW,** any passerby might imagine that here lies a conquering hero who amassed fortune and glory in his lifetime. Certainly, Payne now shares an equal footing with Corcoran, who is buried on the other side of the cemetery.

In fact, having been a writer, Payne was granted a chance at the kind of immortality Corcoran's money could never buy. Eighty-eight years following his death, renewed attention came to Payne's work with the rescue of eleven of his plays from manuscripts and with his publication in *America's Lost Plays* (vol. 5 & 6, 1940). A biographical novel of the man, *John Howard Payne, Skywalker,* by Maude Barragan, followed in 1953, and in 1957 Grace Overmeyer wrote the best biography about Payne's ill-fated life.

Drew Pearson   Author, columnist, broadcaster (1897–1969).

Pearson's famous style, once described by *Time* magazine as a "brand of ruthlessness, theatrical crusading, high-voltage, hypodermic journalism that has made him the most intensely feared and hated man in Washington," brought him daily into the eye of controversy. This also guaranteed that what he wrote got read. His column material was eventually compiled into three wildly successful books.

The incomparable muckraker resided in an 18th-century structure located at **2820 Dumbarton Avenue, NW.** From the comfort of his home, and using a bank of telephones and a teletype machine, Pearson would dispatch his daily column, "Washington Merry-Go-Round." He also tended one of the finest gardens in the nation's capital. His success at gardening perhaps was not so much a green thumb as a nose for shrewd investment in a complementary property, a 450–acre farm overlooking the Potomac River at **13130 River Road,** near the town of **Potomac, MD.**

There, Pearson built a stone mansion in 1937, and was in the habit of going out frequently for relaxation. He also went to check on the state of his lucrative dairy herd. After all, Pearson earned up to $150,000 a year from the sale of manure. Now, *that's* muckraking. The bags read, "Pearson's Best Manure—Better Than The Column—All Cow, No Bull."

Katherine Anne Porter   Novelist, short-story writer, essayist (1890–1980).

Regarded as one of America's finest writers of short stories and novellas, Porter was awarded the Pulitzer Prize and National Book Award in 1966 for her *Collected Stories.* From her astonishing debut in 1930 with the masterful short story collection, *Flowering Judas,* Porter went on to fashion a relatively small but enormously accomplished body of work. Her additional collections, *Noon Wine* (1937) and *Pale Horse, Pale Rider* (1939), solidified her reputation worldwide. Yet it wasn't until 1962 that she would produce her only novel, the commercially and critically successful *Ship of Fools.*

Financial security provided by her novel's success allowed Porter to abandon a demanding routine of delivering guest lectures and moving from one university to another as a visiting instructor. From 1960 to 1975, she resided in her house at **3601 49th Street, NW** near American University in upper northwest Washington, D.C. (still a private residence). She then moved into a condominium in the Westchester Park Apartments at **6100 Westchester Park Drive** in **College Park, MD.** The final year of her life was spent in the **Carriage Hill Nursing Home** at **9101 2nd Avenue** in **Silver Spring, MD.**

In much of her symbol-enriched work, Porter expresses a sense of bewilderment at the strangeness of life's developments. She captures in masterful prose the solid sense and atmosphere of a place, while evoking deep ambivalence about human conduct, particularly people's inclination toward betrayal. Always a passionate writer, she protested the Sacco-Vanzetti case in the Thirties and made that episode the subject of her last book, *The Never Ending Wrong* (1977).

In her collected essays, *The Days Before,* Porter wrote: "I am passionately involved with those individuals who populate all these enormous migrations, calamities, who fight wars and furnish life for the future."

The **University of Maryland Library** has set aside a **Katherine Anne Porter Room,** in which are housed the author's works, her personal library, her papers and personal memorabilia.

Ezra Pound   Poet, critic. editor, translator (1885–1972).

A linguistic genius and gifted critic, Pound commanded the highest respect and attention on the international literary scene during the opening decades of the twentieth century. He crafted poems of great influence, and provided generous assistance to promising writers like T.S. Eliot and Ernest Hemingway. But when World War II ended, Pound was arrested for having made pro-Fascist radio broadcasts in Italy. He was charged with treason.

Prior to his trial in Washington, however, the U.S. attorney declared Pound mentally unfit and had him committed to a mental institution. So, for the next 12 years, Pound became a Washington resident at **2700 Martin Luther King Avenue, SE**—in the **Chestnut Ward** of **St. Elizabeth's Hospital.** He remained incarcerated until 1958, when the indictment was withdrawn. Pound promptly returned to Italy, declaring that "all America is an insane asylum."

Among Pound's best-known books are *Provenca* (1910), *Homage to Sextus Popertius* (1918), and his most famous work, the epic *Cantos* (1917–69).

Jeremiah Eames Rankin   Poet, lyricist, clergyman, educator (1828–1924).

Rankin is best remembered for his hymn, "God Be With You Till We Meet Again." Pastor of the First Congregational Church in Washington, Rankin later became president of **Howard University** from 1889 to 1903. Possessing a command of the Scots dialect, he loved to write verse in that musical tongue.

His work is collected in *The Auld Scotch Mither and Other Poems* (1873) and *Ingleside Rhaims* (1887).

Marjorie Kinnan Rawlings   Novelist, poet, journalist (1896–1953).

Best known for her Pulitzer Prize-winning novel, *The Yearling* (1938), Rawlings began her writing career as a newspaper reporter and gravitated toward the short-story and novel forms. Most of her fiction and nonfiction examines life in backcountry Florida. Many readers also know her nonfiction book, *Cross Creek* (1942), which was made into a feature film.

Born and raised in the District of Columbia, Rawlings displayed her talent in writing from the age of six. For the next decade, she contributed to the children's pages of the city's local newspapers. She attended Western High School. At 15, she submitted her story, "The Reincarnation of Miss Hetty," to *McCall's* Child Authorship Contest and won a prize. Two years later, when her father died, she moved with her mother to Madison, Wisconsin.

In her formative years in Washington, Rawlings lived in a still-standing house at **1221 Newton Street, NE** (not open to the public).

Mary Roberts Rinehart Novelist, short-story writer, playwright (1876–1958).

A successful writer of thrillers and comic novels about the travels and adventures of her spinster character, Tisk, Rinehart lived in Washington from 1920 to 1932. She was conferred a Litt.D. from George Washington University in 1923.

The stock market crash of 1903 drove Rinehart into a writing career in the hopes of earning money. In time, she discovered money and fame through her long and prolific career, and is considered one of the founders of the American mystery and suspense novel. She published 20 novels during her years in Washington.

The literature department of nearby George Mason University administers the Mary Roberts Rinehart Fund, set up in her memory to assist deserving writers in pursuing their craft.

Theodore Roosevelt Author, soldier, 26th President of the United States (1858–1919).

The author of many books, Roosevelt used his popularity as a writer to promote his views—both in and out of politics. In fact, of all U.S. presidents, Roosevelt was closest to functioning as a professional writer. *The Winning of the West* (four volumes, 1889–96) is considered his most significant work.

Roosevelt's first book, *The Naval War of 1812* (1882), served to help land his first elected office. Other important works to follow included: *American Ideals and Other Essays* (1897), *The Rough Riders* (1899) and *African Game Trails* (1910).

At thirty-one years old, Roosevelt moved to Washington in 1889 upon his appointment to the Civil Service Commission by President Harrison. He lived at **1215 19th Street, NW** from 1889 to 1895, shortly before going to war with Spain in Cuba at the head of his famed Rough Riders.

Anne Royall Author, journalist, travel writer (1769–1854).

Unfairly branded "the mother of yellow journalism"

for her caustic, sensational attacks on politicians and other Washington figures, Anne Royall was in fact a champion of the underdog and tirelessly outspoken in her crusades against corruption and political cronyism. Founder of *Paul Pry*, a weekly Washington newspaper, in 1831, she never found herself lacking targets for her railing editorials.

In her time, Anne Royall was the most famous woman in Washington, widely feared and hated by those who had something to hide. Congressmen would find themselves hopelessly cornered by Royall, who never gave way until she got answers to her hard-hitting questions. Tact seemed foreign to her journalistic or personal vocabulary.

But it was not always so. In her initial visits to Washington in the early 1820s, many people found Royall quaintly charming. And when she settled in Washington in 1828, she arrived triumphantly as the author of four successful books: *Sketches, Black Book, Mrs. Royall's Pennsylvania* and *Mrs. Royall's Southern Tour*. To the applause of admiring Senators, Royall became the first woman ever allowed on the Senate floor. How they loved to bask in the glow of a successful author.

But such regard for this talented, quirky writer was short lived. All too soon, public figures discovered Royall relentlessly stalking them and chronicling their questionable behavior. A scourge of religious fanatics, she is the only American to have ever been tried and acquitted on the archaic charge of being a "common scold."

But Royall did more than expose and attack hypocrites in her pages—she championed the causes of ecology, municipal planning and justice for the American Indian. Throughout her years of capital muckraking, the frumpy, limp-legged Royall never flagged in her crusade to get the goods on all the scoundrels populating Capitol Hill. As she once boasted to P.T. Barnum:

"All the Congressmen call on me. They do not dare do otherwise. Enemies and friends all alike, they have to come to me. And why should they not? I made them— every devil of them. You know how I look, ragged and poor, but thank God I am saucy and independent. The whole government is afraid of me, and well they may be. I know them all, from top to toe—I can fathom their rascality."

What made Royall so effective in her work was that

she was utterly above corruption. Her commitment to truth remained unswerving. Anne Royall refused to let her papers become mere political mouthpieces and always spoke her mind. When *Paul Pry* folded in 1836, she promptly started up a new weekly named, appropriately, *Huntress*. She died in 1854, mere weeks following her last editorial.

One of the first insights Royall had upon visiting Washington in 1824—a judgment that today remains deplorably relevant—was that "if you are poor, you have no business in Washington." Throughout her life here, she scrambled for any adequate lodging she could afford, but always managed to live within a stone's throw of the U.S. Capitol.

The first place she stayed was with the Dorret family on Capitol Hill, where she was given a free room. For a time, the secretary of the Supreme Court arranged for her to stay in the **old Brick Capitol Building**, the makeshift structure erected following the destruction of the War of 1812 (now the site of the **Library of Congress, at East Capitol and 1st Streets, SE**).

From 1827 to 1833, through the generosity of her patron Daniel Carroll, she stayed rent free in the old **Bank House** on Capitol Hill, formerly headquarters of the Bank of Washington. Located on what was called Carroll Row on the **east side of 1st Street, between East Capitol and A Streets,** the house was torn down to make way for the **Supreme Court Building.**

Royall then moved to the corner of **East Capitol and Second Streets,** near the old Hill Market. And, in 1838, she moved again to **North B and Third Streets** (now **Constitution Avenue and Third Street, NE**), just down the block from Vice President Richard M. Johnson. Finally, after several more moves, she returned to her favorite house on **B Street between 1st and 2nd Streets, SE** (where the **Madison Building of the Library of Congress** now stands).

Upon her death, she was buried in an unmarked grave in **Congressional Cemetery**, at **1801 E Street, SE.** Fifty-seven years later, a small monument was placed on the gravesite by "a few men from Philadelphia and Washington" with the simple inscription: "Anne Royall, Pioneer Woman Publicist, 1769–1854, 'I Pray That The Union Of These States May Be Eternal.' "

Although Royall's story today remains largely unknown, her colorful personality has been treated in a handful of works: *The Life and Times of Anne Royall*

(1909) by Sarah Harvey Porter, *Seventy-Five Years of White House Gossip* (1926) by Edna M. Colman, *Nymphos and Other Maniacs* (1971) by Irving Wallace and a two-act play, *Mrs. Anne Royall's Black Book* (1988) by Minnesota poet and playwright Bruce Cutler.

Emma Dorothy Eliza Nevitt Southworth   Novelist, short-story writer (1819–1899).

History has not been kind to the memory of Washington native Emma Southworth, who published in her lifetime as E.D.E.N. Southworth. In many ways, her astonishing life story stands as the ironic antithesis to the ill-fated career of John Howard Payne, whom she knew (see his entry). For, while in her day Southworth towered as one of this country's most prolific and widely read novelists, today she is hardly remembered. And, while Payne's career was launched amid praise for his promise as a writing prodigy, Southworth had to overcome the most difficult of circumstances to forge a literary career.

Reared in her early years in St. Mary's County—just south of Washington, D.C.—Southworth moved into Washington when her widowed mother married Joshua Henshaw, who was secretary to Daniel Webster. Henshaw soon established a school for girls in Washington, where Southworth first attended as a pupil and later worked as a teacher.

She was eking out a meager existence in a rowhouse apartment on Capitol Hill when she married Frederick Southworth, who took her to live in a log cabin on the Wisconsin frontier. Frederick worked as a miner, and frequently would leave his wife and children alone for weeks at a time, with wolves howling at night outside the cabin door.

Finding herself and her two children finally abandoned by her husband, Southworth returned to Washington four years after leaving. Teaching didn't pay enough to support her family, so Southworth turned to writing at night to supplement her income.

Her first novel, *Retribution*, made literary history in 1849 when it became one of the first novels to be serialized in the *National Era*, the only abolitionist newspaper in Washington. The novel was enthusiastically received, and Southworth was sufficiently encouraged to venture on her next. By the end of her wildly successful career, she would publish 73 novels.

Many of her books sold over a million copies each.

Southworth used her proceeds to purchase **Prospect Cottage,** located at **36th and Prospect Streets, NW** (**southwest corner**). The "cottage," a 14–room dwelling perched on a bluff in Georgetown overlooking the Potomac River, presented a commanding view of Virginia across the other shore. For half a century, Prospect Cottage became a well-known meeting place for the literary community of Washington. It was even turned into a makeshift hospital for wounded soldiers during the Civil War, and President Lincoln slept there three times on his way to and from the battlefields.

When Harriet Beecher Stowe travelled to Washington to arrange for publication of her novel, *Uncle Tom's Cabin,* in the *Era,* Southworth befriended the budding writer and invited her to stay at Prospect Cottage. They became lifelong friends. Later on, during a trip to England to observe the European publication of one of her books, Southworth befriended Lady Byron.

It is odd and sad to consider that, while in her time Southworth was celebrated as one of the most successful women writers in Victorian America, virtually nothing she wrote is read today. Upon her death in 1899, she was buried in **Oak Hill Cemetery (30th and R Streets, NW**), on the slope of a hill below the chapel. Prospect Cottage was purchased by the National League of the American Pen Women. They decided to demolish Prospect Cottage and construct their national headquarters on the site. The stock market crash of 1903 ended those plans, however.

Prospect Cottage was eventually destroyed in 1941. Today, the spot is occupied by a pair of ordinary brick townhouses, very near the famous steps where the film *The Exorcist* was shot.

James Thurber Short-story writer, humorist, essayist, cartoonist (1894–1961).

Thurber is perhaps equally prized for the sophisticated humor of his short fiction and the hilarious simplicity of his line drawings. He fashioned both, with great success, for *The New Yorker* magazine from 1927 until near his death.

Thurber's most famous story was *The Secret Life of Walter Mitty,* which was turned into a Hollywood movie, as were other of his stories. His collected stories include *My Life and Hard Times* (1933) and *The Thurber Carnival* (1945).

Known to be reclusive and somewhat cranky, Thurber was nonetheless delighted when local writer Elizabeth Acosta sent him her "first fan letter." He was taken by Acosta's wit and charm, and he also remembered her address (323 Maple Avenue) in the City of Falls Church, VA. Here is a portion of Thurber's letter to Acosta, dated November 29, 1958, as it may be found in the Virginia Room of the Falls Church City Public Library:

"I don't think you know about all the houses I lived in, because one of them was a house on Maple Avenue in Falls Church, Virginia. This was fifty-seven years ago, in the summer of 1901, when my father had a job in Washington. My mother couldn't stand the heat of the city and so we rented this house on Maple Avenue, but I can't remember the number now. It was there that, one Sunday, I was struck by an arrow fired by my older brother. He was seven, and I was six, and Robert was four, and I'm sure we all threw up together. My father was on a fishing trip, of course, when I got hurt. It is too late now for you to assassinate Dr. Malone, who must have died years ago, and who did not have the left eye removed soon enough. The operation was finally done by the great Dr. Swann Burnett, whose wife, a dozen years earlier, had written *Little Lord Fauntleroy.*

"When I was a code clerk in the State Department in 1918 I went back to the house on Maple Avenue, and it seemed pretty much the same. We had a big back yard and an apple orchard, and there were some seckel pear trees. Our best apples were big yellow ones called Sheep's Nose. A quarter of a mile from our house was a big estate with a winding driveway, called the Evergreens, and a family named McSween lived there. My brother Robert, now 62—William was 65 in October— still has some photos of the Maple Avenue House, I think, and if he has, I'll send them to you. A lot of good things as well as bad happened in that house. Falls Church was a quiet little village then, and I often wonder what it has become.

"My wife Helen and I both loved your letter, one of the best and funniest I have ever got, and we have shown it to all our friends. I love your loving me, and I love you too. . . ."

After several more letters between them, Acosta and Thurber figured out that the Thurber family rented what was then known as "the Loving cottage" in the summer of 1901 and 1902 at **319 Maple Avenue.** During the winters of those years, the Thurbers lived at **2031 I Street, NW,** just one block from "Bill, Steve and Laura

Benet." In other letters to Acosta, Thurber recalled working in later years with Stephen Vincent Benet in the code rooms of the State Department, and that "Washington was also the home of my favorite American of this century, the late Elmer Davis, to whom I dedicated my last book of fables."

"I always think fondly of Washington and Falls Church," wrote Thurber to Acosta in 1958, "and have enough memories of both places, most of them fond, to fill a book." Mrs. Acosta was pleased, because the house that the Thurber family rented for two summers was directly next door to hers. She exchanged letters and phone calls with Thurber until his death in 1961.

In 1965, the Thurber family cottage and Mrs. Acosta's house were both demolished to make way for twenty townhouses, and Maple Avenue was renamed by the city to . . . **James Thurber Court.**

Mark Twain Novelist, short-story writer, journalist, humorist (1835–1910).

Twain settled into Washington in the fall of 1867, coming here to work for Senator Stewart of Nevada, whom he had gotten to know some years before out West. From the outset, relations between the two men were strained by what seemed an essential difference in temperaments. It also didn't help when the senator came to observe that Twain's attention was chiefly devoted to putting the finishing touches on his new book, *The Innocents Abroad.*

Twain had just returned from his first journey overseas, and was engrossed in the publication arrangements for what promised to be his most nationally popular book. The senator's new aide was also devoting a considerable amount of time toward conducting with William Swinton what he described as "the first Newspaper Correspondence Syndicate that an unhappy world ever saw." The Senator and Twain were on a collision course, and began arguing violently.

Senator Stewart recounted in his autobiography these tempestous months spent with Twain. And Twain himself felt compelled to draft a wry account of his wayward time in Washington, entitled *Washington in 1868.*

Daniel Webster Author, orator, arts patron (1782– 1852).

A prominent figure on the cultural scene in Washington, Webster was an active patron of the arts and an oratorical firebrand who made lasting impressions on those who encountered his colorful personality and persuasive rhetoric. Writers frequently sought Webster's influential intervention with the government and enjoyed his generous financial assistance. Reviewing the history of literary Washington, one is struck at how frequently Webster shows up in the course of writers' lives.

Arriving in Washington first as a New England congressman and then a senator, Webster quickly established his fame as a matchless orator. His talents were soon tapped by Presidents Harrison and Tyler, who appointed him Secretary of State. Among Webster's books are *Discourse in Commemoration of Jefferson and Adams* (1826), and *Writings and Speeches* (1903), collected in 18 volumes. Novelist Honore Willsie Morrow appropriated Webster's colorful life for his 1931 novel *Black Daniel,* and Stephen Vincent Benet would further immortalize the man in his classic story, *The Devil and Daniel Webster* (1939).

While serving as Secretary of State in the 1840s, Webster resided at the northeast corner of **H Street and Connecticut Avenue, NW** (now the **U.S. Chamber of Commerce** building). Although the house was a gift to Webster from his New York and Boston admirers, his extravagant lifestyle forced him to sell it to banker William Corcoran eight years after moving in. He then moved to rented quarters near Judiciary Square, where he died in 1852.

A statue of the great orator now stands at **Scott Circle,** where **Massachusetts Avenue, Rhode Island Avenue** and **N Street, NW** intersect.

Walt Whitman   Poet, journalist, editor (1819–1892).

The editor of *The Brooklyn Times* and other newspapers, Whitman was forty-three years old when he came down to Washington from New York for the first time.

Not long before, *Leaves of Grass* had been praised by Ralph Waldo Emerson as "the most extraordinary piece of wit and wisdom that America has yet contributed." The book was in its third edition, and readers were alternately shocked by its strong ideas and moved by its lush, powerful lyricism.

There was growing interest in Whitman's writing, but the nation was also deeply divided by the Civil War. Among the casualties was Walt's brother George, who was seriously wounded at the first battle of Fredericksburg on December 13th, 1862.

Walt rushed down to his brother's side, and came face-to-face with unimaginable suffering and pain. The field of battle at Fredericksburg was littered with bodies, he later wrote in *Specimen Days,* and "within ten yards of the front of a house, I notice a heap of amputated feet, legs, arms, hands, &c.; a full load for a one-horse cart. Several dead bodies lie near, each cover'd with its brown woolen blanket. In the door-yard, towards the river, are fresh graves, mostly of officers, their names on pieces of barrel-staves or broken boards, stuck in the dirt."

The experience profoundly affected Whitman. He made his way with the wounded from his brother's regiment up to Washington, and took up lodgings in a small boarding house at **1205 M Street** (now torn down). He found a part-time job as an army paymaster, but only to make ends meet, and began writing occasional dispatches for *The New York Times* about wartime Washington.

But, from 1862 until the end of the war, Whitman's main energies were devoted to comforting wounded soldiers in makeshift hospitals throughout the city. He was a daily visitor to the old **Armory Square Hospital,** once located at **6th Street and Independence Avenue, NW.** In *Specimen Days,* he also describes visiting the wounded at **"the Patent-office"** (in what is now the **National Portrait Gallery),** "English street," "H street," "Campbell hospital" and other places around town.

A Washington correspondent for the *New York Herald* gives us this eyewitness account of Whitman during this period:

"I saw him, time and again, in the Washington hospitals, or wending his way there with basket or haversack on his arm, and the strength of beneficence suffusing his face. His devotion surpassed the devotion of woman. . . . Never shall I forget one night when I accompanied him on his rounds . . . there was a smile of affection and welcome on every face, however wan, and his presence seemed to light up the place as it might be lighted by the presence of the God of love.

From cot to cot they called him, often in tremulous tones or in whispers. They embraced him; they touched his hand; they gazed at him. To one he gave a few words of cheer; for another he wrote a letter home; to others he gave an orange, a few comfits, a cigar, a pipe and tobacco, a sheet of paper or a postage stamp . . . from another he would receive a dying message for mother, wife or sweetheart. . . . As he took his way toward the door, you could hear the voices of many a stricken hero calling, 'Walt, Walt, Walt! Come again! Come again!' "

Everywhere he went in Washington, Whitman's presence was known and felt. His friend John Burroughs describes him near the end of the war as "a large slow-moving figure clad in gray, with broad-brimmed hat and gray beard. . . . He had a hirsute, kindly look, but far removed from the finely-cut traditional poet's face."

Unfortunately, Whitman's meager salary and his long vigils brought on a physical breakdown. In 1864, hospital doctors ordered him home to Brooklyn for six months of rest.

The next year—two months before Lee's surrender at Appomattox—Whitman felt well enough to return to Washington. He got a job in the Indian Bureau of the Interior Department, but the job was soon taken away because, it was said, Secretary Harlan disapproved of *Leaves of Grass*.

Whitman's friends were outraged. They found him a job the next day in the Attorney General's Office. Then fellow government official (and novelist) William Douglas O'Connor came to Whitman's defense in a pamphlet called *The Good Gray Poet*. The name of the pamphlet stuck to Whitman himself, and he carried it with him to his grave.

For seven years, Whitman worked and wrote in the nation's capital. His volume of poems, *Drum-Taps* (1865), contained the great odes to Lincoln "When Lilacs Last In The Doorway Bloomed" and "O Captain, My Captain" which were later absorbed into *Leaves of Grass*. A small group of miscellaneous poems, *Passage To India*, came out in pamphlet form. The essay *Democratic Vistas* was published in its entirety in 1871. The prose book *Memoranda During The War*, the journal entries of *Specimen Days* and two volumes of letters (*The Wound Dresser* and *Calamus*) all belong to this period. And, of course, Whitman was intermittently revising, reshaping and rethinking his masterpiece— *Leaves of Grass*.

In 1873, Walt Whitman suffered a sudden paralytic stroke during the night. Unable to work in an office job any longer, he was taken up to his brother George's house in Camden, New Jersey. The "good gray poet" continued writing, lecturing and traveling until his death in 1892.

Woodrow Wilson   Statesman, historian, educator, 28th President of the United States (1856–1925).

Of all our presidents, Wilson stands out as being perhaps the most deeply interested in books. As a writer, Wilson displayed a love of epigrams, a deftness for turning a well-turned phrase and a knack for good storytelling. Altogether, his gifts elevated his prose above the usual benumbing "bureaucratese" infecting most of governmental Washington.

Among Wilson's several works are: *The State* (1889), *Division and Reunion* (1893), *An Old Master and Other Political Essays* (1893) and *A History of the American People* (5 volumes, 1902). Today, the Woodrow Wilson Foundation in Washington serves to further public understanding of international problems and Wilson's ideals of world cooperation.

Still the only President to have retired here in Washington, Wilson in 1921 moved into a red-brick Georgian Revival townhouse located at **2340 S Street, NW,** near **Dupont Circle.** The house today is a National Historic Landmark, and is open to the public for tours (10 am to 4 pm, Tuesday–Saturday, March through December). Visitors will find the home and library richly appointed with virtually all of the original furniture, many books and other personal items belonging to the Wilsons while they were alive.

Upon his death in 1924, Wilson was entombed in **Washington National Cathedral** (**Massachusetts and Wisconsin Avenues, NW**), where today his sarcophagus rests to the right of the Cathedral's main nave, facing the pulpit.

Elinor Wylie   Poet, novelist (1885–1928).

Wylie's rebellion against conventional behavior, particularly her elopement with Horace Wylie in 1910, served to make her a symbolic figure caught up in that era's "American poetic renaissance." Readers found it difficult to separate their feelings about her work from their feelings toward her notorious social behavior.

Wylie's poems were characterized by an interest in things romantic and sensuous. Nevertheless, critic Mary Colum described Wylie as "one of the few important woman poets in any literature. . . . She seemed to write little out of a mood or out of a passing emotion . . . but nearly always out of complete thought." And H. Ludecke wrote of Wylie's work: "Refinement is her essential characteristic as an artist."

Brought up in Philadelphia and Washington, Wylie spent her years here attending **Holton Arms School (7303 River Road**) in **Bethesda, MD.** In her career she wrote four novels (including *Jennifer Lorn,* 1923) and eight volumes of verse, including *Nets to Catch the Wind* (1921) and *Black Armour* (1923). Following her death, her *Collected Poems* were issued in two volumes (1932–33).

Contemporary Authors

"We are all apprentices in a craft where no one ever becomes a master."

—ERNEST HEMINGWAY

"Writers seldom write the things they think. They simply write the things they think other folks think they think."

—ELBERT HUBBARD

"I love being a writer. What I can't stand is the paper-work."

—PETER DEVRIES

There are more working writers per square foot in Washington, D.C. than in any other metropolitan area in the country. Here, where the chief product is paper—all bearing verbiage of one kind or another—it certainly seems plausible that a lot of residents must write to stay working.

And yet, the difference between "writing to work" and calling oneself a "working writer" is substantial. It is often the difference between paying the bills and going flat broke, between finding a style and just banging away on a keyboard.

It's therefore a pleasure to report that we find many of the nation's best "working writers" living and working right here. This book is a celebration of their tenacity, variety and virtuosity, an attempt to offer encouragement, support and some form of recognition to all writers now—when it's needed—and not later on when it may be too late.

In assembling the following list of more than 250 outstanding local book authors, I was surprised by how many accomplished fiction writers live here, particularly in a city so dominated by journalism and facts. I'm also aware that some local authors may have been overlooked, for which I offer apologies and an offer of remedy, if given the chance. Every effort was made to find and include you, as the book's Editorial Board and many others will readily agree.

Now, concerning the listings themselves. All information is current as of January 1989. The book listings for each writer, while thorough, don't always reflect *every* book the author has written. Listed works are, for the most part, hardcover editions of books, unless the book was a paperback original or was issued as a reprint. Only book authors are listed, leaving out the huge pool of local magazine writers, journalists and freelance writers whose articles, essays, poems and short stories have yet to be collected in a volume.

The authors shown live and work somewhere within the following geographic area: from Winchester, VA to Annapolis, MD (west-east) and from just below Baltimore, MD to just above Charlottesville, VA (north-south). Regrettably, this limitation excludes a number of prominent Baltimore and Charlottesville authors who live nearby.

Finally, for those authors who have collaborated with well-known personalities on a book but perhaps didn't get recognition, I have tried to give *you* top billing on the pages that follow. And readers may note that a few authors listed, while they don't live here full-time, still maintain homes in the area and thus qualify for mention here.

FICTION

Vassily Aksyonov Novelist, teacher. Emigrated from U.S.S.R. in 1980; one of Russia's most famous living writers. Professor of creative writing, George Mason University.
  Books: Say Cheese! (Random House, 1989); In Search of Melancholy Baby (RHse, 1987); Our Golden Ironburg (Ardis, 1986); The Burn (RHse, 1984); The Island of Crimea (RHse, 1983); The Steel Bird & Other Stories (Ardis, 1979); Paperscape; A Ticket to the Stars.

Henry Allen Novelist, journalist. Staff writer, *The Washington Post.*
  Books: Fool's Mercy (Carroll & Graf, 1984).

Patrick Anderson Novelist, author, journalist. Former speech writer for Robert Kennedy and President Jimmy Carter.
  Books: The Pleasure Business (Harcourt Brace Jovanovich, 1989); Sinister Forces (Doubleday, 1986); Lords of the Earth (Dday, 1984); First Family (Simon & Schuster, 1978); The President's Mistress (S&S, 1976);

The Approach to Kings (Dday, 1970). *Nonfiction:* High in America (Viking, 1981).

Allen Appel Novelist, photographer, freelance journalist.
Books: Twice Upon a Time (Carroll & Graf, 1988); Time After Time (C & G, 1985); Vengeance Valley (Leisure Books, 1985).

Ellen Argo Novelist.
Books: The Yankee Girl (Putnam, 1980); The Crystal Star (Putnam, 1979); Jewel of the Seas (Putnam, 1977).

Richard Bausch Novelist, short story writer, teacher. Professor of creative writing and literature, George Mason University.
Books: Mr. Field's Daughter (Simon & Schuster, 1989); Spirits & Other Stories (Linden Press/ S & S, 1987); The Last Good Time (Dial, 1984); Take Me Back (Dial, 1981); Real Presence (Dial, 1980).

Robert Bausch Novelist, teacher. Part-time professor of creative writing and literature, George Mason University.
Books: The Lives Of Riley Chance (St. Martin's, 1984); On the Way Home (St. Martin's, 1982).

Elizabeth Benedict Novelist.
Books: The Beginner's Book of Dreams (Knopf, 1988); Slow Dancing (Knopf, 1985).

William Peter Blatty Novelist.
Books: Legion (Simon & Schuster, 1983); The Ninth Configuration (Harper & Row, 1978); I'll Tell Them I Remember You (Norton, 1973); The Exorcist (H & R, 1971); I, Billy Shakespeare (Doubleday, 1965).

Christopher Buckley Novelist, columnist. Former speechwriter, Vice President George Bush.
Books: The White House Mess (Knopf, 1986); Other Lives (Greenfield Review Press, 1985); Steaming to Bamboola (Congdon & Lattes, 1982); Last Rites (Greenfield RPr, 1980).

John Buckley Novelist, journalist. Former press secretary, Jack Kemp's presidential campaign.
Books: Family Politics (Simon & Schuster, 1988).

Alan Cheuse Novelist, radio commentator. Professor of creative writing, George Mason University. Book critic, National Public Radio ("All Things Considered").
Books: The Grandmother's Club (Peregrine Smith, 1986); The Bohemians: John Reed & His Friends Who Shook the World (Applewood, 1982). *Nonfiction:* Fall Out of Heaven: An Autobiographical Journey Across Russia (Gibbs Smith, 1987)

Tom Clancy Novelist. Former insurance salesman, Hartford Insurance Group.
Books: The Cardinal of the Kremlin (Putnam, 1988); Patriot Games (Putnam, 1987); Red Storm Rising (Putnam, 1986); The Hunt For Red October (Naval Institute Press, 1984).

Arnaud de Borchgrave Novelist, journalist, editor. Editor-in-Chief, *The Washington Times.*
Books: Monimbo (with Robert Moss, Simon & Schuster, 1983); The Spike (with Robert Moss, Crown, 1980).

Bruce Duffy Novelist.
Books: The World As I Found It (Ticknor & Fields, 1987).

Gregg Easterbrook Novelist, journalist. Contributing editor, *Newsweek Magazine.*
Books: This Magic Moment (St. Martin's, 1986).

Ellen Ferber Novelist, journalist, poet.
Books: The Gingerbread Man (Doubleday, 1958); Never Smile at Children.

Candida Fraze Novelist.
Books: Renifleur's Daughter (Henry Holt, 1987).

John Rolfe Gardiner Novelist, short-story writer.
Books: In the Heart of the Whole World (Knopf, 1988); Unknown Soldiers (Dutton, 1977); Great Dream From Heaven (Dutton, 1974).

Harold Gershowitz Novelist.
Books: Remember the Dream (Bantam Books, 1988).

Vic Gold Novelist, author, journalist. National correspondent, *Washingtonian Magazine.*

Books: The Body Politic (with Lynne Cheney, St. Martin's, 1988). *Nonfiction:* Looking Forward: The George Bush Story (Doubleday, 1987); PR As in President (Dday, 1977).

Marita Golden Novelist, author, television producer. Founder and president, Afro-American Writers Guild. Former associate producer, WNET-TV, New York.
Books: Long Distance Life (Forthcoming, 1989); A Woman's Place (Doubleday, 1986). *Nonfiction:* Migrations of the Heart (Anchor Press, 1983).

Stephen Goodwin Novelist, teacher. Director of Literature Program, National Endowment for the Arts. Former professor of creative writing and English literature, George Mason University (1979–1987).
Books: Blood of Paradise (Dutton, 1979); Kin (Harper & Row, 1975). *Nonfiction:* The Greatest Masters: The 1986 Masters & Golf's Elite (Harper & Row, 1988).

Jim Grady Novelist, screenwriter. Former staff writer, Jack Anderson.
Books: Steeltown (Bantam Books, 1989); Just A Shot Away (Bantam, 1987); Hard Bargains (Macmillan, 1985); Runner in the Street (Macmillan, 1984); Shadow of the Condor (Putnam, 1975); Six Days of the Condor (Norton, 1974). *T.V. Shows:* D.C. Cop (CBS-TV).

Patricia Griffith Novelist, teacher.
Books: The Great Saturday Night Swindle (1987); Tennessee Blue (Clarkson Potter, 1981); The Future Is Not What It Used To Be (Simon & Schuster, 1970).

Martha Grimes Novelist, mystery writer, poet, teacher. Visiting professor, The Writing Seminars, Johns Hopkins University. Former professor of literature, Montgomery College. Won Nero Wolfe Award in 1983.
Books: The Five Bells & Bladebone (Little, Brown, 1987); I Am the Only Running Footman (L,Br, 1986); The Deer Leap (L,Br, 1985); Help the Poor Struggler (L,Br, 1985); The Dirty Duck (L,Br, 1984); Jerusalem Inn (L,Br, 1984); The Anodyne Necklace (L,Br, 1983); The Old Fox Deceiv'd (L,Br, 1982); The Man With a Load of Mischief (L,Br, 1981).

Doris Grumbach Novelist, essayist, teacher, literary critic. Book critic for National Public Radio. Former literary editor of *The New Republic;* former professor of literature, American University and University of Iowa Writers Workshop. Co-owner (with Sybil Pike) of Wayward Books, a bookstore on Capitol Hill.

Books: The Magician's Girl (Macmillan, 1987); The Ladies (Dutton, 1984); The Missing Person (Putnam, 1981); Chamber Music (Dutton, 1979); The Company She Kept (Coward-McCann, 1967): The Short Throat, The Tender Mouth (Doubleday, 1964); The Spoil of the Flowers (Dday, 1962).

Ann Hood   Novelist. Former flight attendant, TWA Airlines.

Books: Waiting to Vanish (Bantam Books, 1988); Somewhere Off the Coast of Maine (Bantam, 1987).

David Hoof   Novelist.

Books: Foley Effects (New American Library, 1989).

David Ignatius   Novelist, journalist, editor. Editor, Outlook, *The Washington Post.* Former Middle East correspondent, *The Wall Street Journal.*

Books: Agents of Innocence: A Spy Story (Norton, 1987).

Benita Jaro   Novelist, teacher, author.

Books: The Lock (Forthcoming), The Key (Crown, 1988).

Douglas Kiker   Novelist, television journalist. Correspondent, NBC News.

Books: Death at the Cut (Random House, 1988); Murder On Clam Pond (R Hse, 1986).

Michael Kilian   Novelist, author, journalist. Washington columnist, *Chicago Tribune.*

Books: Blood of the Czars (St. Martin's, 1985); Northern Exposure (St. Martin's, 1983); The Valkyrie Project (St. Martin's, 1981). *Nonfiction:* By Order of the President: Who Is Running the United States of America? (St. Martin's, 1986); Who Runs Washington? (with Arnold Sawislak, St. Martin's, 1982).

Larry L. King   Novelist, author, playwright, actor. Won TV Emmy, 1981; Mark Twain Citation, 1969.

Books: Because of Lozo Brown (Viking, 1988); The Old Man & Lesser Mortals (Viking, 1974); The One-

Eyed Man (New American Library, 1966). *Plays:* The Golden Shadows Old West Museum; The Night Hank Williams Died; The Kingfish; Christmas: 1933; The Best Little Whorehouse in Texas. *Nonfiction:* None But a Blockhead: On Being A Writer (Viking, 1986); Warning: Writer at Work (Texas Christian Press, 1985); Of Outlaws, Con Men, Whores, Politicians and Other Artists (Viking, 1980).

Joyce R. Kornblatt Novelist, short-story writer, teacher. Professor of literature and creative writing, University of Maryland.
  Books: Breaking Bread (Dutton, 1987); White Water (Dutton, 1985); Nothing to Do With Love (Viking, 1981).

Aaron Latham Novelist, author, journalist.
  Books: Perfect Pieces (William Morrow, 1987); Orchids For Mother: A Novel (Little, Brown, 1977). *Nonfiction:* Crazy Sundays: F. Scott Fitzgerald In Hollywood (Viking, 1971).

Jim Lehrer Novelist, author, journalist, television news anchor (MacNeil-Lehrer Report, PBS-TV).
  Books: Crown Oklahoma (Putnam, 1989); Kick the Can (Putnam, 1988). *Plays:* Chili Queen.

Kate Lehrer Novelist.
  Books: Best Intentions (Little, Brown, 1987).

Robert Lehrman Novelist. Director of speechwriting, Federal National Mortgage Association.
  Books: Defectors (Arbor House/ Morrow, 1988). *Nonfiction:* Juggling (Putnam, 1984).

Mary Lide Novelist, historian, poet. Won *Romantic Times'* New Historical Fiction Award, 1984.
  Books: Isobelle (Warner Books, 1988); A Royal Quest (Warner, 1987), Gifts of the Queen (Warner, 1985); Ann of Cambray (Warner, 1984).

Arnost Lustig Novelist, short-story writer, playwright, teacher. Professor of creative writing, literature and film history, American University.
  Books: Indecent Dreams (Northwestern University Press, 1988); Diamonds in the Night (Northwestern UPr, 1986); The Unloved: From The Diary of Perla S.

(Arbor House, 1985); Dita Saxova (Harper & Row, 1979); Darkness Casts No Shadow (Inscape, 1976); A Prayer For Katerina Horovitzova (H & R, 1973); Night & Hope (Northwestern UPr); Street of Lost Brothers.

Roderick MacLeish   Novelist, author, commentator (National Public Radio).
Books: Prince Ombra (Congdon & Weed, 1982); The First Book of Eppe: An American Romance (Random House, 1980); The Man Who Wasn't There (R Hse, 1976); A City on the River (Dutton, 1973); The Sun Stood Still (Atheneum, 1967); at least 5 others.

Charles McCarry   Novelist, author, journalist. Editor, *National Geographic Magazine.* Former CIA intelligence officer.
Books: The Bride of the Wilderness (NAL Books, 1988); The Last Supper (Dutton, 1983); The Better Angels (Dutton, 1979); The Secret Lovers (Dutton, 1977); Tears of Autumn (Dutton, 1974); The Miernik Dossier (Saturday Review Press, 1973). *Nonfiction:* For The Record: From Wall Street to Washington (with Donald Regan, Harcourt Brace Jovanovich, 1988); Caveat (with Alexander Haig, Macmillan, 1984); Citizen Nader (Saturday Review Press, 1972).

Abigail McCarthy   Novelist, author, columnist.
Books: A Separate Woman (Forthcoming, 1989); One Woman Lost (with Jane Muskie, Atheneum, 1986); Circles: A Washington Story (Doubleday, 1977). *Nonfiction:* Private Faces, Public Faces (Dday, 1972).

Jane McIlvaine McClary   Novelist, children's fiction writer.
Books: Maggie Royal (Simon & Schuster, 1981); A Portion For Foxes (S & S, 1972). *Children's Books:* Cinta's Challenge (1954); The Sea Sprite (1952); It Happens Every Thursday (1952); Front Page For Jennifer (1950).

Larry McMurtry   Novelist, screenwriter. Co-owner (with Marcia McGhee Carter) of *Booked Up,* a bookstore in Georgetown. Won Pulitzer Prize for Fiction, 1986.
Books: Anything For Billy (Simon & Schuster, 1988); Texasville (S & S, 1987); Lonesome Dove (S & S, 1985); The Desert Rose (S & S, 1983); Cadillac Jack (S & S,

1982); Somebody's Darling (S & S, 1978); Terms of Endearment (S & S, 1975); The Last Picture Show (Dial, 1966); Leaving Cheyenne (Popular, 1963); Horseman, Pass By (Harper & Row, 1961). *Films:* Hud, The Last Picture Show, others. *Nonfiction:* Film Flam: Essays on Hollywood (S & S, 1987).

William McPherson Novelist, book reviewer, editor. Former editor, Book World, *Washington Post* (1972–78); former senior editor, William Morrow & Company (1966–69). Won Pulitzer Prize for Criticism, 1977.
　Books: To the Sargasso Sea (Simon & Schuster, 1987); Testing the Current (S & S, 1984).

Lawrence Meyer Novelist, author, journalist. Editor, National Weekly Edition, *The Washington Post.*
　Books: False Front (Viking, 1979); A Capitol Crime (Viking, 1977). *Nonfiction:* Israel Now: Portrait of a Troubled Land (Delacorte, 1982).

Barbara Michaels Novelist, children's and mystery writer. Frequent book reviewer, *The Washington Post.* Judge, Edgar Awards, Mystery Writers of America. Also writes under the name Elizabeth Peters.
　Books: Shattered Silk (Atheneum, 1986); Be Buried in the Rain (Atheneum, 1985); Someone in the House (Dodd, 1981); The Wizard's Daughter (Dodd, 1980); Ammie Come Home (Meredith, 1968); at least thirty-five others.

James Michener Novelist, author. Won Pulitzer Prize for Fiction, 1948.
　Books: Journey (Random House, 1989); Legacy (R Hse, 1987); Texas (R Hse, 1985); Poland (R Hse, 1983); Space (R Hse, 1982); The Covenant (R Hse, 1980); Chesapeake (R Hse, 1978); Centennial (R Hse, 1974); The Drifters (R Hse, 1971); Iberia (R Hse, 1968); The Source (R Hse, 1965); Caravans (R Hse 1963); Hawaii (R Hse, 1959); The Bridge At Andau (R Hse, 1957); Sayonara (R Hse, 1954); The Floating World (R Hse, 1954); The Bridges At Toko-Ri (R Hse, 1953); The Fires of Spring (R Hse, 1949); Tales of the South Pacific (Macmillan, 1947).

Faye Moskowitz Short-story writer, essayist, teacher. Assistant professor, Department of English, George Washington University.

Books: Whoever Finds This, I Love You (David Godine, 1988); A Leak in the Heart (D Godine, 1985).

Kermit Moyer Novelist, author, teacher. Professor of English, American University.
Books: Tumbling (University of Missouri Press, 1988).

Phyllis Reynolds Naylor Novelist, author, children's and juvenile fiction writer.
Books: Unexpected Pleasures (Putnam's, 1986); Revelations (St. Martin's, 1979); In Small Doses (Atheneum, 1977); No Easy Circle (Follett, 1972). *Children's Books:* Beetles, Lightly Toasted (Macmillan, 1987); The Baby, the Bed & the Rose (Clarion, 1987); The Year of the Gopher (Atheneum, 1987); The Agony of Alice (Atheneum, 1985); The Dark of the Tunnel (Atheneum, 1985); Eddie, Incorporated (Atheneum, 1980); at least nineteen others. *Nonfiction:* How I Came to be a Writer (Atheneum, 1978); Crazy Love: An Autobiographical Account of Marriage and Madness (William Morrow, 1977).

Peter Ognibene Novelist, author, columnist.
Books: The Big Byte (Ballantine, 1984). *Nonfiction:* Scoop; The Life & Politics of Henry M. Jackson (Stein & Day, 1975).

Mark Olshaker Novelist, author.
Books: Unnatural Causes (William Morrow, 1986); Einstein's Brain (Evans, 1981). *Nonfiction:* The Instant Image: Edwin Land & The Polaroid Experience (Stein & Day, 1978).

Michele Orwin Novelist.
Books: Waiting For Next Week (Henry Holt, 1988).

Sally Quinn Novelist, journalist. Staff writer, Style Section, *The Washington Post;* former co-anchor, CBS Morning News.
Books: Regrets Only (Simon & Schuster, 1986). *Nonfiction:* We're Going To Make You A Star.

William Prochnau Novelist, author, journalist. Staff writer, *The Washington Post.* Alicia Patterson Fellow, 1988.
Books: Trinity's Child (Putnam, 1983). *Nonfiction:* A

Certain Democrat: Senator Henry M. Jackson, A Political Biography (Prentice Hall, 1972).

Barbara Raskin   Novelist, short-story writer, teacher. Former adjunct professor of creative writing, American University. Past president, Washington Independent Writers.
 Books: Hot Flashes (St. Martin's, 1987); Out of Order (Simon & Schuster, 1979); National Anthem (Dutton, 1977); Loose Ends (1973).

Robert Reiss   Novelist, author, journalist. Former reporter, *The Chicago Tribune*. Staff associate, Bread Loaf Writers' Conference, 1983.
 Books: Saltmaker (Viking, 1988); Divine Assassin (Berkeley, 1987); The Casco Deception (Little, Brown, 1983); Summer Fires (Simon & Schuster, 1980). *Nonfiction:* Franco Harris (Signet, 1977).

Marilyn Sharp   Novelist. Former editorial assistant, *The New Yorker*.
 Books: Firebird (Dutton, 1987); Falseface (St. Martin's, 1984); Masterstroke (R Marek, 1981); Sunflower (R Marek, 1979).

Sam Shepard   Playwright, poet, actor, film director.
 Books: Chicago & Other Plays (Applause Theater Books, 1988); Rolling Thunder Logbook (Limelight Editions, 1987); Fool For Love & Other Plays (Bantam, 1984); Hawk Moon: A Book of Short Stories, Poems & Monologues (PAJ Publications, 1981). *Films:* Far North; Paris, Texas; Zabriskie Point. *Plays:* Tooth of Crime, True West, Curse of the Starving Class, Fool For Love, Buried Child, Lie of the Mind.

Susan Richards Shreve   Novelist, children's and short-story writer, teacher. Professor of creative writing, George Mason University; visiting professor, Columbia University.
 Books: A Country of Strangers (Simon & Schuster, 1989); Queen of Hearts (S & S, 1987); Dreaming of Heroes (William Morrow, 1984); Children of Power (Macmillan, 1979); Loveletters (Knopf, 1978); A Woman Like That (Atheneum, 1977); A Fortunate Madness (Houghton Mifflin, 1974); Miracle Play. *Children's Books:* Lucy Forever & Miss Rosetree (Henry Holt, 1987); The Flunking of Joshua T. Bates (Knopf, 1984);

The Bad Dreams of a Good Girl (Knopf, 1982); at least nine others.

William Stevenson   Novelist, author, journalist, television writer and producer.
  Books: Boobytrap (Doubleday, 1987); Eclipse (Dday, 1986); The Ghosts of Africa (Harcourt Brace Jovanovich, 1980). *Nonfiction:* Intrepid's Last Case (Villard, 1984); A Man Called Intrepid (HBJ, 1980); The Bormann Brotherhood (HBJ, 1973); Zanek!: A Chronicle of the Israeli Air Force (Viking, 1971).

Judith Viorst   Novelist, poet, author, children's fiction writer.
  Books: Necessary Losses (Simon & Schuster, 1986); Love & Guilt & The Meaning Of Life (S & S, 1979). *Poetry:* When Did I Stop Being 20 & Other Injustices: Selected Poems From Single to Mid-Life (S & S, 1987); How Did I Get to be Forty & Other Atrocities (Caedmon, 1978); It's Hard to be Hip Over Thirty & Other Tragedies of Married Life (New American Library, 1968); at least two others. *Children's Books:* Alexander & the Terrible, Horrible, No Good, Very Bad Day (Atheneum, 1972); The Tenth Good Thing About Barney (Atheneum, 1971); I'll Fix Anthony (Harper & Row, 1969); at least five others.

James Webb, Jr.   Novelist, author, government official. Secretary of the Navy, 1987–88.
  Books: A Country Such as This (Doubleday, 1983); A Sense of Honor (Prentice Hall, 1981); Fields of Fire (Pr Hall, 1978).

Les Whitten   Novelist, author, poet, journalist. Former staff writer, *The Washington Post;* former associate reporter, Jack Anderson.
  Books: The Lost Disciple (Atheneum, 1989); A Day Without Sunshine (Atheneum, 1985); A Killing Pace (Atheneum, 1983); The Alchemist (Charterhouse, 1983); Sometimes a Hero (Doubleday, 1979); Conflict of Interest (Dday, 1976); Moon of the Wolf (Dday, 1967); Flowers of Evil.

Herman Wouk   Novelist, playwright, author. Won Pulitzer Prize for Fiction, 1952.
  Books: Inside, Outside (Little, Brown, 1985); War and Remembrance (L,Br, 1978); The Winds of War

(L,Br, 1971); Don't Stop the Carnival (Doubleday, 1965); Youngblood Hawke (Dday, 1962); This Is My God (Dday, 1959); Marjorie Morningstar (Dday, 1955); The Caine Mutiny: A Novel of World War II (Dday, 1952); The City Boy: The Adventures of Herbie Book-binder (Dday, 1950); Aurora Dawn (Simon & Schuster, 1947).

HUMOR

Russell Baker   Author, columnist ("All Things Considered," *New York Times*). Won two Pulitzer Prizes—Commentary (1979) and Autobiography (1983). Also won Frank Sullivan Award (1976) and George Polk Award (1979).

Books: The Good Times (William Morrow, 1989); The Norton Book of Light Verse (Norton, 1986, ed.); Growing Up (Congdon & Weed, 1982); The Rescue of Miss Yaskell & Other Pipe Dreams (Thorndike Press, 1981); So This Is Depravity (Congdon & Lattes, 1980); Poor Russell's Almanac (Doubleday, 1972); All Things Considered (Lippincott, 1965); No Cause For Panic (Lippincott, 1964); An American in Washington (Knopf, 1961).

Art Buchwald   Author, columnist, children's story writer. Won Pulitzer Prize for Commentary, 1982. Former Paris columnist, *NY Herald Tribune*.

Books: I Think I Don't Remember (Putnam, 1987); You *Can* Fool All of the People All of the Time (Putnam, 1985); While Reagan Slept (Putnam, 1983); Laid Back in Washington (Putnam, 1981); The Buchwald Stops Here (Putnam, 1978); Down the Seine & Up the Potomac with Art Buchwald (Putnam, 1977); "I Am Not A Crook" (Putnam, 1974); I Never Dreamed At The White House (Putnam, 1973); Getting High in Government Circles (Putnam, 1971); Counting Sheep (Putnam, 1970); The Establishment Is Alive & Well in Washington (Putnam, 1969); Have I Ever Lied to You? (Putnam, 1968); . . . And Then I Told the President (Putnam, 1965); I Chose Capitol Punishment (World Publications, 1963); at least five others. *Children's Books:* The Bollo Caper: A Furry Tail for Children of All Ages (Putnam, 1983).

Herblock   Author, editorial cartoonist. Cartoonist, *The Washington Post*, since 1946. Former editorial cartoonist, *Chicago Daily News.* Won Pulitzer Prize for Editorial Cartooning three times (1942, 1954 and 1979). Also has won Elijah Lovejoy Award (1986), Franklin Roosevelt Freedom Medal (1987) and many other honors.

Books: Herblock at Large (Pantheon, 1987); Herblock Through the Looking Glass (Norton, 1984); Herblock on All Fronts (New American Library, 1980); Herblock's State of the Union (Simon & Schuster, 1972); Herblock Special Report (Norton, 1974); The Herblock Gallery (S & S, 1968); Herblock's Special for Today (S & S, 1958); The Herblock Book (Beacon Press, 1952).

Jeff MacNelly   Author, editorial cartoonist. Created comic strip "Shoe." Won Pulitzer Prize for Editorial Cartooning three times (1972, 1978 and 1985).

Books: Shoe Goes to Wrigley Field (Bonus Books, 1988); Too Old For Summer Camp & Too Young to Retire (St. Martin's, 1988); The Greatest Shoe on Earth (Henry Holt, 1985); The Shoe Must Go On (Holt, 1984); A Shoe For All Seasons (Holt, 1983); On with the Shoe (Holt, 1982); The New Shoe (Avon, 1981); The Other Shoe (Avon, 1980); The Very First Shoe Book (Avon, 1978).

Judith Martin   Author, novelist, columnist ("Miss Manners"); children's writer.

Books: Common Courtesy (Atheneum, 1985); Miss Manners' Guide to Rearing Perfect Children (Atheneum, 1984); Miss Manners' Guide to Excrutiatingly Correct Behavior (Atheneum, 1982). *Fiction:* Style & Substance (Atheneum, 1986); Gilbert: A Comedy of Manners (Atheneum, 1982). *Children's Books:* I Won't Take A Bath (Paper Bag, 1987); Everybody, Everybody (Paper Bag, 1987); Reasons to be Cheerful (Paper Bag, 1985).

Diana McClellan   Author, columnist, editor. Washington editor, *Washingtonian Magazine.* Former gossip columnist, "Washington Ear."

Books: Ear On Washington: A Chrestomathy of Scandal, Rumor and Gossip Among the Capital's Elite (Arbor House, 1982).

Patrick Oliphant   Author, editorial cartoonist. Won Pulitzer Prize for Editorial Cartooning, 1967.

Books: Nothing Basically Wrong (Andrews & McNeel, 1988); Up to Here in Alligators (A&M, 1987);

Between a Rock and a Hard Place (A&M, 1986); But Seriously Folks (A&M, 1983); Ban This Book! (A&M, 1982); Oliphant! A Cartoon Collection (A&M, 1980); An Informal Gathering (Simon & Schuster, 1978); The Oliphant Book (S&S, 1969).

P.J. O'Rourke   Author, journalist, travel writer. Former editor-in-chief, *National Lampoon.*
Books: Modern Manners: An Etiquette Book for Rude People (Atlantic Monthly Press, 1989); Holidays in Hell: In Which Our Intrepid Reporter Travels to the World's Worst Places & Asks "What's Funny About This?" (Atlantic MPr, 1988); Republican Party Reptile (Atlantic MPr, 1987); The Bachelor Home Companion: A Practical Guide to Keeping House Like a Pig (Pocket Books/ Simon & Schuster, 1987).

Arnold Sawislak   Author, journalist. News Editor, *United Press International.*
Books: Dwarf Rapes Nun, Flees in UFO (St. Martin's, 1985); Who Runs Washington? (with Michael Kilian, St. Martin's, 1982).

Michelle Slung   Author, columnist. Editor, American Women Writers Series (NAL/ Plume). Former columnist, Book World, *The Washington Post.*
Books: The Only Child Book (Ballantine, 1989); Momilies & More Momilies (Ballantine, 1988); Crime on Her Mind (Pantheon, 1987); Momilies: As My Mother Used to Say (Ballantine, 1985); The Absent-Minded Professor's Memory Book.

NONFICTION

Bill Adler, Jr.   Author, journalist, book packager (Bill Adler, Jr. Publishing). President, Washington Independent Writers, 1988–89.
Books: How to Profit From Public Auctions (William Morrow, 1989); Smoking Wars: Nonsmokers' Rights In America (Wm Morrow, 1989); Outwitting Squirrels (Chicago Review Press, 1988); The Student's Memory Book (Doubleday, 1988); The Wit and Wisdom of Wall Street (with Bill Adler, Sr., Dow Jones-Irwin, 1984); The Home Buyer's Guide (Simon & Schuster, 1984); at least four others.

Thomas B. Allen Author, novelist, journalist, editor. Former book editor, *National Geographic Magazine.*
 Books: Merchants of Treason (with Norman Polnar, Delacorte, 1988); War Games (McGraw Hill, 1987); Rickover (with Norman Polnar, Simon & Schuster, 1982). *Fiction:* Ship of Gold (Macmillan, 1987); A Short Life (Putnam, 1978); The Last Inmate (Charterhouse, 1973).

Joseph Alsop Author, journalist.
 Books: F.D.R., 1882–1945: A Centenary Remembrance (Viking, 1982); From The Silent Earth: A Report on the Greek Bronze Age (Harper & Row, 1964); The Reporter's Trade (Reynal, 1958).

Susan Alsop Author, biographer.
 Books: Yankees at the Court: The First Americans In Paris (Doubleday, 1982); The Congress Dances (Harper & Row, 1984); Lady Sackville: A Biography (Dday, 1978).

Jack Anderson Author, investigative journalist, novelist, columnist. Won Pulitzer Prize for National Reporting, 1972.
 Books: Fiasco (Times Books, 1983); Confessions of a Muckraker (Random House, 1979); Inside Story (with Brit Hume, Doubleday, 1974); The Anderson Papers (R Hse, 1973). *Novels:* Control (Forthcoming); The Cambodia File (with Bill Pronzini, Doubleday, 1981).

Trevor Armbrister Author, journalist. Washington editor, *Reader's Digest.*
 Books: A Time to Heal (with Pres. Gerald Ford, Harper & Row, 1979); O Congress! (with Sen. Don Riegle, Doubleday, 1972); Act of Vengeance: The Yablonski Murders & Their Solution (Saturday Review Press, 1975); A Matter of Accountability: The True Story of the Pueblo Affair (Coward, 1970).

Scott Armstrong Author, journalist. Executive director, National Security Archives. Former staff writer, *The Washington Post.* Former senior investigator, Senate Select Committee on Presidential Campaign Practices.
 Books: The Brethren: Inside The Supreme Court (with Bob Woodward, Simon & Schuster, 1979)

Rick Atkinson Author, journalist. Staff writer, *The Washington Post.*
  Books: The Long Gray Line (Houghton Mifflin, 1989).

Donald C. Bacon Author, journalist. Assistant managing editor, *U.S. News & World Report.* Former staff writer, *The Washington Star, Wall Street Journal* and *Newhouse News Service.*
  Books: Rayburn: A Biography (with D.B. Hardeman, Madison Books, 1989); Congress & You; The New Millionaires; Reminiscences of D. B. Hardeman.

Michael Barone Author, journalist.
  Books: The Almanac of American Politics (National Journal, 1987).

Beryl Lieff Benderly Author, journalist.
  Books: The Myth of Two Minds: What Gender Means and Doesn't Mean (Doubleday, 1987); Dancing Without Music: Deafness in America (Anchor Press, 1980); Thinking About Abortion (Dial Press, 1984); Discovering Culture.

Lisa L. Berger Author, journalist. Former president, Washington Independent Writers.
  Books: Mind Flight (William Morrow, Forthcoming); Cashing In (Warner Books, 1988).

Michael R. Beschloss Author, historian. Adjunct historian, The Smithsonian Institution. Senior associate member, St. Anthony's College, Oxford.
  Books: Mayday: Eisenhower, Kruschev and the U–2 Affair (Harper & Row, 1986); Kennedy & Roosevelt: The Uneasy Alliance (Norton, 1980).

Tom Bethell Author.
  Books: The Electric Windmill (Regnery Gateway, 1987); Television Evening News Covers Inflation (Media Institute, 1980); George Lewis: A Jazzman from New Orleans (University of California Press, 1977).

Richard N. Billings Author, journalist, editor. Former editor, *Life* magazine and *Congressional Quarterly.*
  Books: Shirra (with Walter M. Schirra, Quinlan Press, 1988); So Close to Greatness: A Biography of William C. Bullitt (with Will Brownell, Macmillan, 1987); Sara

& Gerald: Villa America and After (with Honoria Donnelly, Henry Holt, 1984); The Plot to Kill the President (with G. Robert Blakey, Times Books, 1981); Power to the Public Worker (R.B. Luce, 1974).

Sidney Blumenthal   Author, journalist, columnist. Staff writer, *Washington Post*. Former writer, *The New Republic*.
   Books: Our Long National Daydream: A Political Pageant of the Reagan Era (Harper & Row, 1988); The Rise of the Counter-Establishment: From Conservative Ideology To Political Power (Times Books, 1986); The Permanent Campaign: Inside the World of Elite Political Operatives (Beacon Press, 1980).

Daniel Boorstin   Author, historian. Librarian of Congress (1975–87). Won Pulitzer Prize for History, 1974; many other honors.
   Books: Hidden History: Exploring Our Secret Past (Harper & Row, 1989); Image: A Guide to Pseudo-Events in America (Atheneum, 1988); The Discoverers: A History of Man's Search to Know His World & Himself (Random House, 1983); American Civilization: A Portrait for the 20th Century (McGraw Hill, 1972); The Americans: The Democratic Experience (R Hse, 1973); The Decline of Radicalism: Reflections on America Today (R Hse, 1969); The Americans: The National Experience (R Hse, 1965); The Americans: The Colonial Experience (R Hse, 1958); at least eight others.

Tom Boswell   Author, journalist, columnist. Sportswriter, *The Washington Post*. Won American Society of Newspaper Editors Award, 1981.
   Books: The Heart of the Order (Doubleday, 1989); Strokes of Genius (Dday, 1987); Why Time Begins on Opening Day (Dday, 1984); How Life Imitates the World Series: An Inquiry Into the Game (Dday, 1982).

Benjamin Bradlee   Author, editor, journalist. Executive editor, *The Washington Post*.
   Books: Conversations with Kennedy (Norton, 1974).

Howard Bray   Author, journalist. Former executive director, Fund For Investigative Journalism. Past president, Washington Independent Writers.
   Books: Pillars of the Post: The Making of a News Empire in Washington (Norton, 1980).

David Brinkley   Author, journalist, television news commentator ("This Week With David Brinkley," ABC-TV). Former co-anchor, The Huntley-Brinkley Report; former co-anchor (with John Chancellor), NBC Nightly News. Has won 10 Emmy Awards and three George Foster Peabody Awards.
   Books: Washington Goes to War (Knopf, 1988).

David Broder   Author, journalist. Staff writer, *Washington Post;* member of *Washington Post Writers Group.* Won Pulitzer Prize for Commentary, 1973.
   Books: Behind the Front Page: A Candid Look at How the News is Made (Simon & Schuster, 1987); Changing of the Guard: Power & Leadership in America (S & S, 1980); The Pursuit of the Presidency (Putnam, 1980); The Party's Over: The Failure of Politics in America.

Patrick Brogan   Author, journalist. Former Washington bureau chief, *London Times;* former editorial writer, *NY Daily News.*
   Books: Deadly Business: Sam Cummings, Interarms & the Arms Trade (Norton, 1983); Spiked.

Patrick J. Buchanan   Author, journalist, television commentator ("The McLaughlin Group" & Cable News Network).
   Books: Right from the Beginning (Little, Brown, 1988); Conservative Votes, Liberal Victories: Why the Right Has Failed (Quadrangle, NY Times, 1975).

David Burnham   Author, journalist. Former reporter, *The New York Times.*
   Books: Book on Internal Revenue Service (Forthcoming); The Rise of the Computer State (Random House, 1983).

Sophy Burnham   Author.
   Books: The Landed Gentry (Putnam, 1978); The Art Crowd (D. McKay, 1973). *Fiction:* The Dogwalker (Warner, 1979).

Jeremy Campbell   Author, journalist. Washington correspondent, *The London Evening Standard.*
   Books: Winston Churchill's Afternoon Nap: A Wide-Awake Inquiry into the Nature of Time (Simon &

Schuster, 1987); Grammatical Man: Information, Entropy, Language & Life (S & S, 1982).

Lou Cannon Author, journalist. Staff writer, *Washington Post;* member, Washington Post Writers Group.
   Books: Reagan (Putnam, 1982); Reporting: An Inside View (California Journal Press, 1977); The McCloskey Challenge (Dutton, 1972); Ronnie & Jesse: A Political Odyssey (Doubleday, 1969).

Lincoln Caplan Author, journalist.
   Books: The Tenth Justice: The Solicitor General and the Rule of Law (Knopf, 1987); The Insanity Defense and the Trial of John W. Hinckley, Jr. (D. Godine, 1984).

Jean Carper Author, journalist, columnist. Former television correspondent and producer, Cable News Network.
   Books: The Food Pharmacy: Dramatic New Evidence That Food Is Your Best Medicine (Bantam Books, 1988); Jean Carper's Total Nutrition Guide (Bantam, 1987); The All-In-One Calorie Counter (Bantam, 1987); Health Care USA (Prentice Hall, 1987); The National Medical Directory (Pr Hall, 1986).

Hodding Carter Author, journalist, television commentator. Former spokesperson, U.S. State Department.
   Books: The South (Bantam Books, Forthcoming); The Reagan Years (Braziller, 1988); The Angry Scar: The Story of Reconstruction (Greenwood, 1974); Their Words Were Bullets: The Southern Press in War (University of Georgia Press, 1969).

Nien Cheng Author. Widow of Chinese oil company executive; imprisoned in solitary confinement for seven years during Chinese Cultural Revolution.
   Books: Life & Death In Shanghai (Grove Press, 1986).

William S. Cohen Author, novelist, poet and U.S. Senator (R-Maine).
   Books: Men of Zeal: A Candid Story of the Iran-Contra Hearings (with Sen. George J. Mitchell, William Morrow, 1988); Of Sons & Seasons (Hamilton Press, pbk, 1987); Roll Call: One Year in the U.S. Senate (Simon & Schuster, 1981). *Fiction:* The Double Man (with Gary Hart, William Morrow, 1985).

James Conaway   Author.
Books: The Texans (Knopf, 1976); Judge: The Life and Times of Leander Perez (Knopf, 1973). *Fiction:* World's End (Knopf, 1976).

A. Craig Copetas   Author, journalist. National correspondent, *Regardie's* magazine.
Books: Metal Men: Marc Rich and the $10 Billion Scam (Putnam, 1985).

Marcus Cunliffe   Author, historian.
Books: American Presidents and the Presidency (HM, 1986); The Literature of the United States (4th edition, Penguin, 1986); The Age of Expansion, 1848–1917 (Merriam, 1979); The Ages of Man: From Savage to Sewage (Heritage, 1971); at least 5 others.

Nicholas Daniloff   Author, journalist. Former Moscow correspondent, *U.S. News & World Report.*
Books: Two Lives, One Russia (Houghton Mifflin, 1988); The Kremlin & the Cosmos (Knopf, 1972).

Leon Dash   Author, journalist. Staff writer, *The Washington Post.*
Books: When Children Want Children: The Urban Crisis of Teenage Childbearing (William Morrow, 1989).

Deborah Davis   Author, journalist.
Books: Katherine the Great: Katherine Graham and *The Washington Post* (National Press, 1987); The Children of God: The Inside Story (Zondervan Publishing, 1984).

Mollie Dickenson   Author, journalist.
Books: Thumbs Up!: The Life & Courageous Comeback of White House Press Secretary Jim Brady (with Jim Brady, William Morrow, 1987).

Paul Dickson   Author, journalist. Former president, Washington Independent Writers.
Books: The Dickson Baseball Dictionary (Facts on File, 1989); Family Words: The Dictionary for People Who Don't Know a Frone from a Brinkle (Addison-Wesley, 1988); On Our Own (Facts On File, 1985); The Great American Ice Cream Book (Atheneum, 1972); Think Tanks (Atheneum, 1971); The Official Rules (De-

lacorte, 1978); The Library In America (Facts on File, 1986); at least twenty others.

John Dinges   Author, journalist.
Books: Assassination on Embassy Row (with Saul Landau, Pantheon, 1980).

Jeane Dixon   Author, astrologer.
Books: Yesterday, Today, Forever (Andrews & Mc-Meel, 1987); Horoscopes for Dogs (Houghton Mifflin, 1979); Jeane Dixon's Astrological Cookbook (William Morrow, 1976); The Call to Glory: Jeane Dixon Speaks of Jesus (Wm Morrow, 1971); My Life & Prophecies (Wm Morrow, 1969).

Dusko Doder   Author, journalist. Former Moscow bureau chief, *The Washington Post.*
Books: Shadows & Whispers: Power Politics Inside The Kremlin from Brezhnev to Gorbachev (Random House, 1986); The Yugoslavs (R Hse, 1978).

Sam Donaldson   Author, journalist, television news reporter. White House correspondent, ABC-TV News.
Books: Hold On, Mr. President! (Random House, 1987).

Robert J. Donovan   Author, journalist. Former bureau chief, *The Los Angeles Times* and *The New York Herald Tribune.*
Books: The Second Victory: The Marshall Plan & The Postwar Revival of Europe (Madison Books, 1987); Nemesis: Truman & Johnson in the Coils of War in Asia (St. Martin's, 1984); Tumultuous Years: The Presidency of Harry S. Truman, 1949–53 (Norton, 1982); Conflict & Crisis: The Presidency of Harry S. Truman, 1945–48 (Norton, 1977); The Future of the Republican Party (New American Library, 1964); PT–109: John F. Kennedy in World War II (McGraw Hill, 1961); Eisenhower: The Inside Story (Harper & Row, 1956); The Assassins (H & R, 1955).

Len Downie   Author, editor, journalist. Managing editor, *The Washington Post.*
Books: The New Muckrakers (New Republic Books, 1976); Justice Denied: The Case for Reform of the Courts (Praeger, 1971); Mortgage on America (Praeger, 1971).

Elizabeth Drew   Author, journalist, television commentator (Inside Washington). Regular contributor to *The New Yorker;* former Washington editor, *Atlantic Monthly.*
  Books: Election Journal: The Political Events of 1987–88 (Macmillan, 1988); Campaign Journal: The Political Events of 1983–84 (Macmillan, 1985); Politics & Money: The New Road to Corruption (Macmillan, 1983).

Pete Earley   Author, journalist. Former staff writer, *The Washington Post.*
  Books: Family of Spies: Inside the John Walker Spy Ring (Bantam Books, 1988); The Keys to the Kingdom (Bantam, 1988).

Terry Eastland   Author, journalist, editor. Resident scholar, National Legal Center for the Public Interest.
  Books: Counting by Race: Equality from the Founding Fathers to Bakke and Weber (with William Bennett, Basic Books, 1979); The Conservative Paradox.

Laura Elliott   Author, journalist. Senior writer, *Washingtonian Magazine.*
  Books: Shattered Dreams (with Charlotte Fedders, Harper & Row, 1987).

Steven Emerson   Author, journalist, editor. Senior editor, *U.S. News & World Report.* Won Investigative Reporters & Editors Award (1988).
  Books: Secret Warriors: Inside the Covert Operations of the Reagan Era (Putnam, 1988); The American House of Saud: The Secret Petrodollar Connection (Franklin Watts, 1985).

James Fallows   Author, journalist, editor. Washington editor, *The Atlantic.* Former editor, *The Washington Monthly;* former associate editor, *Texas Monthly.* Former chief speechwriter, President Jimmy Carter. Won American Book Award, 1981.
  Books: Human Capital (Houghton Mifflin, 1989); More Like Us: Making America Great Again (H Mifflin, 1989); National Defense (Random House, 1981).

John Feinstein   Author, journalist. Sportswriter, *Sports Illustrated.* Former sportswriter, *The Washington Post.*
  Books: A Season Inside: One Year in College Basketball (Villard Books, 1988); A Season on the Brink: A

Year with Bob Knight & the Indiana Hoosiers (Macmillan, 1986).

Suzanne Fields   Author.
Books: Like Father, Like Daughter: How Father Shapes the Woman His Daughter Becomes (Little, Brown, 1983).

Randall Fitzgerald   Author, journalist. Staff writer, *Reader's Digest.* Founding editor, *Second Look Magazine.* Former reporter, Jack Anderson & Capitol Hill News Service.
Books: When Government Goes Private: Successful Alternatives to Public Services (Universe Books, 1988); Porkbarrel (with Gerald Lipson, Cato Institute Press, 1984); The Complete Book of Extraterrestrial Encounters (Collier Bks, 1979).

Linda Bird Francke   Author, journalist, editor. Former contributing editor, *New York Magazine;* former editor, *Newsweek.*
Books: A Woman of Egypt (with Jihan Sadat, Simon & Schuster, 1987); Ferraro: My Story (with Geraldine Ferraro, Bantam Books, 1985); First Lady From Plains (with Rosalynn Carter, Houghton Mifflin, 1984); Growing Up Divorced: Children of the 80's (S & S, 1983); The Ambivalence of Abortion (Random House, 1978).

Jon Franklin   Author, teacher, science writer. Professor of journalism, University of Maryland. Won two Pulitzer Prizes—Feature Writing (1979) and Explanatory Journalism (1985). Also won James T. Grady Medal (1975) & Helen Carringer Award (NMHA, 1984).
Books: Molecules of the Mind: The Brave New Science of Molecular Psychology (Atheneum, 1987); Shock-trauma (with Alan Doelp, St. Martin's, 1980); Guinea Pig Doctors.

Frank Getlein   Author, journalist, editor.
Books: John Safer (J.J. Bimms, 1982); Mary Cassatt (Abbeville, 1980); The Washington, DC Art Review: The Art Explorer's Guide to Washington (Vanguard Press, 1980); Chaim Gross (Abrams, 1974); at least 7 others.

Georgie Anne Geyer   Author, journalist.
Books: Buying the Night Flight: the Autobiography

of a Woman Foreign Correspondent (Delacorte Press, 1983); The Young Russians (ETC Publications, 1975).

Jack Gillis   Author, consumer advocate, teacher. Communications department, Consumer Federation Of America. Part-time faculty, George Washington University.
   Books: The Car Book 1989 (Perennial Library/ Harper & Row, 1988); The Used Car Book 1989 (P Lib/ H & R, 1988); The Armchair Mechanic (with Tom Kelly, H & R, 1988); How to Keep Your Car Almost Forever (Putnam, 1987); The Childwise Catalog (with Mary Fise, Pocket Books, 1986).

Ronald L. Goldfarb   Author, attorney, literary agent.
   Books: The Writer's Lawyer: Essential Legal Advice for Writers and Editors In All Media (with Gail Ross, Times Books, 1989); Jails: The Ultimate Ghetto (Anchor Press, 1975); After Conviction (Simon & Schuster, 1973); Crime and Publicity (with Alfred Friendly, 20th Century Fund, 1967).

James M. Goode   Author, historian. Curator, Smithsonian Institution Building.
   Books: Best Addresses: A Century of Washington's Distinguished Apartment Houses (Smithsonian Institution Press, 1988); Capital Losses: A Cultural History of Washington's Destroyed Buildings (Sm InstPr, 1979); The Outdoor Sculpture of Washington, DC: A Comprehensive Historical Guide (Sm InstPr, 1974).

Hays Gorey   Author, journalist. Washington correspondent, *Time* magazine.
   Books: Pepper, Eyewitness to a Century (with Rep. Claude Pepper, Harcourt Brace Jovanovich, 1987); Mo: A Woman's View of Watergate (with Maureen Dean, Simon & Schuster, 1975); Nader & The Power of Everyman (Grosset & Dunlap, 1975).

Joseph Goulden   Author, journalist. Former reporter, *Dallas News;* former Washington bureau chief, *Philadelphia Inquirer.*
   Books: Fit To Print: A.M. Rosenthal & His Times (Lyle Stuart, 1988); Dictionary of Espionage (as Henry Sabecket, Stein & Day, 1986); The Death Merchant (Simon & Schuster, 1984); Korea: The Untold Story of the War (Times Books, 1982); The Best Years (Athe-

neum, 1976); The Superlawyers (Weybright & Talley, 1972); Meany (Atheneum, 1972); Truth is the First Casualty (Rand McNally, 1969); Monopoly (Putnam, 1968).

John Greenya   Author, journalist, novelist.
Books: Blood Relations: The Exclusive Inside Story of the Benson Family Murders (Harcourt Brace Jovanovich, 1987); Are You Tough Enough? (with Anne Burford, McGraw Hill, 1986); The Real David Stockman (St. Martin's, 1986); Guns Don't Die, People Do (with Pete Shields, Arbor House, 1981); Maxine Cheshire, Reporter (with Maxine Cheshire, Houghton Mifflin, 1978); For the Defense (with F. Lee Bailey, Atheneum, 1975); at least four others. *Fiction:* The Fifty Ford; One Punch Away; Love Four; Mystery in the Lower Case.

William Greider   Author, journalist, columnist. Contributing editor, *Rolling Stone.* Former assistant managing editor, *The Washington Post.*
Books: Secrets of the Temple: How the Federal Reserve Runs the Country (Simon & Schuster, 1987); The Education of David Stockman & Other Americans (Dutton, 1982).

Jerry Hagstrom   Author, journalist. Contributing editor, *National Journal.*
Books: Beyond Reagan: The New Landscape of American Politics (Norton, 1988); The Book Of America (with Neal Pierce, Norton, 1983).

Gilbert Harrison   Author, editor, biographer. Former owner and editor, *The New Republic.*
Books: The Enthusiast: A Life of Thornton Wilder (Ticknor & Fields); A Timeless Affair: The Life of Anita McCormick Blaine (University of Chicago Press, 1979); The Critic As Artist: Essays on Books, 1920–70 (Liveright, 1972); Gertrude Stein's America (R.B. Luce, 1965).

Robin Marantz Henig   Author, journalist, medical writer. Regular contributor, "Body & Mind," *New York Times Magazine.*
Books: How A Woman Ages (Ballantine, 1985); Your Premature Baby (Rawson Associates, 1983); The Myth of Senility: The Truth About the Brain & Aging (Doubleday, 1981).

Carl F. H. Henry   Author, theologian.

Books: Christian Countermoves in a Decadent Culture (Multnomah, 1986); Horizons of Science: Christian Scholars Speak Out (Harper & Row, 1978); God, Revelation and Authority (Word Books, 1976); Baker's Dictionary of Christian Ethics (Baker Book House, 1973); Christianity Today, (Holt, 1962); at least 10 others.

John Herbers   Author.

Books: The New Heartland: America's Flight Beyond the Suburbs and How it is Changing Our Future (Times Books, 1986); No Thank You, Mr. President (Norton, 1976); The Black Dilemma (Stein & Day, 1973); The Lost Priority: What Happened to the Civil Rights Movement in America? (Funk, 1970).

Seymour M. Hersh   Author, journalist. Former reporter for United Press International and *The New York Times* (1972–79). Contributing editor, *Atlantic Monthly.* Won Pulitzer Prize for International Reporting, 1970; four George Polk Awards (1970, 1974, 1975 and 1981).

Books: "The Target is Destroyed": What Really Happened To Flight 007 & What America Knew About It (Random House, 1986); The Price of Power: Kissinger in the White House (Summit Books, 1983); Coverup: The Army's Secret Investigation of the Massacre At My Lai 4 (Random House, 1972); Chemical & Biological Warfare: America's Hidden Arsenal (Bobbs Merrill, 1968).

Mark Hertsgaard   Author, journalist.

Books: On Bended Knee: The Press & The Reagan Presidency (Farrar, Straus & Giroux, 1988); Nuclear Inc.: The Men & the Money Behind Nuclear Energy (Pantheon, 1983).

Roy Hoopes   Author, journalist. Washington bureau chief, *Modern Maturity Magazine.* Former editor, *Washingtonian Magazine, National Geographic* and *High Fidelity.*

Books: The Making of a Mormon Apostle: A Biography of Rudger Clawson (Madison Books, 1989); Ralph Ingersoll: A Biography (Atheneum, 1985); Cain: A Biography of James M. Cain (Holt, 1982); Political Campaigning (Franklin Watts, 1979); Americans Remember the Home Front (Hawthorne, 1977); The Peace Corps Experience (Clarkson Potter, 1968).

Russell Warren Howe   Author, novelist, journalist. Former foreign correspondent, *The Washington Post*. President, Foreign Policy Correspondents Association.
   Books: The Koreans: Passion and Grace (Harcourt Brace Jovanovich, 1988); Mata Hari—The True Story (Dodd Mead, 1986); Weapons: The International Game of Arms, Money & Diplomacy (Doubleday, 1980); The Power Peddlers (Dday, 1977); Black Africa; The African Revolution (Barnes & Noble, 1968). *Novels:* The Siberian Riviera (Forthcoming).

Mark Hulbert   Author, columnist, editor, publisher. Editor, *The Hulbert Financial Digest* and president, Minerva Books. Regular columnist, *Forbes Magazine* ("The Wall Street Irregular").
   Books: The Hulbert Guide to Financial Newsletters (Probus Publishing, 1989); Interlock: The Untold Story of American Banks, Oil Interests, The Shah's Money, Debts & The Astounding Connection Between Them (Richardson & Snyder, 1982).

Brit Hume   Author, journalist, television news reporter. White House correspondent, ABC-TV News.
   Books: Inside Story (Doubleday, 1974); Death & The Mines: Rebellion & Murder in the United Mine Workers (Grossman, 1971).

James Humes   Author, journalist, public speaker, actor. Former White House speech writer.
   Books: Bully Pulpit: Presidential Speeches that have Shaped History (Forthcoming); Standing Ovation: How to be an Effective Speaker and Commentator (Harper & Roe, 1988); Churchill: Speaker of the Century (Stein & Day, 1980); Talk Your Way to the Top (McGraw-Hill, 1980); How to Get Invited to the White House . . . And Over One-Hundred Impressive Gambits, Foxy Face Saves & Clever Maneuvers (Crowell, 1977); at least 4 others.

Brooks Jackson   Author, journalist.
   Books: Honest Graft: Big Money & The Political Process (Knopf, 1988).

John Jenkins   Author, journalist.
   Books: The Litigators (Doubleday, 1989).

Haynes Johnson Author, journalist, television commentator ("Washington Week in Review"). Won Pulitzer Prize for National Reporting, 1966.

Books: The Reagan Revolution; In the Absence of Power: Governing America (Viking, 1980); The Working White House (Praeger, 1975); Lyndon (with Richard Harwood, Praeger, 1973); Army in Anguish (Pocket Books, 1972); Fulbright: The Dissenter (Doubleday, 1968); The Bay of Pigs: The Leader's Story of Brigade 2506 (Norton, 1964). *Fiction:* The Landing: A Novel of Washington & WW II (with Howard Simons, Villard, 1986).

Rochelle Jones Author. Press secretary/ health care advisor, Rep. Claude Pepper (D-Fla).

Books: The Super Meds: How Private For-Profit Medical Organizations Are Controlling Our Health Care & What to do About It (Scribner's, 1987); The Big Switch: New Careers, New Lives After 35 (McGraw Hill, 1980); The Private World of Congress (with Peter Woll, Free Press, 1979); The Older Generation: The New Power of Older People (Prentice Hall, 1977).

Larry Kahaner Author, journalist.

Books: Cults That Kill: Probing The Underworld of Occult Crime (Warner Books, 1988); On the Line: The Men of MCI Who Took on AT & T, Risked Everything And Won! (Warner, 1986); The Phone Book: The Most Complete Guide to the Changing World of Telephones (Penguin, 1983).

Robert Kaiser Author, journalist. Staff writer, *The Washington Post.*

Books: Russia from the Inside (Dutton, 1980); Great American Dreams: A Portrait of the Way We Are (Harper & Row, 1979); Russia: The People & The Power (Atheneum, 1976); Cold Winter, Cold War (Stein & Day, 1974).

Fred Kaplan Author, biographer, historian.

Books: Dickens: A Biography (Morrow, 1988); Sacred Tears: Sentimentality in Victorian Literature (Princeton University Press, 1987); The Wizards of Armageddon: Strategists of the Nuclear Age (Simon & Schuster, 1983); Thomas Carlyle: A Biography (Cornell University Presss, 1983); Dubious Specter: A Skeptical Look at the Soviet Nuclear Threat (Institute for Policy Studies, rev.

ed. 1980); Dickens and Mesmerism: The Hidden Springs of Fiction (Princeton University Press, 1975); Miracles of Rare Device: The Poet's Sense of Self in Nineteenth-Century Poetry (Wayne State University Press, 1972).

Stanley Karnow   Author, journalist, columnist. Columnist, King Features. Former reporter for *Time, Washington Post, New Republic* and NBC News.
   Books: In Our Image: America's Empire in the Phillipines (Random House, 1989); Vietnam: A History (Viking, 1983); Mao & China: From Revolution to Revolution (Viking, 1972).

Walter Karp   Author, historian.
   Books: Liberty Under Seige: American Politics, 1976–88 (Henry Holt, 1988); The Politics of War (Harper & Row, 1979); Indispensable Enemies: The Politics of Misrule in America (Saturday Review Press, 1973); The Smithsonian Institution (American Heritage, 1965).

Kitty Kelley   Author, journalist, celebrity biographer. Former staffer, *The Washington Post.* Won Outstanding Author Award, American Society of Journalists & Authors (1987). Also won Philip M. Stern Award, Washington Independent Writers (1987)
   Books: Unauthorized biography of Nancy Reagan (Simon & Schuster, Forthcoming); His Way: The Unauthorized Biography of Frank Sinatra (Bantam Books, 1986); Elizabeth Taylor: The Last Star (S & S, 1981); Jackie Oh! (Lyle Stuart, 1978); The Glamour Spas.

Brian Kelly   Author, editor, journalist. Editor, *Regardie's* magazine.
   Books: Amazon (with Mark London, Harcourt Brace Jovanovich, 1983); The Four Little Dragons.

Marguerite Kelly   Author, journalist, columnist ("The Family Almanac").
   Books: The Mother's Almanac II: Your Child From 6–12 (Doubleday, 1989) The Mother's Almanac (with Ella Parsons, Doubleday, 1975).

Tom Kelly   Author, journalist, editor. Feature writer, *The Washington Times.* Former reporter and contributing editor, *Washingtonian Magazine* and *Washington Daily News* (1954–65).
   Books: The Imperial Post: The Meyers, The Grahams

& The Paper That Rules Washington (William Morrow, 1983); Murders: Washington's Most Famous Murder Stories (Washingtonian Books, 1976).

Ronald Kessler   Author, journalist. Former staff writer, *The Washington Post.*
   Books: Moscow Station: How The KGB Penetrated The American Embassy (Scribners, 1989); Spy vs. Spy: Stalking Soviet Spies in America (Scribner's, 1988); Adnan Khashoggi: The Story of the World's Richest Man (Warner Books, 1986); The Life Insurance Game (Holt, 1985).

James J. Kilpatrick   Author, journalist, columnist, television commentator ("Inside Washington").
   Books: A Bestiary of Bridge (Andrews & McMeel, 1986); The Writer's Art (A & M, 1985); The Ear Is Human: A Handbook of Homophones & Other Confusions (A & M, 1985); The Smut Peddlers (Greenwood, 1973).

Florence King   Author, novelist.
   Books: Confessions of a Failed Southern Lady (St. Martin's, 1985); He: An Irreverent Look at the American Male (Stein & Day, 1978); Wasp, Where is Thy Sting? (Stein & Day, 1977); Southern Ladies and Gentlemen (Stein & Day, 1975). *Fiction:* When Sisterhood was in Flower, Viking, 1982).

Larry King   Author, television & radio talk show host, columnist.
   Books: Mr. King, You're Having a Heart Attack (with B.D. Colen, Delacorte, 1989); Tell it to the King (with Peter Occhiogrosso, Putnam, 1988); Larry King (with Emily Yoffe, Simon & Schuster, 1982).

Michael Kinsley   Author, journalist, columnist. Editor, *The New Republic.*
   Books: Curse of the Giant Muffins & Other Washington Maladies (Summit Books, 1987).

Philip Klass   Author, journalist. Senior editor, *Aviation Week & Space Technology.*
   Books: UFO Abductions: A Dangerous Game (Prometheus Books, 1988); UFOs: The Public Deceived

(Prometheus, 1986); UFOs Explained (Random House, 1975); UFOs Identified (Random House, 1968).

Philip Kopper   Author, journalist, editor of WETA's *Dial* magazine. Former staff reporter, *The Washington Post*.
   Books: The Smithsonian Book of North American Indians: Before the Coming of the Europeans (Abrams/ Smithsonian, 1986); Colonial Williamsburg (Abrams, 1986); The National Museum of Natural History (Abrams, 1982); The Wild Edge: Life and Lore of the Great Atlantic Beaches (Times Books, 1979).

Mary Lynn Kotz   Author, journalist. Contributing editor, *Artnews*. Former reporter, UPI.
   Books: Rauschenberg Himself (Abrams, 1988); Marvella: A Personal Journey (with Marvella Bayh, Harcourt Brace Jovanovich, 1979); Upstairs at the White House (with J.B. West, Coward, 1973); A Passion for Equality (with Nick Kotz, Norton, 1977).

Nick Kotz   Author, journalist, teacher. Professor of journalism, American University School of Communications. Former staff writer, *The Washington Post*. Won Pulitzer Prize for National Reporting, 1968; National Magazine Award, 1983.
   Books: Wild Blue Yonder: Money, Politics and the B–1 Bomber (Pantheon, 1987); A Passion for Equality (with Mary Lynn Kotz, Norton, 1977); Let Them Eat Promises: The Politics of Hunger in America (Prentice Hall, 1969).

Charles Krauthammer   Author, journalist, columnist. Regular contributor, *Time* magazine. Won Pulitzer Prize for Commentary, 1987.
   Books: Cutting Edges: Making Sense of the '80s (Random House, 1985); Intervention & The Reagan Doctrine (Carnegie, 1985).

Irving Kristol   Author, political analyst.
   Books: Reflections of a Neoconservative: Looking Back, Looking Ahead (Basic Books, 1983); Two Cheers for Capitalism (Basic Books, 1978); The American Commonwealth (Basic Books, 1976); The Americans (Lexington Books, 1976); America's Continuing Revolution (American Enterprise Institute, 1975); On the Democratic Idea in America, Harper & Row, 1972).

Donald Lambro   Author, journalist, political analyst.
   Books: Land of Opportunity: The Entrepreneurial Spirit in America (LB, 1986); Washington, City of Scandals: Investigating Congress and Other Big Spenders (LB, 1984); Fat City: How Congress Wastes Your Taxes (Regnery Gateway, 1980); The Conscience of a Young Conservative (Random House, 1976); The Federal Rathole (Random House, 1975).

Michael Ledeen   Author, journalist. Former governmental consultant in international affairs.
   Books: Perilous Statecraft (Scribners, 1989); West European Communism and American Foreign Policy (Transaction Books, 1987).

Matthew Lesko   Author, journalist, information specialist. President, Information USA.
   Books: The Investor's Information Sourcebook (Harper & Row, 1988); Getting Yours: The Complete Guide to Government Money (Penguin, 1987, 3rd ed.); Information USA (Viking, 1986); Lesko's New-Tech Sourcebook (Harper & Row, 1986); The Marketing Sourcebook (with Wendy Lesko, Warner Books, 1984).

Neil C. Livingstone   Author, commentator.
   Books: The Cult of Counterterrorism (Warner Books, 1989); Fighting Back (Lexington Books, 1986); The War Against Terrorism (Lexington, 1982).

Milton Lomask   Author, biographer & historian, teacher.
   Books: The Biographer's Craft (Harper & Row, 1986); The Spirit of 1787: The Making of Our Constitution (Farrar, Straus & Giroux, 1980); Aaron Burr: Conspiracy & Years of Exile (FSG, 1982); Aaron Burr: The Years from Princeton to Vice President (FSG, 1979); Andrew Johnson: President on Trial (FSG, 1960); Seed Money: The Guggenheim Story; at least twelve others.

Edward Luttwak   Author, military historian. Former Pentagon official.
   Books: Strategy: The Logic of War & Peace (Harvard University Press, 1987); On the Meaning of Victory: Essays on Strategy (Simon & Schuster, 1986); The Pentagon and the Art of War (S&S, 1985); The Grand Strategy of the Soviet Union (St. Martins Press, 1983); at least 6 others.

Kenneth Lynn   Author, literary biographer.
Books: Hemingway (Simon & Schuster, 1987); A Divided People (Greenwood Press, 1977); Visions of America: Eleven Literary Historical Essays (Greenwood Press, 1973); William Dean Howells: An American Life (HBJ, 1971); The American Society (Braziller, 1963); at least 4 others.

Joel Makower   Author, journalist, book packager (Tilden Press).
Books: Woodstock: The Oral History (Doubleday, 1989); The Map Catalog (Random/Vintage, 1987); Trend Watching: How The Media Create Trends And How to be the First to Uncover Them (with John E. Meriam, Amacom, 1988); Boom!: Talkin' 'Bout Our Generation (Contemporary Books, 1986); Office Hazards: How Your Job Can Make You Sick (Tilden Press, 1981).

Frank Mankiewicz   Author, journalist.
Books: Television & The Manipulation of American Life (Times Books, 1978); With Fidel: A Portrait of Castro & Cuba (Playboy Press, 1975); The U.S. vs. Richard Nixon: The Final Crisis (Quadrangle, 1975); Perfectly Clear: Nixon from Whittier to Watergate (Quadrangle, 1973).

Victor Marchetti   Author, novelist, intelligence officer. Former special assistant to the Deputy Director, Central Intelligence Agency.
Books: The CIA & The Cult of Intelligence (with John Marks, Knopf, 1974). *Fiction:* The Rope Dancer (Grosset & Dunlap, 1971).

David C. Martin   Author, novelist, journalist.
Books: Best Laid Plans: The Inside Story of America's War Against Terrorism (with John Walcott, Harper & Row, 1988). *Fiction:* A Wilderness of Mirrors (Harper & Row, 1980).

Christopher Matthews   Author, journalist, columnist, television & radio commentator (CBS Morning News, Mutual Broadcasting). Washington bureau chief, *San Francisco Examiner*. Columnist, King Features. Former senior aide, House Speaker Tip O'Neill.
Books: Hardball: How Politics is Played, Told by One Who Knows the Game (Summit Books, 1988).

Barbara Matusow Author, journalist, editor, television producer (NBC-TV & CBS-TV). Senior writer, *Washingtonian Magazine*. Former senior editor, *Washington Journalism Review*.
Books: The Evening Stars: The Making of the Network News Anchor (Houghton Mifflin, 1983).

Kathleen Maxa Author, journalist.
Books: The Prize Pulitzer: The Scandal That Rocked Palm Beach (with Roxanne Pulitzer, Villard Books, 1988); "This is Judy Woodruff at the White House" (with Judy Woodruff, Addison-Wesley, 1982).

Rudy Maxa Author, journalist. Senior writer, *Washingtonian Magazine*.
Books: Dare to be Great (William Morrow, 1977); Public Trust, Private Lust (with Marion Clark, Wm Morrow, 1977).

Jane Mayer & Doyle McManus Jane Mayer is a former White House correspondent for *The Wall Street Journal;* Doyle McManus is a Washington correspondent for *The Los Angeles Times*.
Book: Landslide: The Unmaking of the President, 1984–1988 (Houghton Mifflin, 1988).

Coleman McCarthy Author, journalist, columnist (*The Washington Post*).
Books: Involvements: One Journalist's Place in the World (Acropolis, 1984); The Pleasures of the Game: The Theory Free Guide to Golf (Dial Press, 1977); Inner Companions (Acropolis, 1975); Disturbers of the Peace: Profiles in Nonadjustment (HM, 1973).

Eugene McCarthy Author, poet, columnist, politician. Former U.S. Senator (D-Mn.) from 1959–71, former Presidential candidate (1968).
Books: Required Reading: A Decade of Political Wit & Wisdom (Harcourt Brace Jovanovich, 1988); Up 'Til Now: A Memoir of the Decline of American Politics (HBJ, 1987); The Ultimate Tyranny: The Majority Over The Majority (HBJ, 1980); at least ten others. *Poetry:* Ground Fog & Night: Poems (HBJ, 1979).

David McCullough Author, historian, journalist. Host, Smithsonian World TV series (from 1984); Chairman, Advisory Board, *American Heritage* magazine. Former staff writer, *Time* magazine, 1956–61. Won National Book Award for History, 1977; American Book Award for Biography, 1982.

Books: Mornings on Horseback (Simon & Schuster, 1981); The Path Between the Seas: The Creation Of The Panama Canal, 1870–1914 (S & S, 1977); The Great Bridge (S & S, 1972); The Johnstown Flood (S & S, 1968).

Luree Miller   Author, journalist, historian.

Books: Late Bloom: New Lives for Women (Grossett & Dunlap, 1979); On Top of the World: Five Women Explorers In Tibet (G & D, 1976). *Children's Books:* The Black Hat Dances: Two Buddhist Boys in the Himalayas (Dodd, Mead, 1987).

Nathan Miller   Author, journalist, historian and biographer.

Books: Spying for America: the Hidden History of U.S. Intelligence (Paragon House, 1989); F.D.R.: An Intimate History (Doubleday, 1983); The Roosevelt Chronicles (Dday, 1979); The U.S. Navy: An Illustrated History (American Heritage, 1977); The Founding Finaglers (D McKay, 1976); The Belarus Secret.

William Minter   Author, journalist. Contributing editor, Africa News Service.

Books: Operation Timber: Pages From the Savimbi Dossier (Africa World, 1988); King Solomon's Mines Revisited: Western Interests and the Burdened History of South Africa (Basic Books, 1986); The Imperial Brain Trust (with Lawrence Sharp, Monthly Review Press, 1977); Portuguese Africa & the West (Monthly RPr, 1974).

Morton Mintz   Author, journalist.

Books: President Ron's Appointment Book (with Margaret Mintz, St. Martins, 1988); Quotations from President Ron (with Margaret Mintz, St. Martin's, 1987); At Any Cost: Corporate Greed, Women and the Dalkon Shield (Pantheon, 1985); at least 3 others.

Dan E. Moldea   Author, journalist. Former president, Washington Independent Writers.

Books: Ashes to Ashes (Forthcoming); Dark Victory: Ronald Reagan, MCA & The Mob (Viking, 1986); The Hunting of Cain: A True Story of Money, Greed &

Fratricide (Atheneum, 1983); The Hoffa Wars: Teamsters, Rebels, Politicians & the Mob (Paddington Press, 1978).

John S. Monagan Author, biographer.
Books: The Grand Panjandrum: Mellow Years of Justice Holmes (University Press of America, 1988); Horace: Priest of the Poor (Georgetown University Press, 1985).

Edmund Morris Author, biographer. Won Pulitzer Prize for Biography, 1980.
Books: Forthcoming biography of Ronald Reagan (Random House, Forthcoming); Theodore Rex (Random House, 1988); The Rise of Theodore Roosevelt (Putnam, 1979).

Sylvia Morris Author, biographer.
Books: Biography of Clare Boothe Luce (Houghton Mifflin, Forthcoming); Edith Kermit Roosevelt: Portrait of a First Lady (Coward, 1980).

Daniel P. Moynihan Author, journalist, U.S. Senator (D-NY).
Books: Loyalties (Harcourt, Brace Jovanovich, 1989); Came the Revolution: Argument in the Reagan Era (HBJ, 1988); Family and Nation (HBJ, 1986); Counting Our Blessings: Reflections on the Future of America (Little, Brown, 1980); A Dangerous Place (LB, 1978); Coping: Essays on the Practice of Government (Random House, 1973); Toward a National Urban Policy (Basic Books, 1970); at least 10 others.

Bruce Allen Murphy Author.
Books: Fortas: The Rise & Ruin of a Supreme Court Justice (William Morrow, 1987); The Brandeis/ Frankfurter Connection: the Secret Political Activities of Two Supreme Court Justices (Oxford University Press, 1982).

Ralph Nader Author, lawyer, consumer advocate.
Books: More Action For A Change: Students Serving the Public Interest (Dembner Books, 1987); The Big Boys: Power & Position in American Business (with William Taylor, Pantheon, 1986); Who's Poisoning America? (Sierra Club Books, 1981).

John Naisbitt   Author, columnist, trend analyst.
Books: Megatrends Revisited (Forthcoming, 1989); Reinventing the Corporation: Transforming Your Job & Your Company for the New Information Society (with Patricia Aburdene, Warner Books, 1985); Megatrends: Ten New Directions Transforming Our Lives (Warner Books, 1982).

Robert A. Nisbet   Author, historian.
Books: The Present Age: Progress and Anarchy in Modern America (Harper & Row, 1988); Roosevelt and Stalin: The Failed Courtship (Regnery Gateway,1988); Conservation: Dream and Reality (University of Minnesota Press, 1986); History of the Idea of Progress (Basic Books, 1980); Twilight of Authority (Oxford University Press, 1975); The Social Philosophers (Cornell, 1973); Social Change and History (Oxford University Press, 1975).

Michael Novak   Author, columnist, novelist. George Frederick Jewitt Scholar in Religion & Public Policy, American Enterprise Institute.
Books: Free Persons & the Common Good (Madison Books, 1988); Will It Liberate? (Paulist Press, 1987); Human Rights & the New Realism: Strategic Thinking in a New Age (Freedom House, 1986); Toward A Theology of the Corporation (American Enterprise Press, 1981). *Novels:* Naked I Leave (Macmillan, 1970); The Tiber Was Silver.

Jerry Oppenheimer   Author, journalist.
Books: Biography of Barbara Walters (St. Martin's, Forthcoming); Rock Hudson.

Judy Oppenheimer   Author, journalist.
Books: Private Demons: The Life of Shirley Jackson (with Shirley Jackson, Putnam, 1988).

Robert Pack   Author, journalist, poet, literary critic. Senior writer, *Washingtonian Magazine.*
Books: Speaking Out (with Larry Speakes, Scribner's, 1988); Edward Bennett Williams for the Defense (Harper & Row, 1983); Jerry Brown: The Philosopher-Prince (Stein & Day, 1978).

John Pekkanen   Author, journalist. Senior writer, *Washingtonian Magazine.*

Books: M.D.: Doctors Talk About Themselves (Delacorte, 1988); My Father, My Son (with Elmo Zumwalt Sr. & Jr., Macmillan, 1986); Donor: How One Girl's Death Gave Life to Others (Little, Brown, 1986).

Mark Perry Author, journalist, editor. Editor, *The Veteran*, Vietnam Veterans Association of America. Former editor, *City Paper*. Former president, Washington Independent Writers.
Books: Four Stars: The Joint Chiefs of Staff and the American Military (Houghton Mifflin, 1989).

Joseph Persico Author, novelist, historian. Former chief speechwriter for Nelson A. Rockefeller; former Foreign Service officer.
Books: Biography of William Casey (Viking, Forthcoming); Edward R. Murrow: An American Original (McGraw Hill, 1988); The Imperial Rockefeller (Simon & Schuster, 1982); Piercing the Reich (Viking, 1979); My Enemy, My Brother: Men & Days of Gettysburg (Viking, 1977). *Fiction:* The Spiderweb (Crown, 1979).

Charles Peters Author, journalist, editor. Editor, *The Washington Monthly.*
Books: Tilting at Windmills: An Autobiography (Addison-Wesley, 1988); How Washington Really Works; Inside the System; Blowing the Whistle; The System.

Neal Pierce Author, journalist, columnist. Contributor and co-founder, *National Journal.*
Books: The Book of America (with Jerry Hagstrom, Norton, 1983); The Megastates of America; The People's President (Simon & Schuster, 1968).

Norman Polnar Author, biographer, naval expert.
Books: Merchants of Treason: America's Secrets for Sale (with Thomas B. Allen, Delacorte Press, 1988); Ship of Gold (wth Thomas B. Allen, Macmillan, 1987); Guide to the Soviet Navy (Naval Institute Press, 1983); Rickover: Controversy and Genius (with Thomas B. Allen, Simon & Schuster, 1982); Death of the Thresher (Chilton, 1964); Atomic Submarines (Van Nostrand, 1963).

John Prados Author, journalist, intelligence expert.
Books: Pentagon Games (Harper & Row, 1987); Pres-

idents' Secret Wars: CIA & Pentagon Covert Operations Since World War II (William Morrow, 1986); The Soviet Estimate: U.S. Intelligence & Soviet Strategic Forces (Princeton University Press, 1986); The Sky Would Fall—Operation Vulture: The U.S. Bombing Mission in Indochina, 1954 (Dial Press, 1983).

Peter Prichard   Author, journalist, editor. Editor, *USA Today*.
   Books: The Making of McPaper: The Inside Story of USA Today (Andrews & McMeel, 1987).

Daniel Rapoport   Author, journalist, publisher (Farragut Publishing). Former president, Washington Independent Writers.
   Books: Inside the House: An Irreverent Guided Tour Through the House of Representatives, from the Days of Adam Clayton Powell to those of Peter Rodino (Follett, 1975).

Richard Rashke   Author, journalist, screenwriter.
   Books: Runaway Father (Harcourt Brace Jovanovich, 1988); Capitol Hill in Black and White (with Robert Parker, Jr., Dodd Mead, 1986); Stormy Genius: The Life of Aviation's Maverick Bill Lear (Houghton Mifflin, 1985); Escape From Sobibor (H Mifflin, 1982); The Killing of Karen Silkwood (H Mifflin, 1981).

Coates Redmon   Author, journalist, editor. Executive director, Robert F. Kennedy Journalism Awards. Former producer, Children's Television Workshop; former speechwriter, Rosalynn Carter.
   Books: Come As You Are: The Peace Corps Story (Harcourt Brace Jovanovich, 1986).

Richard M. Restak   Author, psychiatrist, radio commentator (National Public Radio).
   Books: The Mind (Bantam Books, 1988); The Infant Mind (Doubleday, 1986); The Brain (Bantam, 1985); The Self Seekers (Dday, 1982); Premeditated Man: Bioethics & The Control of Future Human Life (Viking, 1975).

Roger Rosenblatt   Author, editor, journalist. Editor, *US News & World Report*.
   Books: Children of War (Anchor Press/Doubleday, 1983); Black Fiction (Howard University Press, 1974).

David Richards   Author, journalist. Drama critic, *The Washington Post.*
Books: Biography of William Inge (Forthcoming); Played Out: The Jean Seberg Story (Random House, 1981); George Buckner and the Birth of Modern Dance (State University of New York Press, 1977).

Gail Ross   Author, attorney, literary agent.
Books: The Writer's Lawyer: Essential Legal Advice for Writers and Editors In All Media (with Ronald Goldfarb, Times Books, 1989).

Betty Ross   Author, journalist, travel writer.
Books: Museum Guide of Washington, DC (Americana Press, 1988); How to Beat the High Cost of Travel (US News & World Report Books, 1977).

Carl T. Rowan   Author, columnist, television news commentator ("Inside Washington"). Former U.S. ambassador to Finland, director of the U.S. Information Agency and National Security Council official.
Books: You Can't Get There From Here (Little, Brown, 1986); Just Between Us Blacks (Random House, 1974); Wait Till Next Year (Random House, 1960); The Pitiful & the Proud (R Hse, 1956); South of Freedom (Knopf, 1952).

Richard Rubenstein   Author, teacher, political historian. Professor, George Washington University.
Books: Alchemists of Revolution: Terrorism in the Modern World (Basic Books, 1987); Great Courtroom Battles (Simon & Schuster, 1973); Left Turn: Origins of the Next American Revolution (Little Brown, 1973); Rebels in Eden: Mass Political Violence in the US (LB, 1970); The Lives of Asher Lev.

William Safire   Author, novelist, columnist. Writes political commentary and "On Language" column, *The New York Times.* Won Pulitzer Prize for Commentary, 1978.
Books: Take My Word For It (Times Books, 1986); I Stand Corrected: More on Language (Times Books, 1984); Before The Fall (Doubleday, 1975). *Novels:* Freedom (Doubleday, 1987), Full Disclosure (Doubleday, 1977).

Jerrold Schechter Author, journalist. Former correspondent, *Time* magazine. Former official, National Security Council.
Books: The Palace File (with Nguyen Tien Hung, Harper & Row, 1986); An American Family in Moscow (Little, Brown, 1975); The New Face of Buddha (Coward, 1967).

David Scheim Author, journalist.
Books: Contract On America: The Mafia Murder of President John F. Kennedy (Shapolsky Publishers, 1988).

Andrew Bard Schmookler Author, poitical analyst. Policy adviser, Search for a Common Ground.
Books: Out of Weakness: Healing The Wounds That Drive Us to War (Bantam Books, 1988); The Parable Of The Tribes: The Problem of Power in Social Evolution (Houghton Mifflin, 1986).

Martin Schram Author, journalist, television commentator (Cable News Network). National editor, *Washingtonian Magazine*. Former Washington bureau chief, Newsday; former White House correspondent, *The Washington Post*.
Books: The Great American Video Game: Presidential Politics in the Television Age (William Morrow, 1987); Running for President, 1976 (Stein & Day, 1977).

Meryle Secrest Author, journalist. Former reporter, *The Washington Post*.
Books: Salvador Dali (Dutton, 1986); Kenneth Clark: A Biography (Holt, 1984); Being Bernard Berenson: A Biography (Holt, 1979); Between Me & Life: A Biography of Romaine Brooks (Doubleday, 1974).

Tom Shales Author, critic, columnist. Television critic, *The Washington Post*. Movie reviewer, National Public Radio. Won Pulitzer Prize for Criticism, 1988.
Books: Legends: Remembering America's Greatest Stars (Random House, 1989); On the Air! (Summit Books, 1982); The American Film Heritage (Acropolis, 1972).

Elaine Shannon Author, journalist. Washington bureau reporter, *Time* magazine.

Books: Desperados: Latin Drug Lords, U.S. Lawmen & the War America Can't Win. (Viking, 1988).

Deborah Shapley   Author, journalist.
Books: Robert McNamara: Soldier of the American Century (William Morrow, 1986); The Seventh Continent: Antarctica in a Resource Age (Resources for the Future, 1986).

Neil Sheehan   Author, journalist. Former Vietnam bureau chief, United Press International (1962–64); former reporter for *The New York Times.* Won Pulitzer Prize for Nonfiction (1988), National Book Award for Nonfiction (1988), Investigative Reporters & Editors Award (1988), Page One Award, Drew Pearson Award and many others.
Books: A Bright Shining Lie: John Paul Vann & America in Vietnam (Random House, 1988); The Arnheiter Affair (Random House, 1971); The Pentagon Papers (Bantam Books, 1971).

Susan Sheehan   Author, journalist. Staff writer, *The New Yorker.* Won Pulitzer Prize for Nonfiction, 1983.
Books: A Missing Plane (Putnam, 1986); Kate Quinton's Days (Houghton Mifflin, 1984); Is There No Place on Earth for Me? (H Mifflin, 1982); A Prison & A Prisoner (H Mifflin, 1978); A Welfare Mother (H Mifflin, 1976); Ten Vietnamese (Knopf, 1967).

Christopher Simpson   Author, journalist. Assistant director, documentary film *Hotel Terminus* (1989 Academy Award winner). Won Investigative Reporters & Editors Award and Present Tense Award for History, *Present Tense Magazine* (both in 1988).
Books: Blowback: America's Recruitment of Nazis & Its Effect on the Cold War (Weidenfeld & Nicolson, 1987).

Patsy Sims   Author, journalist.
Books: Can Somebody Shout Amen! (St. Martin's, 1988); The Klan (Stein & Day, 1978); Cleveland Benjamin's Dead (Dutton, 1981).

Hedrick Smith   Author, journalist, television commentator (PBS series, "The Power Game"). Chief Washington correspondent, *The New York Times.* Won Pulitzer Prize for International Reporting, 1974.

Books: The Power Game: How Washington Really Works (Random House, 1987); The Russians (Times Books, 1983); Reagan the Man, the President (Macmillan, 1980).

Duncan Spencer Author, journalist, editor. Managing editor, *Fathers Magazine.* Former staff writer, *The Washington Star.*
Books: Facing The Wall: Americans at the Vietnam Veteran's Memorial (Macmillan, 1986); Conversations with the Enemy (with Winston Groom, Putnam's, 1983); Love Gone Wrong (New American Library).

James Srodes Author, journalist. Former president, Washington Independent Writers.
Books: Takeovers (with Ivan Fallon, Pantheon, 1987); Dream Maker: The Rise and Fall of John Z. Delorean (with Ivan Fallon, Putnam, 1983).

Susan Stamberg Author, journalist, National Public Radio host ("Weekend Edition"). Former NPR evening host, "All Things Considered."
Books: Every Night at Five (Pantheon, 1982).

Philip Stern Author, journalist. Former deputy assistant Secretary of State. Founder, Center for Public Financing of Elections. Founding member, Washington Independent Writers.
Books: The Best Congress Money Can Buy (Pantheon, 1988); Lawyers on Trial (Times Books, 1980); The Rape of the Taxpayer (Random House, 1973); The Oppenheimer Case (Harper & Row, 1969); O Say Can You See (Acropolis, 1968); The Shame of a Nation (with George de Vincent, Astor-Honor, 1965); The Great Treasury Raid (Random House, 1962).

I.F. Stone Author, journalist, publisher, editor. Former publisher and editor, *I. F. Stone Weekly.*
Books: The Trial of Socrates (Little, Brown, 1988); The War Years, 1939–1945 (L, Br, 1988); The Truman Era (L, Br, 1988); Underground to Palestine (Pantheon, 1978); Polemics and Prophecies, 1967–70 (Random House, 1970); In a Time of Torment (R Hse, 1967).

Michael Straight Author, novelist, art historian. Former arts administrator, National Endowment for the Arts.

Books: Nancy Hanks: An Intimate Portrait (Duke, 1988); After Long Silence (Norton, 1983); Caravaggio (Devon Press, 1979); Trial by Television and Other Encounters (Devon Press, 1979). *Fiction:* A Very Small Remnant (Knopf, 1963).

Paul N. Strassels Author, columnist, editor, tax expert. Former editor-in-chief, *Washington Tax & Business Report.* Former official, Internal Revenue Service.
Books: Money Matters: The Hassle-Free, Month-By-Month Guide to Money Management (with William B. Mead, Addison-Wesley, 1986); Paul Strassels' Quick & Easy Guide to Tax Management (Dow Jones-Irwin, 1986); The 1986 Tax Reform Act (Dow JIr, 1986); Strassel's Tax Savers (Times Books, 1985); All You Need to Know About The IRS (with William B. Mead).

Harry G. Summers Author, journalist, editor. Editor, *Vietnam Magazine.* Former military correspondent, *U.S. News & World Report.*
Books: On Strategy: A Critical Analysis of the Vietnam War (Presidio Press, 1982); The Vietnam War Almanac (Facts On File, 1985).

Joel Swerdlow Author, novelist, journalist.
Books: To Heal a Nation (with Jan Scruggs, Harper & Row, 1985); Beyond Debate: A Paper on Televised Presidential Whites (Priority Press, 1984); Remote Control (with Frank Mankiewicz, Times Books, 1978). *Fiction:* Code Z (Putnam, 1979).

Tad Szulc Author, journalist. Former foreign correspondent, *New York Times* (1953–72).
Books: Fidel: A Critical Portrait (William Morrow, 1986); The Illusion of Peace: Foreign Policy in the Nixon Years (Viking, 1978); The Winds of Revolution. *Fiction:* Diplomatic Immunity (Simon & Schuster, 1981).

Strobe Talbott Author, journalist, television commentator. Washington bureau chief, *Time* magazine.
Books: The Master of the Game: Paul Nitze and the Nuclear Peace (Knopf, 1988); Reagan & Gorbachev (with Michael Mandelbaum, Random House, 1987); Deadly Gambits: The Reagan Administration & the Stalemate in Nuclear Arms Control (Knopf, 1984); The Russians & Reagan (with Cyrus Vance, R Hse, 1984);

Endgame: The Inside Story of SALT II (Harper & Row, 1979).

Wallace Terry   Author, journalist, editor, radio and television commentator.
Books: Bloods: An Oral History of the Vietnam War (Random House, 1984).

Phyllis Theroux   Author, columnist (*Parents* magazine). Regular contributor, *New York Times* & *The Washington Post.*
Books: Night Lights: Bedtime Stories for Parents in the Dark (Viking, 1987); Peripheral Visions (William Morrow, 1982); California & Other States of Grace (Wm Morrow, 1980).

Evan Thomas & Walter Isaacson   Evan Thomas is Washington bureau chief of *Newsweek* magazine; Walter Isaacson is a senior editor of *Time* magazine.
Books: The Wise Men: Six Friends and the World They Made (Simon & Schuster, 1986).

Susan & Martin Tolchin   Susan Tolchin is professor of public administration at George Washington University; Martin Tolchin is a reporter for *The New York Times.*
Books: Buying Into America: How Foreign Money is Changing The Face of Our Nation (Times Books, 1988); Dismantling America: The Rush to Deregulate (Houghton Mifflin, 1983).

William Triplett   Author, journalist, playwright. Board member, Washington Independent Writers.
Books: Flowering of the Bamboo: A Bizarre International Mystery (Woodbine House, 1985).

Sheldon Tromberg   Author, teacher, screenwriter.
Books: Making Money, Making Movies (Vision Books, 1980).

Patrick Tyler   Author, journalist. Staff writer, *The Washington Post.*
Books: Running Critical: The Silent War, Rickover And General Dynamics (Harper & Row, 1986).

Morris K. Udall   Author, politician, U.S. Representative (D-Ariz). Former Presidential candidate, 1976.
Books: Too Funny to be President: Notes From the

Life of a Politician (Henry Holt, 1988); The Job of the Congressman (with Donald Tacheron, Bobbs Merrill, 1966).

Sanford J. Ungar   Author, journalist, teacher. Dean of the School of Journalism, American University.
Books: Estrangement: America and the World (Oxford University Press, 1985); Africa: The People and Politics of an Emerging Continent (Simon & Schuster, 1985); FBI (Little, Brown, 1976); The Papers and The Papers: The Legal and Political Battle Over the Pentagon Papers (Dutton, 1972); at least 2 others.

Jack Valenti   Author, journalist, association executive. Executive Director, Motion Picture Association of America. Former aide and speechwriter, President Lyndon Johnson.
Books: Speak with Confidence: How to Prepare, Learn & Deliver Effective Speeches (William Morrow, 1982); A Very Human President (Norton, 1975); The Bitter Taste of Glory (World Publications, 1971).

Milton Viorst   Author, journalist. Former staff writer, *Washington Post.* Former chairman, Fund for Investigative Journalism.
Books: Sands of Sorrow: Israel's Journey From Independence to Client State (Harper & Row, 1987); Fire in the Streets: America in the Nineteen Sixties (Simon & Schuster, 1981); Making a Difference: The Peace Corps at Twenty-Five (Wiedenfeld & Nicholson, 1986).

Marta Vogel   Author, journalist. Former president, Washington Independent Writers.
Books: The Babymakers (with Diana Frank, Carroll & Graf, 1988); Hassle-free Homework (Doubleday, 1989).

Nicholas Von Hoffman   Author, journalist. Former columnist, *The Washington Post.* Former reporter, *Chicago Daily News* and King Features Syndicate.
Books: Citizen Cohn: The Life & Times of Roy Cohn (Doubleday, 1988); Organized Crimes (Harper & Row, 1984); We Are the People Our Parents Warned Us Against (Elephant Books, 1989).

Ben J. Wattenberg   Author, novelist, editor, columnist. Senior Fellow, American Enterprise Institute. Co-editor, *Public Opinion* magazine. Radio commentator, CBS-Radio ("Spectrum").

Books: The Birth Dearth (Pharos Books, 1987); The Good News is the Bad News is Wrong (Simon & Schuster, 1984); The Real America: A Surprising Examination of the State of the Union (Doubleday, 1974); This USA (Dday, 1965). *Fiction:* Against All Enemies (with Ervin Duggan, Dday, 77).

Michael J. Weiss   Author, journalist. Contributing editor, *Washingtonian* magazine.

Books: The Clustering of America (Harper & Row, 1988).

Tim Wells   Author, columnist. Writes "Capital Pages" column, *Dossier* magazine.

Books: Uneasy Verdicts: A Narrative History of the 1968 Democratic National Convention (Viking, 1989); 444 Days: The Hostages Remember (Harcourt Brace Jovanovich, 1985).

George F. Will   Author, journalist, columnist, television news commentator (Inside Washington). Contributing editor, *Newsweek*. Won Pulitzer Prize for Commentary, 1977.

Books: Men at Work (Macmillan, Forthcoming); How We Lost the Cold War (Simon & Schuster, 1988); The Morning After: American Successes & Excesses, 1981–86 (Free Press, 1986); Statecraft as Soulcraft: What Government Does (S & S, 1983).

Juan Williams   Author, journalist, columnist. Staff writer, *The Washington Post.*

Books: Eyes on the Prize: America's Civil Rights Years, 1954–1965 (Viking, 1987).

George C. Wilson   Author, journalist. Staff writer, *The Washington Post.*

Books: Mud Soldiers: Life Inside the New American Army (Scribner's, 1989); Supercarrier: An Inside Account of Life Aboard the World's Most Powerful Ship, the USS John F. Kennedy (Macmillan, 1986).

David Wise   Author, novelist, journalist. Intelligence & espionage expert. Former Washington bureau chief, *New York Herald Tribune*. Won George Polk Award, 1974, Page One Award, 1969.

Books: The Spy Who Got Away: The Inside Story of Edward Lee Howard, The CIA Agent Who Betrayed His Country's Secrets & Escaped to Moscow (Random House, 1988); The Invisible Government (with Thomas B. Ross, 1964). *Fiction:* The Samarkind Dimension (Doubleday, 1987); The Children's Game (St. Martin's, 1983); Spectrum (St. Martin's, 1981).

Jules Witcover   Author, journalist, columnist (with Jack Germond, *Baltimore Evening Sun*). Former reporter, Newhouse Newspapers, *The Los Angeles Times* and *The Washington Post.*
   Books: Whose Broad Stripes & Bright Stars?: The Trivial Pursuit of the Presidency, 1988 (with Jack Germond, Warner Books, 1989); 85 Days: The Last Campaign of Robert Kennedy; The Resurrection of Richard Nixon; White Knight: The Rise of Spiro Agnew; Marathon: The Pursuit of the Presidency, 1972–76. *Fiction:* A Heartbeat Away.

Elder Witt   Author, journalist. Reporter, Congressional Quarterly. Won American Book Award, 19—.
   Books: A Different Justice: Reagan & The Supreme Court (Congressional Quarterly, 1985); Education for a Nation (CQtly, 1972); Crime & The Law (CQtly, 1971).

Bob Woodward   Author, journalist. Assistant Managing Editor, Investigative Staff, *The Washington Post.* Won George Polk Award, 1972.
   Books: Veil: The Secret Wars of the CIA, 1981–1987 (Simon & Schuster, 1987); Wired: The Short Life & Fast Times of John Belushi (Simon & Schuster, 1984); The Brethren (with Scott Armstrong, S & S, 1979); The Final Days (with Carl Bernstein, S & S, 1976); All the President's Men (with Carl Bernstein, S & S, 1974).

Jonathan Yardley   Author, literary critic. Book critic, Book World, *The Washington Post.* Won Pulitzer Prize for Criticism, 1981.
   Books: Our Kind of People: The Story of an American Family (Weidenfeld & Nicolson, 1989); Ring: A Biography of Ring Lardner (Random House, 1977).

POETRY

Carl Bode   Poet, author, teacher, journalist.
   Books: Sacred Seasons: Poems (AMS Press, 1953/ Reprint); Practical Magic: Poems (Swallow/Ohio Uni-

versity Press, 1981). *Nonfiction:* H.L. Menken: A Biography (Johns Hopkins, 1986); Highly Irregular: The Newspaper Columns of Carl Bode (Southern Illinois University Press, 1974); The Man Behind You (Dutton, 1969); at least 8–10 others.

Grace Cavalieri   Poet, author, radio host. Hosts "The Poet & The Poem," WPFW-FM Radio.
Books: Bliss (Hillmunn Roberts, 1986); Creature Comforts (Word Works, 1982); Swan Research (W Works, 1979).

Eric Cheyfitz   Poet, teacher. Instructor, Georgetown University.
Books: Bones & Ash (Cymric Press, 1977). *Nonfiction:* The Trans-Parent: Sexual Politics in the Language of Emerson (Johns Hopkins University Press, 1981).

Ann Darr   Poet, author.
Books: Do You Take This Woman? (Washington Writers' Publishing House, 1986); Riding with the Fireworks (Alicejamesbooks, 1981); Cleared for Landing (Dryad Press, 1978); The Myth of a Woman's Fist (William Morrow, 1973); Saint Ann's Gut (W Morrow, 1971).

Ralph De Toledano   Poet, author.
Books: Poems: You & I (Pelican, 1978); Lament for a Generation (Farrar, Straus & Giroux, 1960).

Roland Flint   Poet, teacher, author. Instructor, Georgetown University.
Books: Sicily (Wesleyan Press, 1987); Resuming Green: Selected Poems 1965–1982 (Dial Press, 1983); Say It (Dryad Press, 1979); And Morning (Dryad Press, 1975).

Carolyn Forche   Poet, teacher. Instructor, George Mason University.
Books: The Country Between Us (Harper & Row, 1982); Gathering the Tribes (Yale University Press, 1976).

O.B. Hardison, Jr.   Poet, editor, author, teacher. Professor of literature, Georgetown University. Former director, Folger Shakespeare Library.

Books: Pro Musica Antiqua: Poems (Louisiana State University Press, 1977); Lyrics and Elegies (1958). *Nonfiction:* The Princeton Handbook of Poetry (Princeton University Press, 1986); Entering the Maze: Identity & Change in Modern Culture (Oxford University Press, 1981); at least two others.

Anthony Hecht   Poet, literary critic, teacher. Professor of creative writing and literature, Georgetown University. Consultant in Poetry, Library of Congress (1982–84). Won Pulitzer Prize for Poetry, 1968.
Books: A Love for Four Voices (Penmaen Press, 1983); The Venetian Vespers (Atheneum, 1979); Millions of Strange Shadows (Atheneum, 1977); The Hard Hours: Poems (Atheneum, 1967). *Nonfiction:* Obbligati: Essays In Criticism (Atheneum, 1986); Jiggery-Pokery: A Compendium of Double Dactyls (Atheneum, 1966).

Philip K. Jason   Poet, author.
Books: Near the Fire (Dryad Press, 1983); Thawing Out (Dryad, 1979; Shaping: New Poems in Traditional Prosodies (Dryad, 1978).

Rod Jellema   Poet, author, teacher. Professor, University of Maryland.
Books: Eighth Day: New and Selected Poems (Dryad Press, 1984); Something Tugging The Line (1974).

Beth Joselow   Poet, author.
Books: The April Wars (SOS Books, 1983); Gypsies (Washington Writers Publishing House, 1979).

Peter Klappert   Poet, teacher. Professor of creative writing and literature, George Mason University.
Books: The Idiot Princess of the Last Dynasty (Knopf, 1984); Fifty-Two Pick-Up (Orchises Press, 1984); Circular Stairs, Distress in the Mirrors (Griffin Press, 1975); After the Rhymer's Guild (New Collage, 1972); Lugging Vegetables to Nantucket (Yale University Press, 1971).

Merrill Leffler   Poet, publisher, teacher. Publisher, Dryad Press.
Books: Partly Pandemonium, Partly Love (Dryad Press, 1982).

Chris Llewelyn   Poet. Won 1986 Walt Whitman Award, Academy of American Poets.

Books: Fragments from the Fire: The Triangle Shirt-waist Company Fire of March 25, 1911 (Viking, 1987).

William Meredith   Poet. Won Pulitzer Prize for Poetry, 1988.
Books: Partial Accounts: New & Selected Poems (Knopf, 1987); The Cheer (Knopf, 1980); Hazard, the Painter (Knopf, 1975); Earth Walk: New & Selected Poems (Knopf, 1970); Love Letter from an Impossible Land (AMS Press, 1944).

E. Ethelbert Miller   Poet, teacher. Director, Afro-American Studies Resource Center, Howard University.
Books: Where Are the Love Poems for Dictators? (Open Hand, 1987); Season of Hunger-Cry of Rain (Lotus, 1982); Migrant Worker (Washington Writers Publs, 1978); Synergy; An Anthology of Washington, DC Blackpoetry (editor, Energy Blacksmith Press, 1975).

May Miller   Poet, author.
Books: The Ransomed Wait (Lotus, 1983); Halfway to the Sun (Washington Writers Pub, 1981); Dust of Uncertain Journey (Lotus, 1975); The Clearing and Beyond (Charioteer, 1974); Not That Far (Solo Press, 1973).

Linda Pastan   Poet, teacher. Professor of creative writing and literature, American University. Regular instructor at Bread Loaf Writers Conference.
Books: The Imperfect Paradise (Norton, 1988); A Fraction of Darkness (Norton, 1985); PM/AM: New & Selected Poems (Norton, 1982); Waiting for My Life (Norton, 1981); The Five Stages of Grief (Norton, 1978); Aspects of Eve (Liveright, 1975); On the Way to the Zoo (1975); A Perfect Circle of Sun (1971).

Richard Peabody   Poet, editor, publisher. Editor, *Gargoyle* magazine; editor & publisher, Paycock Press.
Books: Echt & Ersatz (Paycock Press, 1985); I'm In Love with the Morton Salt Girl (Paycock Press, 1979). *Anthologies:* Fiction/ 86, 84 & 82 (co-editor/ with Gretchen Johnsen, Paycock Press). *Nonfiction:* Mavericks: Nine Independent Publishers (Paycock Press, 1983).

Stanley Plumly   Poet, essayist, teacher. Professor of English, University of Maryland.
Books: Summer Celestial (Ecco Press, 1983); Out-of-the-Body Travel (Ecco Press, 1976). *Essays:* Sentimental Forms.

Susan Sonde   Poet, author. Won Capricorn Poetry Prize, 1986.
Books: In the Longboats with Others (1988); Whose Woods These Are (Word Works, 1984); Inland is Parenthetical (Dryad Press).

Bradley Strahan   Poet, author.
Books: Poems (Barbara Allen, 1982); Love Songs for an Age of Anxiety (Black Buzzard Press, 1986).

Henry Taylor   Poet, author, teacher. Professor of creative writing and literature, American University. Won Pulitzer Prize for Poetry, 1986.
Books: The Flying Change (Louisiana State University Press, 1985); Desperado (1979), An Afternoon of Pocket Billiards (University of Utah Press, 1975); Breakings (1971); The Horseshow at Midnight (1966).

Susan Tichy   Poet, author, teacher. Professor, George Mason University.
Books: The Hands in Exile (Random House, 1983); A Smell of Burning Starts the Day (Wesleyan University Press, 1988).

Reed Whittemore   Poet, author, teacher. Editor, *Delos.* Professor emeritus, English Department, University of Maryland. Former literary editor, *The New Republic.* Former Consultant in Poetry, Library of Congress (1964–65). Award of Merit, American Academy of Arts & Letters.
Books: The Feel of the Rock: Poems of Three Decades (Dryad, 1982); Fifty Poems Fifty (Univ of Minnesota Press, 1970); Heroes & Heroines (1946); An American Takes a Walk; The Self-Made Man; The Boy From Iowa; The Fascination of the Abomination; The Mother's Breast and the Father's House (1974). *Nonfiction:* Pure Lives: The Early Biographers (Johns Hopkins Press, 1988); William Carlos Williams: Poet From Jersey (Houghton Mifflin, 1975).

Katharine Zadravec Poet, author, journalist, teacher. Former columnist, *The Washington Post* ("Anne's Reader Exchange" for thirty years.). Former administrator, PEN-Faulkner Award for Fiction.

Books: Imitations (1988); How to Travel (SCOP Publications, 1987); Shewski's Ladder.

Book Publishers

Publishers are to writers what wells are to underground rivers: someone has to put up the money to dig down and tap that water so we can drink.

This is not to suggest that, like water, all publishing houses are essentially alike. Each house, in fact, is quite unique, reflecting the tastes and interests of the people who run them. A writer or reader can learn a lot about a publisher by studying the kinds of books the publisher chooses to print. Some publishers stake out a limited market with specialized titles (military, business, poetry, etc.). Other publishers are generalists, choosing to span the entire spectrum of book categories as general or "trade" publishers and selling their books primarily through bookstores.

Locally, we enjoy a growing number of excellent book publishers in all categories: general trade, academic and public policy, literary, mail order/specialty and professional/business. With so deep a pool of writing talent here, this is not surprising. I expect the total number of local trade publishers to at least double within the next five years.

For a writer to be selected by any of these local houses for publication is an achievement. As for *how* a book gets published, distributed and promoted, each house operates by its own methods and tastes. Which is to say that, in this imperfect world, writers may face some tough decisions.

A particular publishing house may have an astute "acquiring" editor but not a lauded "editing" editor.

The house may be unimaginative in the design of its books and use inferior materials, but it may very well have a track record that shows it really knows how to place and promote books. Furthermore, submitting writers should make certain that their manuscripts complement what a publisher has brought out in the past or has a mind to pursue.

In recent years, major New York publishers have taken a stronger interest in the wealth of book ideas and writers in Washington. Simon & Schuster has recently opened a branch office here (headed by vice president and senior editor Marie Arana-Ward), and other major New York houses have acquiring editors who live and work here. Additionally, some Big Apple publishers like Random House send certain editors (David Rosenthal, Peter Osnos) down to Washington regularly to seek out good material.

In most cases, however, writers do a better job of finding publishers than the other way around. I hope this list helps. And if, for some unfortunate reason, your manuscript gets returned, just remember what Edna St. Vincent Millay said about all publishers:

> A person who publishes a book willfully appears before the populace with his pants down. . . . If it is a good book, nothing can hurt him. If it is a bad book, nothing can help him.

GENERAL TRADE

Acropolis Books   Nonfiction (current issues, leisure & family, self-help, fashion & beauty, contemporary education, biography). Hardcover and paperback originals; adult titles only. Averages 25 books p/year.

John R. Hackl, President & Publisher, Colortone Building, 2400 17th Street, NW, Washington, DC 20009; (202) 387-6805/(800) 451-7771.

Bartleby Press   Nonfiction (history, some international affairs) Hardcover and some paperback originals; adult and young adult titles. Averages 4 books p/year.

Jeremy Kay, Publisher, 11141 Georgia Avenue, Ste. A6, Silver Spring, MD 20902; (301) 949-2443.

Joseph J. Binns Publisher   Nonfiction (general topics, foreign co-publishing, hardcover reprints of classics).

Hardcover and paperback originals; adult titles only. Averages 10 books p/year. Distributed by Robert B. Luce, Inc.

Joseph J. Binns, President & Editor, 6919 Radnor Road, Bethesda, MD 20817; (301) 320-3327/(800) 243-2790.

Corkscrew Press Nonfiction (cookbooks, how-to books, humor) and some fiction. Paperback originals; adult titles only. Averages 4 books p/year.

Richard Lippmann, President, 2915 Fenimore Road, Silver Spring, MD 20902; (301) 933-0407.

EPM Publications Nonfiction (Americana, history, cookbooks, crafts, quilt books, self-help, social sciences, recreation, regional guides). Hardcover and paperback originals; adult and children's titles. Averages 8–10 books p/year.

Evelyn Metzger, President & Editor, 1003 Turkey Run Road, McLean, VA 22101; (703) 442-7810.

Farragut Publishing Nonfiction (cookbooks, regional guides, politics, general interest subjects). Paperback originals; adult titles only. Averages 1–2 books p/year.

Dan Rapoport, Publisher, 3804 Jenifer Street, NW, Washington, DC 20015; (202) 364-8093.

Great Ocean Publishers Nonfiction (literature, biography, health, philosophy, crafts, music, how-to, illustrated books, reference, self-help). Hardcover and trade paperback originals, reprints; adult titles only. Averages 3–5 titles p/year.

Mark Esterman, President & Editor-in-Chief, 1823 North Lincoln Street, Arlington, VA 22207; (703) 525-0909.

Gryphon House Nonfiction (educational activity books, teaching materials, how-to projects). Paperback originals; children's titles only (ages 1–5). Distributor for a number of smaller presses, including Building Blocks Press, First Teacher Press and others. Averages 4–5 titles p/year.

Larry Rood, President & Editor, 3706 Otis Street, Mt. Rainier, MD 20712; (301) 779-6200/(800) 638-0928.

Hero Books Nonfiction (military history, national security, political science, history and military science,

Russian studies). Hardcover and paperback originals, some reprints; adult titles only. Distributor for Dixie Publishing Company and Seven Locks Press. Averages 40 books p/year.

Guy P. Clifton, Publisher, 10392 Democracy Lane, Fairfax, VA 22030; (703) 591-6109.

Kar-Ben Copies Nonfiction (Jewish life-cycle, holidays and customs, Judaica) and fiction (Jewish adventure, fantasy, historical and religious). Hardcover and paperback originals; children's and juvenile titles only. Averages 8–10 books p/year.

Judyth Groner, President, 6800 Tildenwood Lane, Rockville, MD 20852; (301) 984-8733. Madeline Wikler, Vice President.

Madison Books Nonfiction (history, biography, popular culture, contemporary affairs, the social sciences, trade reference). Hardcover and paperback originals, reprints; adult titles only. Divisions include Hamilton Press. Subsidiary of University Press of America. Distributed by Kampmann National Book Network. Averages 20 books p/year.

James E. Lyons, Publisher, 4720 Boston Way, Lanham, MD 20706; (301) 459-5308. Charles Lean, Associate Publisher.

Mage Publishers Nonfiction and fiction (illustrated bilingual books of short stories, poetry, short fiction, art and history). Hardcover and paperback originals, reprints; adult and children's titles. Averages 6 books p/year.

Mohammad Batmanglij, Publisher & Editor, 1032 29th Street NW, Washington, DC 20007; (202) 342-1642/(800) 962-0922.

National Press Nonfiction (law and legislation, cookbooks, sports, recreation, children's books of all kinds and humor) and fiction (adventure, contemporary, historical, mainstream, regional, suspense/ mystery, translations). Hardcover and paperback originals, reprints; adult and children's titles. Imprints include Garlic Press, Beach Books, Pandemonium Books, Venith Editions. Averages 12–14 books p/year.

Joel Joseph, President, 7201 Wisconsin Avenue, Ste. 720, Bethesda, MD 20814; (301) 657-1616/(800) 622-6657. Karen McComas, Submissions Editor.

Naval Institute Press Nonfiction (naval and maritime subjects—professional, engineering, science, history, texts, technical and trade, Institute proceedings) and some fiction (naval adventure, history or war themes). Hardcover originals; adult titles only. Averages 35–50 books p/year.

Thomas Epley, Press & Editorial Director, U.S. Naval Institute, Annapolis, MD 21402; (301) 268-6110/ (800) 233-USNI. Deborah Guberti-Estes, Acquisitions Editor.

Red Brick Press Nonfiction (food, beer and related travel). Hardcover and paperback originals; adult titles only. Magazine focused on same topics being started in 1990. Averages 3–4 books p/year.

Jack Erickson, Publisher, P.O. Box 2184, Reston, VA 22090; (703) 476-6420.

Regnery Gateway Nonfiction (politics, biography, current affairs, philosophy, economics, religion). Hardcover and paperback originals, reprints; adult titles only. Imprint: Gateway Editions. Subsidiaries include Cahill & Company Reader's Catalogue and American Citizen Reader's Catalogue. Distributed by Kampmann & Company. Averages 25 books p/year.

Alfred S. Regnery, Publisher, 1130 17th Street, NW, Ste. 620, Washington, DC 20036; (202) 457-0978/ (800) 448-8311. Harry Crocker, Editor.

Seven Locks Press Nonfiction (biography, reference, politics, history, business and economics, international relations, journalism, nature, religion, sociology, regional guides, art and Americana). Hardcover and paperback originals, reprints; adult titles only. Imprint: Isidore Stephanus Sons Publishing. Distributed by Hero Books. Averages 6–9 books p/year.

James McGrath Morris, President & Publisher, P.O. Box 27, Cabin John, MD 20818; (301) 320-2130. Jane Gold, Editor.

Simon & Schuster (D.C. Office) Nonfiction (politics, history, contemporary issues, biography and autobiography, arts and music, true crime) and fiction (commercial and literary). Hardcover originals only; adult titles only. Averages 20 books p/year.

Marie Arana-Ward, Vice President & Senior Editor,

1819 L Street, NW, Ste. 400, Washington, DC 20036; (202) 293-0202. Ellen Butts, Editorial Assistant.

Starrhill Press   Nonfiction (art & architecture, gardens and weather, classic literary day books, travel, performing arts, decoration, reference). Paperback originals; adult titles only. Averages 4 books p/year.

Elizabeth Hill & Marty Starr, Co-Presidents, P.O. Box 32342, Washington, DC 20007; (202) 686-6703.

Stone Wall Press   Nonfiction (nature, ecology, recreation, outdoors, health and fitness, hunting and fishing, natural history). Hardcover and paperback originals; adult titles only. Averages 3–4 books p/year.

Henry C. Wheelwright, President & Publisher, 1241 30th Street, NW, Washington, DC 20007; (202) 333-1860. Theresa Sullivan, Assistant Publisher.

Three Continents Press   Nonfiction (African, Caribbean, Asian and Middle Eastern literature and criticism, translations, Third World histories) and some fiction (poetry, novels, short story collections, plays and translations by non-Western authors only). Hardcover and paperback originals, reprints; adult titles only.

Imprints include Critical Perspectives and Sun-Lit Books. Distributor of several foreign publishers, including Graham Brash Singapore, Forest Books (London), Heinemann (Modern Arab Writers) and others. Averages 12–15 books p/year.

Donald Herdeck, Publisher & Editor-in-Chief, 1636 Connecticut Avenue NW, Ste. 501, Washington, DC 20009; (202) 332-3885. Norman Ware, Managing Editor.

TJ Publishers   Nonfiction and fiction (books and videotapes for hearing-impaired children, adults and teachers—sign language, deafness, rehabilitation of disabled, biography). Hardcover and paperback originals, reprints, videotapes and other materials; adult and children's titles.

Distributor for other publishers, including Bantam Books, Gallaudet College Press, Houghton Mifflin Company, Random House, St. Martin's Press and a dozen more. Averages 5–7 published books p/year.

Ramon F. Rodriguez, President, 817 Silver Spring Avenue, Silver Spring, MD 20910; (301) 585-4440.

Twenty-First Century Books   Nonfiction (biography, history, hobbies, nature and the environment, geography, travel, social issues for children and teens) and some fiction (illustrated children's books). Hardcover and paperback originals; children's and juvenile titles only. Subsidiary of University Publications of America. Averages 8–10 books p/year.

  Jeffrey Shulman, President, 38 South Market Street, Frederick, MD 21701; (301) 698-0210. Gretchen Super, Editor.

USA Today Books   Nonfiction (collections of articles that have appeared in USA Today, with additional information). Hardcover and paperback originals; adult and young adult titles. A division of Gannett Company. Thirteen books published since 1986.

  Susan Bokern, Director of Sales & Marketing, Gannett New Media, PO Box 450, Washington, DC 20044; (703) 276-5948.

Woodbine House   Nonfiction (biography, reference, travel, self-help, Americana, health, history, parents' guides for special needs children). Hardcover and trade paperback originals; adult titles only. Averages 4–8 books p/year.

  Irvin Shapell, Publisher, 10400 Connecticut Avenue, NW, Ste. 512, Kensington, MD 20895; (301) 949-3590. Susan Stokes, Editor. Jim Peters, Director of Marketing.

ACADEMIC & PUBLIC POLICY

The Alban Institute   Nonfiction (religious, ecumenical and congregational subjects). Paperback originals; adult titles only. Averages 7 books p/year.

  Celia A. Hahn, Director of Publications, 4125 Nebraska Avenue, NW, Washington, DC 20016; (202) 244-7320.

American Enterprise Institute   Nonfiction (economics, foreign affairs, defense issues, government, politics, law, education, energy, health policy, philosophy, religion, tax policy). Hardcover and paperback originals; adult titles only. Distributed by University Press of America. Averages 40 books p/year.

  Christopher C. DeMuth, President, 1150 17th Street,

NW, Washington, DC 20036; (202) 862-5800. Edward Styles, Publications Director.

The Brookings Institution Nonfiction (economics, government affairs, foreign policy). Hardcover and paperback originals; adult titles only. Averages 40 books p/year.

Bruce K. MacLaury, President, 1775 Massachusetts Avenue NW, Washington, DC 20036; (202) 797-6000. Robert L. Faherty, Director of Publications; Caroline Lalire, Managing Editor.

CQ Press Nonfiction (politics and political science, various aspects of government, some college textbooks). Hardcover and paperback originals; adult titles only. Imprint of Congressional Quarterly. Averages 3–5 books p/year.

Joanne Daniels, Director, 1414 22nd Street, NW, Washington, DC 20037; (202) 887-8642.

Catholic University of America Press Nonfiction (history, biography, languages and literature, philosophy, religion, church-state relations, political theory, social sciences and other subjects). Hardcover and paperback originals; adult titles only. Averages 20 books p/year.

Dr. David J. McGonagle, Director, 620 Michigan Avenue, NE, Washington, DC 20064; (202) 635-5052.

Chadwyck-Healey Nonfiction (scholarly books, reference works and academic microform publications). Hardcover and paperback originals, some reprints; adult titles only. Distributes Avero Publications. Averages 15 books p/year.

Charles Chadwyck-Healey, Owner, 1101 King Street, Ste. 180, Alexandria, VA 22314; (703) 683-4890. Susan Severtson, President.

Ethics & Public Policy Center Nonfiction (foreign policy, education/ business/ religion and society). Hardcover and paperback originals, some reprints; adult titles only. Averages 5 books p/year. Distributed by University Press of America.

Tim Kunes, Publications Manager, 1030 15th Street, NW, Ste. 300, Washington, DC 20005; (202) 682-1200.

Gallaudet University Press Nonfiction (scholarly, educational and general interest books on deafness and hearing impairments) and some fiction. Hardcover and paperback originals; adult, juvenile and children's titles. Imprints include Clerc Books and Kendall Green Publications. Averages 12–15 books p/year.

Elaine Costello, Director & Editor-in-Chief, Gallaudet University, 800 Florida Avenue, NE, Washington, DC 20002; (202) 651-5488/(800) 451-1073. Ivey Pittle, Managing Editor.

George Mason University Press Nonfiction (scholarly books on various subjects in the humanities, social sciences and sciences). Hardcover and paperback originals, reprints; adult titles only. Averages 10 books p/year. Distributed by University Publishing Associates, Inc.

Mark Carroll, Director, George Mason University, 4400 University Drive, Fairfax, VA 22030; (703) 323-3785.

Georgetown University Press Nonfiction (scholarly and educational books on linguistics, languages, ethics, theology and other subjects). Hardcover and paperback originals; adult titles only. Averages 15 books p/year.

John B. Breslin, Director, Georgetown University, Intercultural Center, Ste. 111, Washington, DC 20057; (202) 687-5912. Eleanor Waters, Senior Editor.

GP Publishing Nonfiction (physics, the sciences, reference and technical). Hardcover and paperback originals, software; adult titles only. Subsidairy of General Physics Corporation. Imprints include GP Courseware and Nichols Publishing. Averages 50 titles p/year.

Robert Healy, Editorial Director, 10650 Hickory Ridge Road, Columbia, MD 21044; (301) 964-6253/(800) 638-3838.

Heritage Books Nonfiction (histories, genealogies, how-to and reference). Hardcover and paperback originals, reprints; adult titles only. Averages 60 books p/year.

Laird Towle, Editorial Director, 1540 East Pointer Place, Bowie, MD 20716; (301) 390-7708.

Howard University Press Nonfiction (history, sociology, education, literature and other subjects). Hardcover and paperback originals; adult titles only. Averages 5 books p/year.

Renee Mayfield, Managing Editor, Howard University, 2900 Van Ness Street, NW, Washington, DC 20008; (202) 686-6696. Fay Acker, Senior Editor.

Library of Congress Nonfiction (scholarly books about the Library and its collections: catalogs, bibliographies, guides, checklists, etc.). Hardcover and paperback originals; adult titles only. Averages 30–35 books p/year. Distributed by U.S. Government Printing Office. (No unsolicited manuscripts).

Dana J. Pratt, Director of Publishing, Library of Congress—Madison Building, Independence Avenue & 1st Streets, SE, Rm 604, Washington, DC 20540; (202) 707-5093.

Maryland Historical Press Nonfiction (biography, history and other subjects for children and young adults). Some trade titles. Hardcover and paperback originals; children's and juvenile titles. Averages 4 books p/year.

Vera Rollo, Publisher, 9205 Tuckerman Street, Lanham, MD 20706; (301) 577-5308.

National Academy Press Nonfiction (health, science and technology). Hardcover and paperback originals; adult tiles only. Division of the National Academy of Sciences. Averages 45 books p/year.

Virginia B. Martin, Director, 2101 Constitution Avenue NW, Washington, DC 20418; (202) 334-3318. Betsy Turvene, Executive Editor.

The Preservation Press Nonfiction (architecture and architectural history, building restoration and historic preservation). Some trade books. Hardcover and paperback originals; adult titles only. Imprints include Building Watchers Series, Great American Series Places, Landmark Reprint Series and others. Averages 6–10 books p/year.

Diane Maddex, Director, National Trust For Historic Preservation, 1785 Massachusetts Avenue, NW, Washington, DC 20036; (202) 673-4058/673-4061. Margaret Bryne Heimbold, VP & Publisher.

Public Affairs Press Nonfiction (political science, foreign affairs, social sciences; mostly reference). Hardcover and paperback originals; adult titles only. Averages 15 books p/year.

M. B. Schnapper, Executive Director, 2908 Woodstock Avenue, Silver Spring, MD 20910; (301) 544-3024.

Rowman & Littlefield Publishers Nonfiction (business and economics, computer science, environmental studies, geography, government, law, social and biological sciences, health services, medical and nursing research, philosophy, policy studies, statistics, women's studies, technical and reference). Hardcover and paperback originals; adult titles only. Division of University Press of America. Averages 40 books p/year.

James E. Lyons, Publisher, 8705 Bollman Place, Savage, MD 20763; (301) 306-0400. Dr. George Zimmar, Editor-in-Chief.

Smithsonian Institution Press Nonfiction (American history, natural science, anthropology, history of science & technology, aeronautics and astronautics, art and art history, regional interest, musicology and many other subjects). Hardcover and paperback originals, direct mail books, reprints; adult titles only.

Imprint is Smithsonian Books. Divisions are: University Press Division (44 books p/year), Direct Mail Division (2 books p/year), Federal Series Division (35 books p/year), Smithsonian/ Folkways Recordings. Averages 85 books p/year.

Felix C. Lowe, Director, 955 L'Enfant Plaza, Rm 2100, Washington, DC 20560; (202) 287-3738/(800) 678-2675. Daniel Goodwin, Editorial Director. Amy Pastan, Acquisitions Editor, University Press Division.

University Press of America Nonfiction (scholarly monographs; college and graduate level textbooks on history, economics, business, psychology, political science, African studies, philosophy, religion, sociology, music, art, literature, drama and education; conference proceedings). Hardcover and paperback originals, reprints; adult titles only.

Imprints include Abt Books and RF Publishing. Subsidiaries include Madison Books, Hamilton Press, Rowman & Littlefield, Barnes & Noble Books, Littlefield, Adams Quality Paperbacks and Kampmann National Book Network. Divisions include British American Publishing Company, UPA Co-Publishing and UPA Publishers' Reprints. Through KNBN, distributes for a number of prominent American publishers. Averages 450–500 books p/year.

James E. Lyons, Publisher, 4720 Boston Way, Lanham, MD 20706; (301) 459-3366.

University Publications of America Nonfiction (monographs, microforms, research collections and looseleafs). Hardcover and paperback originals, reprints; adult titles only. Subsidiaries: Twenty-First Century Books. Averages 200 books p/year. An imprint of Congressional Information Service.

Paul P. Massa, President, 44 North Market Street, Frederick, MD 21701; (301) 694-0100/(800) 692-6300. Betsey Covell, Managing Editor.

Urban Institute Press Nonfiction (economics, government, public policy, social sciences). Hardcover and paperback originals; adult titles only. Distributed by University Press of America. Averages 25 books p/year.

William Gorham, President, 2100 M Street, NW, Washington, DC 20037; (202) 857-8724. Felicity Skidmore, Director.

Wilson Center Press Nonfiction (social sciences and the humanities). Hardcover and paperback originals; adult titles only. Distributed by University Press of America. Averages 5 books p/year.

Shaun Murphy, Assistant Director for Publishing, Woodrow Wilson International Center for Scholars, 1000 Jefferson Drive, SW, Washington, DC 20560; (202) 287-3000.

LITERARY

Dryad Press Fiction (poetry, short stories, translations) and selected literary nonfiction. Paperback originals, reprints; adult titles only. Averages 3–5 books p/year.

Merrill Leffler, President, 15 Sherman Avenue, Takoma Park, MD 20912; (301) 454-8809/891-3729.

The Galileo Press Fiction (poetry and short story collections, novellas, children's stories) and nonfiction. Hardcover and paperback originals; adult and children's titles. Averages 3–5 books p/year.

Julia Wendell & Jack Stephens, Editors, 15201 Wheeler Lane, Sparks, MD 21152; (301) 771-4544.

Orchises Press Fiction (poetry) and nonfiction (general trade). Paperback originals; adult titles only. Averages 2–3 books p/year.

Roger Lathbury, Publisher, P.O. Box 20602, Alexandria, VA 22030; no phone listed.

Paycock Press Fiction (poetry, novels, short story collections, translations—contemporary, literary, experimental, humor/satire). Paperback originals, reprints; adult titles only. Imprints include *Gargoyle Magazine*. Averages 1–2 books p/year.

Richard Peabody, Jr., Publisher & Editor, P.O. Box 30906, Bethesda, MD 20814; (301) 656-5146.

Sibyl-Child Press Fiction (poetry, short story collections, novellas). Paperback and chapbook originals; adult titles only. Averages 2–3 books p/year.

Saundra Maley and Nancy Prothro, Editors, P.O. Box 1773, Hyattsville, MD 20788; (301) 267-3423.

Washington Writers' Publishing House Writers' collective which selects books by local poets to publish each year. Paperback originals; adult titles only. Averages 1–2 books p/year.

Editorial Board, P.O. Box 50068, Washington, DC 20004; (202) 546-1020.

The Word Works Nonprofit literary organization which publishes "contemporary poetry in single author editions, usually in collaboration with a visual artist."

Also starting new series called "The Capital Collection," books of poetry by area poets. Paperback originals, occasional anthologies; adult titles only. Averages 1–2 books p/year.

Karren Alenier/J.H. Beall/Robert Sargent, Poetry Editors, P.O. Box 42164, Washington, DC 20015.

MAIL ORDER & SPECIALTY

Columbia Books Nonfiction (local reference guides, political subjects, current affairs). Hardcover originals; adult titles only. Averages 6 books p/year.

Arthur Close, President, 1350 New York Avenue, NW, Ste. 207, Washington, DC 20005; (202) 737-3777. John Russell, Vice President.

Denlinger's Publishers Nonfiction (books about dogs and dog breeding). Hardcover and paperback originals, reprints; adult titles only. Averages 12 books p/year.

William Denlinger, Publisher, P.O. Box 76, Fairfax, VA 22030; (703) 830-4646.

Hatier Publishing Nonfiction (French language arts publisher and distributor). Hardcover and paperback originals; adult titles only. Subsidiary of Librarie Hatier. Distributor for Didier, Foucher, Hatier and Hatier-Didier USA. Averages 4 titles p/year.

Martha Dupecher, Vice President, 3160 O Street, NW, Washington, DC 20007; (202) 333-4435.

National Geographic Books Nonfiction (books, maps and atlases with a focus on geography, travel, natural sciences, natural history and the history of human civilization).

Charles Hyman, Director, 1145 17th Street, NW, Washington, DC 20036; (202) 857-7000.

Peeking Duck Books Nonfiction (personalized children's name books). Hardcover originals; children's titles only. Available by direct mail, mail order through catalogs and select children's specialty stores. Division of PD Children's Products.

Orin R. Heend, President, P.O. Box 207, Arlington, VA 22201; (703) 525-2378.

Time-Life Books Nonfiction (art, cooking, crafts, gardening, health, history, home repair, nature, photography, science, reference and other subjects of general interest). Hardcover originals; adult and children's titles. Subsidiary of Time, Inc. Division: Time-Life Music. Distributed by Little, Brown & Company and others. Averages 50–60 books p/year.

Christopher T. Linen, President & CEO, 777 Duke Street, Alexandria, VA 22314; (703) 838-7000/(800) 621-7026. George Constable, Managing Editor.

PROFESSIONAL & BUSINESS

American Institute of Architects Press Nonfiction (illustrated books of historical and contemporary architecture, construction technology, research, statistics, interior design). Hardcover and paperback originals; adult titles only. Averages 7 books p/year.

John Ray Hoke Jr., Publisher, AIA, 1735 New York

Avenue, NW, Washington, DC, 20006; (202) 626-7000.
Cynthia G. Ware, Managing Editor.

American Psychiatric Press Nonfiction (psychiatry, behavioral and social sciences, medicine, reference and college texts). Hardcover and some paperback originals, some reprints; adult titles only. Averages 40 books p/year.

Ron McMillan, General Manager, APA, 1400 K Street, NW, Ste. 1101, Washington, DC 20005; (202) 682-6262. Tim Clancy, Editorial Director.

American Psychological Association Nonfiction (psychology, mental health, scholarly works for professionals in field). Hardcover and paperback originals; adult titles only. Averages 30 books p/year.

Publications and Communications Office, APA, 1200 17th Street, NW, Washington, DC 20036; (202) 955-7600.

Aspen Publishers Nonfiction (health care, nursing, medicine, special education, allied health, physical and occupational therapy, gerontology, speech and hearing, psychology, family therapy, business and professional, law text and reference). Hardcover and paperback originals; adult titles only. Member of Worldwide Wolters-Kluwer Group. Imprint: Health Law Center. Averages 90 books p/year.

Michael Brown & Kenneth Killion, VPs & Publishers, 1600 Research Blvd, Rockville, MD 20850; (301) 251-5000/(800) 638-8437. Margot Raphael, Executive Managing Editor.

BNA Books Nonfiction (law & legal practice, taxation, finance, management, arbitration, labor & employee relations, environment & safety). Hardcover and paperback originals; adult titles only. Division of The Bureau of National Affairs. Subsidiaries include BNA International (London). Averages 40 books p/year.

William Beltz, President & Editor-in-Chief, Bureau of National Affairs, 1231 25th Street, NW, Washington, DC 20037; (202) 452-4276. Timothy Darby, Managing Editor.

Communications Press Nonfiction (broadcast, radio, satellite cable television, reference books on communications subjects). Hardcover, trade paperback and professional/text paperback originals; adult titles only. Imprint of Broadcasting Publications. Averages 10–15 books p/year.

David Dietz, Manager, 1705 DeSales Street, NW, Washington, DC 20036; (202) 659-2340.

Computer Science Press   Nonfiction (computer science, computer engineering, computer chess, electrical and biomedical engineering, computers and math, telecommunications). Hardcover and paperback originals, software; adult titles only. Imprint of W.H. Freeman & Company. Averages 18–20 books p/ year.

Arthur & Barbara Friedman, Editors-in-Chief, 1803 Research Blvd, Rockville, MD 20850; (301) 251-9050.

Congressional Staff Directory   Nonfiction (directories covering all aspects of the federal government, reference books and other materials). Hardcover and paperback originals; adult titles only. Averages 6 books p/year.

Bruce Brownson, President, P.O. Box 62, Mount Vernon, VA 22121; (703) 765-3400.

Gifted Education Press   Nonfiction (adult literacy, education of the gifted, psychology, philosophy, parenting). Mass market paperback originals; adult titles only. Averages 5 books p/year.

Maurice Fisher, Publisher, The Reading Tutorium, 10201 Yuma Court, P.O. Box 1586, Manassas, VA 22110; (703) 369-5017.

Government Institutes   Nonfiction (environmental law, health, safety, personnel, energy, reference and technical). Hardcover and paperback originals; adult titles only. Averages 24 books p/year.

David Williams, VP Publishing, 966 Hungerford Drive, Ste. 24, Rockville, MD 20850; (301) 251-9250. Jerome Frumkin, Acquisitions Editor.

Information Resources Press   Nonfiction (health planning, information and library science, reference and technical). Hardcover originals; adult titles only. Division of Herner & Company. Averages 6 books p/year.

Gene Allen, VP & Publisher, Ste. 700, 1700 N. Moore Street, Arlington, VA 22209; (703) 558-8270.

International Library-Law Book Publishers Nonfiction (law books in the fields of advertising, insurance, business, finance, energy, government, political science, public utilities, tax and labor). Hardcover and paperback originals; adult titles only. Divisions include International Law Library and Law Book Publishers. Averages 12–15 books p/year.

Donald J. Hoyes, President, 7315 Wisconsin Avenue, Ste. 229E, Bethesda, MD 20814; (301) 961-8850.

Island Press Nonfiction (books for resource conservation professionals and activists). Hardcover and paperback originals; adult titles only. Averages 15 books p/year.

Charles Savitt, President, 1718 Connecticut Avenue, NW, Ste. 300, Washington, DC 20009; (202) 232-7933. Barbara Dean, Executive Editor.

Lomond Publications Nonfiction (science policy and business management for professionals). Hardcover originals; adult titles only. Averages 3 books p/year.

Lowell Hattery, President & Publisher, P.O. Box 88, Mount Airy, MD 21771; (301) 829-1496/(800) 443-6299. Thomas Hattery, Vice President.

Mackechnie (McWare Products) Nonfiction (books about microcomputers and software). Paperback originals; adult titles only. Averages 3 books p/year.

Robert McKechnie, President, P.O. Box 2784, Fairfax, VA 22031; (703) 323-1212.

Minerva Books Nonfiction (financial newsletter performance ratings, investment trends and other related subjects). Hardcover and paperback originals, reprints; adult titles only. Averages 2–3 books p/year.

Mark Hulbert, President & Publisher, 316 Commerce Street, Alexandria, VA 22314; (703) 683-5905.

National Health Publishing Nonfiction (health and nursing administration, long-term care, health finance and law, adult day care, organ procurement). Hardcover and paperback originals; adult titles only. Division of Williams & Wilkins. Imprints include National Law Publishing, AUHPA Press and others. Averages 15–20 books p/year.

Sara Sides, Acquisitions Editor, 99 Painters Mill

Road, Owings Mill, MD 21117; (301) 363-6400. Jacqueline Karkos, President.

Octameron Associates Nonfiction (post-secondary education subjects, career guides, college admission information). Paperback originals; adult titles only. Imprints: Octameron Press. Subsidiaries include Educational Access. Distributed by Longman Trade. Averages 15 books p/year.

Anna Leider, Publisher, 4805 A Eisenhower Avenue, Alexandria, VA 22304; (703) 823-1882.

Literary Agents & Book Producers

> "Then there's the one about the two agents, Jack and Morty, who fall off the boat and find themselves treading water. Jack suddenly points and screams: 'MORTY, IT'S A SHARK—WE'RE DONE FOR!!!' The shark comes straight for them, but at the last minute turns away.
> 'What do you make of that?' says Jack.
> 'Professional courtesy,' says Morty, flashing a smile."
>
> **—WRITER'S JOKE**

Popular lore holds that *all* literary agents are sharks, but this may be an exaggeration. We're like the professionals one finds in any other specialized field—and, believe it or not, we do make mistakes.

Sometimes an agent can meet an author's needs, sometimes he or she cannot. There are "managing agents," those who take the long view with their clients, and "selling agents," who push hard to sign quick deals without always considering long-term consequences. While most agents work on contingency—on the promise of future royalty returns—some agents insist on charging reading and other up front fees before going to work. And there is always the vague doubt among writers that agents take far too much for what they do (although, as you might expect, any self-respecting agent would disagree).

What do agents do for authors? They help focus book ideas, submit manuscripts to sympathetic editors, negotiate book/movie/TV contracts, secure promotional and advertising considerations (before, during and after release), review royalty and residual statements for accuracy and much more. Nine-tenths of all agents seek manuscripts with "trade potential," meaning they hope to interest a "trade" (general interest) publisher in acquiring rights to the manuscript. For all they do, agents typically request commissions of between 10–15% on all advances, royalties and other revenues their authors receive.

A new kind of "super-agent," the book producer, also provides design, production and sometimes even printing services to publishers after collaborating with an author to write, edit and sell a manuscript. Book producers, because of their higher overhead costs, usually request higher commissions than agents.

To contact any local agent or book producer, writers should send a query letter, book proposal or short manuscript sample along with a self-addressed, stamped envelope. Don't send entire manuscripts (unless specifically asked to do so), don't call and, above all, don't show up on anyone's doorstep.

If what you write rings true, chances are someone will hunt you down.

LITERARY AGENTS

Jannell Walden Agyeman Adult nonfiction and fiction titles (trade only).

Jannell Walden Agyeman, 2509 22nd Street, NE, Washington, DC 20018; (202) 635-8113. Washington representative, Marie Brown Associates Literary Agency.

Robert B. Barnett Adult nonfiction and fiction titles (trade only).

Williams & Connolly, Hill Building, 839 17th Street, NW, Washington, DC 20006; (202) 331-5034.

BSW Literary Agency Adult fiction titles (trade only).

Betsy Sarah Wouk, 3255 N Street, NW, Washington, DC 20007; (202) 333-2669.

David Cutler & Associates Adult nonfiction and fiction titles (trade only).

David Cutler, 2983 Oakleigh Lane, Oakton, VA 22124; (703) 255-2886. Zak Mettger, Associate.

Anne Edelstein Literary Agency Adult nonfiction and fiction titles (trade only).

Anne Edelstein, 3039 Q Street, NW, Washington, DC 20007; (202) 333-8881.

Evelyn Freyman Adult nonfiction and fiction titles (trade only).

Evelyn Freyman, 1660 L Street, NW, Suite 1000, Washington, DC 20036; (202) 775-1041.

Ronald Goldfarb   Adult nonfiction and fiction titles; feature films/plays/television shows. Public relations services and lecture bookings for authors (Newsmakers, Inc).

Ronald Goldfarb, Esq., 918 16th Street, NW, Washington, DC 20006; (202) 466-3030. Terry Joyce, Executive Director, Newsmakers; (202) 785-5089.

Larry Kaltman Literary Agency   Adult nonfiction and fiction titles (trade only).

Larry Kaltman, 1301 South Scott Street, Arlington, VA 22204; (703) 920-3771.

Literary Agency of Washington   Adult & juvenile nonfiction and fiction titles (trade only), short stories, magazine fiction, articles for national magazines.

David Richards, Editorial Director, 2025 I Street, NW, Ste. 606, Washington, DC 20006; (202) 639-8214. Fred Reinstein, Fiction Editor.

Muriel Nellis   Feature films/plays/television shows; adult nonfiction and fiction titles (trade only).

Muriel Nellis, 3539 Albemarle Street, NW, Washington, DC 20008; (202) 362-4688.

Eleanor Roszel Rogers   Adult & juvenile nonfiction and fiction titles; feature films/television shows.

Eleanor Roszel Rogers, 1487 Generals Highway, Crownsville, MD 21032; (301) 987-8166.

Gail Ross   Adult nonfiction and fiction titles (trade only); feature films/plays/television shows.

Lichtman, Trister, Singer & Ross, 1666 Connecticut Avenue, NW, Ste. 501, Washington, DC 20009; (202) 328-1666. Elaine English, Associate.

The Sagalyn Literary Agency   Adult nonfiction and fiction titles (trade only).

Raphael Sagalyn, 1717 N Street, NW, Washington, DC 20036; (202) 835-0320. Lisa Di Mona, Agent.

Leona Schechter   Adult nonfiction and fiction titles (trade only).

Leona Schechter, 3748 Huntington Street, NW, Washington, DC 20015; (202) 362-9040.

Sodsisky & Sons Adult nonfiction and fiction titles (trade only).

Roberta Sodsisky, 5914 Greentree Road, Bethesda, MD 20817; (301) 897-8444.

Ann Tobias Children's and juvenile nonfiction and fiction titles (trade only).

Ann Tobias, 307 South Carolina Avenue, SE, Washington, DC 20003; (202) 543-1043.

Audrey Adler Wolf Adult nonfiction and fiction titles (trade only); feature films/plays/television shows.

Audrey Adler Wolf, 1001 Connecticut Avenue, NW, Washington, DC 20036; (202) 659-0088. Affiliated with The Lantz Agency (New York & California).

BOOK PRODUCERS

Bill Adler, Jr. Publishing The owner, WIW's president from 1988–89, offers book production services from conception through design on a variety of adult trade titles (hardcover and paperback).

Bill Adler, Jr., 3021 Macomb Street, NW, Washington, DC 20008; (202) 363-7410.

Educational Challenges Provides a full-range of book development services, from concept through camera-ready mechanical. Specializes in student-oriented, elementary and high school textbooks on the social sciences, history, geography and other subjects.

Peg Paul, President, 1009 Duke Street, Alexandria, VA 22314; (703) 683-1500.

Fastback Press Develops series ideas and provides full production services from manuscript to printed books. Specializes in mass market paperbacks.

Linda Williams Aber & Louise Colligan, 9905 Doubletree Court, Potomac, MD 20854; (301) 279-2027.

Dianne Johansson-Adams Specializes in creating and producing directories. Services include product development, research, compilation, database planning, editorial services and book production and delivery.

Dianne Johansson-Adams, President, 2059 Huntington Avenue, Ste. 1407, Alexandria, VA 22303; (703) 960-5810.

Redefinition   Undertakes series projects, from concept through final production and printing. Specializes in gardening, illustrated books and other blends of text and pictures.

Edward Brash, President, 700 North Fairfax Street, Alexandria, VA 22314; (703) 739-2110.

Alvin Rosenbaum Projects   Illustrated art and gift books, produced with great attention to detail and beautifully designed, are the hallmarks of this full-service book production company. Also handles popular reference, design and other titles (hardcover and paperbacks).

Alvin Rosenbaum, President, 1200 18th Street, NW, Ste. 206, Washington, DC 20036; (202) 223-1616.

Strawtown Associates   Specializes in developing books for children (8–13 years old), including mass market paperbacks, trade books, activity books, humor and premiums. Full development services, from concept to camera-ready mechanicals.

Linda Williams Aber, 9905 Doubletree Court, Potomac, MD 20854; (301) 279-2027.

Tilden Press   Produces trade hardcover and paperback books on reference, business and consumer topics. Handles projects from concept to camera-ready boards; also offers publishing consulting and marketing services.

Joel Makower, President, 1001 Connecticut Avenue, NW, Ste. 201, Washington, DC 20036; (202) 659-5855.

Literary, Media & Writers' Organizations

"Americans of all ages, all stations in life and all types of disposition are forever forming associations."
—ALEXIS DE TOCQUEVILLE

Writers can't do it alone. They never could. In addition to publishers, who serve to deliver writers' works to the public, writers can seek out and find invaluable services provided them by professional literary, media and writers' organizations.

There are a sizable number of such organizations here in the nation's capital, working to help, support and serve authors, screenwriters, editors, reporters, publishers and others concerned with communicating the written word to diverse national and international audiences.

In this section, readers will also find listings for a number of groups that help promote the better manufacture and dissemination of books, films, magazines, newspapers, software and other literary products. Certain foundations and other organizations which recognize achievements in writing or journalism with awards, grants and other kinds of support have also been included, along with key media organizations which protect First Amendment rights, copyright issues or offer legal services and counsel to working editors and journalists.

To join the right organization is to find solidarity and a sense of security in a typically insecure, unstable profession. Members get moral support, advice, technical assistance, educational opportunities and a chance to mingle with and learn from other people in their field.

Accuracy In Media A media watchdog organization which receives complaints from the public on factual errors made by news organizations. If and when such errors are confirmed, AIM asks that news organizations publicly correct the errors in subsequent reports.

Donald K. Irvine, Executive VP, 1275 K Street, NW, Washington, DC 20005; (202) 371-6710.

Afro-Hispanic Institute   Promotes the study of Afro-Hispanic literature and culture. Assists in the research of blacks in Spanish-speaking nations.

Dr. Stanley A. Cyrus, President, 3306 Ross Place, NW, Washington, DC 20008; (202) 966-7783.

American Agricultural Editors Association   Comprised of editors and editorial staff members of farm publications, AGEA's affiliate members are agricultural public relations and advertising personnel and state and local officials. Members: 625.

Paul Weller, Executive Secretary, American Agricultural Association, 1629 K Street, NW, Ste. 1100, Washington, DC 20006; (202) 785-6710.

American Association of Disability Communicators   Members are communications professionals—including editors, freelance writers, broadcasters, columnists and reporters—concerned with disability issues. Members: 1,000.

Robert Ruffner, President, 910 16th Street, NW, Ste. 600, Washington, DC 20006; (202) 293-5960.

American Association of Sunday & Feature Editors   Specialized media group, whose members are Sunday and feature newspaper editors; bestows awards. Members: 120.

Mary Nahan, Administrative Secretary, Newspaper Center, P.O. Box 17407, Dulles Airport, Washington, DC 20041; (703) 648-1286.

American Copyright Council   Serves to educate the public about the value of copyrights and the harm caused by copyright infringement. Coalition of film, law, magazine, computer, publishing, music, recording and television organizations. Members: 25.

Fritz Attaway, VP & Secretary, 1600 I Street, NW, Washington, DC 20006; (202) 293-1966.

American Film Institute   Nonprofit corporation dedicated to preserving and developing the nation's artistic and cultural resources in film. Goals are to increase recognition and understanding of the moving image as an art form, to assure preservation of the art form and to identify, encourage and develop talent. Members: 140,000.

Jean Firstenberg, Director, John F. Kennedy Center

For The Performing Arts, Washington, DC 20566; (202) 828-4000.

American Intellectual Property Law Association
Voluntary bar association of lawyers practicing in the fields of patents, trademarks and copyrights. Dedicatd to aid in the operation and improvement of U.S. patents, trademark and copyright systems. Offers placement service and maintains 25 committees. Members: 5,500.

Michael Blommer, Executive Director, 2001 Jefferson Davis Highway, Ste. 203, Arlington, VA 22202; (703) 521-1680.

American International Book Development Council
Established to promote access to American books abroad and foreign literature in the United States. Also known as Helen Dwight Reid Educational Foundation.

William M. Childs, Executive Director, 4000 Albemarle Street, NW, Washington, DC 20016; (202) 362-8131. Evron M. Kirkpatrick, President.

American Medical Writers Association Dedicated to the advancement and improvement of medical communication. Sponsors annual medical book awards and over fifty workshops at annual conference. Members: 2,700.

Lillian Sablack, Executive Director, 9650 Rockville Pike, Bethesda, MD 20814; (301) 493-0003.

American News Womens' Club Members are women who write news for all media, as well as government agencies, nonprofit organizations and freelance. Encourages friendly understanding between members and their sources. Members: 450.

M. Virginia Daly, Executive Director, 1607 22nd Street, NW, Washington, DC 20008; (202) 332-6770.

American Newspaper Publishers Association Serves newspapers and newspaper executives by working to advance the cause of a free press; to encourage the efficiency and economy of the newspaper publishing business in all departments and aspects; to engage in and promote research of use to newspapers; to gather and distribute among its member newspapers accurate, reliable and useful information about newspapers and their environment and to promote the highest standard in journalism. Members: 1,400.

Jerry W. Freidheim, President, The Newspaper Center, P.O. Box 17407, Dulles Airport, Washington, DC 20041; (703) 648-1000.

American Philatelic Society Writers Unit   Members are editors, writers and columnists who specialize in covering stamps and stamp collecting. Members: 400.

George Griffenhagen, Secretary/Treasurer, 2501 Drexel Street, Vienna, VA 22180; (703) 560-2413.

American Press Institute   Educational center dedicated to the continuing education and management training of newspaper men and women in the United States and Canada.

William L. Winter, Executive Officer, 11690 Sunrise Valley Drive, Reston, VA 22091; (703) 620-3611.

American Society of Newspaper Editors   Represents interests of directing editors who determine editorial and news policy on daily newspapers. Members: 1,000.

Lee Stinnett, Executive Director, 11600 Sunrise Valley Drive, Reston, VA 22091; (703) 620-6087.

American Women in Radio & Television   Members are women in administrative, creative or executive positions in the broadcasting industry (radio, television, cable and networks). Members: 3,000.

Susan K. Finn, President, 1101 Connecticut Avenue, NW, Suite 700, Washington, DC 20036; (202) 429-5102.

Armed Forces Broadcasters Association   Former and current military and commercial broadcasters. Conducts seminars and provides job information center. Members: 600.

Robert P. Bubniak, Executive VP, P.O. Box 12013, Arlington, VA 22209; (609) 924-3600.

Association for the Study of Afro-American Life & History   Historians, scholars and students interested in the research and study of black people as a contributing factor in civilization. Encourages the study of black history and training in the social sciences, history and other disciplines. Members: 2,200.

Karen Robinson, Executive Director, 1401 14th Street, NW, Washington, DC 20005; (202) 667-2822.

Association of American Publishers (D.C. Office) Monitors and promotes the U.S. publishing industry. Members are actively engaged in the creation, publication and production of books or types of prints and AV materials. Members: 300.

Judith Platt/Diana Rennert/Carol Risher, Directors, 2005 Massachusetts Avenue, NW, Washington, DC 20036; (202) 232-3335. Nicholas A. Veliotes, President (Main Office-NY).

Association of Area Business Publications Works to encourage high journalistic standards among area business publications across the nation. Acts as a forum for the exchange of ideas and information. Members: 95.

Lewis Conn, Executive Director, 202 Legion Avenue, Annapolis, MD 21401; (301) 263-0015.

Association of Railway Communicators Members are editors of house organs for the railroad industry and rail labor. Presents annual achievement awards. Members: 90.

J. Ronald Shumate, Secretary Treasurer, c/o Association of American Railroads, 50 F Street, NW, Washington, DC 20001; (202) 639-2526.

Bookbuilders of Washington Members concerned with all phases of book production, including typesetting, design, printing, binding and specialized techniques.

Richard E. Farkas, President, c/o American Psychiatric Press, 1400 K Street, NW, Suite 1101, Washington, DC 20005; (202) 682-6273.

Cable Television Information Center Provides cable television resource and information center for local governments across the nation, and works to help local officials make informed decisions about cable television. Members: 180.

Harold E. Horn, President, 1500 N. Beauregard Street, Ste. 205, Alexandria, VA 22311; (703) 845-1705.

Capital Press Club Seeks to expand opportunities for minorities within the news industry, and acts as a platform for leaders to convey opinions on issues affecting minorities in the U.S. Members are black communications professionals from newspapers and news services nationwide. Members: 200.

Claryce Handy, President, P.O. Box 19403, Washington, DC 20036; (202) 429-5497.

Capital Press Women   Runs monthly meetings and annual conference to help foster professional development among local women journalists. Publishes quarterly newsletter, honors Women of Achievement at annual spring dinner and fosters opportunities to build networks of associates. Members: 50.

Ruthann Saenger, President, 1448 Duke Street, Alexandria, VA 22314; (703) 684–6988.

Center for the Book   Established by law in 1977, the Center for the Book uses the influence and resources of The Library of Congress to stimulate public interest in books and reading and to encourage the study of books. Its program of symposia, projects, lectures, exhibitions and publications is supported by tax-deductible contributions from corporations and individuals.

The Center has chapters in many U.S. states and in countries overseas. Sponsors PLUS literacy campaign on national television, and many other worthwhile programs.

John Y. Cole, Director, The Library of Congress, Washington, DC 20540; (202) 287-5221. Simon Michael Bessie, Chairman.

Center for Media & Public Affairs   Conducts random surveys to determine media impact on public opinion; does in-depth and rapid response media surveys.

Dr. S. Robert Lichter, Co-Director, 2101 L Street, NW, Washington, DC 20037; (202) 223-2942.

Chesapeake Regional Area Book Sellers (CRABS)   An alliance of bookstore owners in the Washington/Baltimore area which sponsors programs and publishes materials designed to increase public awareness of the many outstanding bookstores and book-related operations throughout the region. Members: 75.

Liz Steingraber, President, 11 Sparrow Valley Court, Gaithersburg, MD 20879; (301) 840–9074.

Children's Book Guild of Washington   Provides contact and exchange among authors, illustrators and specialists in children's literature. Holds monthly luncheon meetings. Members include established writers and illustrators of trade books, specialists in children's literature, school and public library systems, bookstores and appropriate local and national organizations. Members: 70.

Patricia Markun, Public Relations Coordinator; (202) 965–0403.

City & Regional Magazine Association CRMA White Awards Competition, The University of Kansas William Allen White School of Journalism; city & regional magazine competition, professional development seminars, annual conference (43 members).

Brandi Sullivan, 335 Commerce Street, Alexandria, VA 22314; (703) 548-5016.

Construction Writers Association Members are writers and editors for media in the construction field; associate members include public relations and advertising personnel connected with construction. Members: 122.

E.E. Halmos, Jr., Secretary-Treasurer, P.O. Box 259, Poolesville, MD 20837.

Department of State Correspondents Association Newspaper, magazine, wire service, radio and television news correspondents who cover the U.S. State Department are members. Members: 130.

Norman Kempster, President, 2201 C Street, NW, Rm. 2310, Washington, DC 20520; (202) 293-4650.

Dog Writers' Association of America Provides information about dogs (sport breeding and ownership) and assists writers in gaining access to exhibitions. Members: 300.

Harold Sundstrom, President, 9800 Flint Rock Road, Manassas, VA 22111; (703) 369-2384.

Education Writers Association Dedicated to improving the quality of education reporting nationwide and in helping to attract top-notch writers and reporters to the education field. Provides members with conferences, seminars, publications, employment services, freelance referral, workshops and national awards. Members: 450.

Lisa J. Walker, Executive Director, 1001 Connecticut Avenue, NW, Suite 310, Washington, DC 20036; (202) 429-9680.

Federal Publishers' Committee Promotes (and studies) cost-effective publications management in the federal government, including planning, marketing, writing, design, printing, distribution and other areas of publishing. Conducts symposia, offers speakers' bureau, maintains placement service, compiles statistics. Members are representatives of executive and legislative branches involved in publishing. Members: 511.

John E. Mounts, Chairman, National Center for Health Statistics, 3700 East-West Highway, Rm I–57, Hyattsville, MD 20782; (301) 436-8586.

Freedom of Information Clearinghouse Assists citizens seeking information from the government. Collects and disseminates information on state and federal Freedom of Information statutes.

Patti Goldman, Executive Director, 2000 P Street, NW, P.O. Box 19367, Washington, DC 20036; (202) 785-3704.

Fund for Investigative Journalism The Fund's mission is to increase knowledge about the concealed, obscure or complex aspects of matters significantly affecting the public. Makes grants to writers to enable them to probe abuses of authority and other abuses of power—more than 35 books have been written with Fund support.

John Hanrahan, Executive Director, 1755 Massachusetts Avenue, NW, Washington, DC 20036; (202) 462-1844.

Fund for Objective News Reporting Nonpartisan organization working to correct biases in major news media. Provides grants to journalists doing media research.

713 D Street, SE, Washington, DC 20003; (202) 547-9404.

Guild of Book Workers A national nonprofit organization founded in 1906 to foster the hand book arts: binding, calligraphy, illumination, paper decorating, etc. Sponsors exhibits, lectures and workshops. Members: 650.

Frank Mowery, President, Folger Shakespeare Library, 201 East Capitol Street, SE, Washington, DC 20003; (202) 544-4600.

International Association of Business Communicators (DC Chapter) Dedicated to helping members apply skills and improve professionalism. Most members of the Washington chapter work for area associations, with more than half in management and ten percent serving as consultants and freelancers. Holds monthly luncheons. Members: 450.

Nancy Johnson, Chair, 3801 Mount Vernon Avenue, Alexandria, VA (703) 684-7079.

International Copyright Information Center   Assists publishers in developing countries to contact U.S. publishers regarding the licensing of translation and English-language reprint rights to U.S. books. One of several national information centers on copyright clearance in major publishing countries throughout the world.

Carol Risher, Director, Association of American Publishers (D.C. Branch Office), 2005 Massachusetts Avenue, NW, Washington, DC 20036; (202) 232-3335.

Jesuits in Communications in the United States   Through this association, U.S. members of the Society of Jesus (Jesuits) can learn more about various areas of communication, including writing, editing, radio and television.

James J. Conn, Executive Secretary, 1424 16th Street, NW, Ste. 300, Washington, DC 20036; (202) 462-0400.

Lewis Carroll Society of North America   Members are collectors, authors, publishers and others interested in the life and works of Charles Lutwidge Dodgson (1832–1898), who wrote under the pen name of Lewis Carroll. Purpose is to encourage study of the author, to publish journals and books about him and to become the center for Carroll studies. Members: 350.

Edward Guiliano, President, 617 Rockford Road, Silver Spring, MD 20902; (301) 593-7077.

Literary Friends of the D.C. Public Library   Active group of community book lovers who promote interest in and appreciation of the written word while helping to support and further operations of the D.C. Public Library. Sponsors many outstanding programs; organized and continues to promote the Washington Writers Collection displayed in the library's Washingtoniana Room. Members: 650.

Mari Francis Hardison, President, DC Public Library, 901 G Street, NW, Washington, DC 20001; (202) 727-1101.

Media Access Project   Public-interest law firm working to assure that the media inform the public fully and fairly on important national issues. Participates in conferences and seminars, advises local and national organizations and represents those groups in their efforts to gain access to media.

Andrew Jay Schwartzman, Executive Director, 2000 M Street, NW, Washington, DC 20036; (202) 232-4300.

The Media Institute Promotes understanding of the American media and communications, conducts research into various aspects of the media and communications industry, maintains program of research and conferences focusing on media performance, role of new technologies, and communications policy issues; sponsors luncheon discussion series on media topics and maintains speakers' bureau. Members: 4,300.

Patrick D. Maines, Executive Director, 3017 M Street, NW, Washington, DC 20007; (202) 298-7512.

Motion Picture Association of America (D.C. Office) Trade association for the major motion picture producers and distributors. Administers motion picture industry's system of self-regulation and seeks to further production and distribution of motion pictures for theatrical, home video and television use in the United States. Members: 60.

Jack Valenti, President, 1600 I Street, NW, Washington, DC 20006; (202) 293-1966.

Beatrice M. Murphy Foundation Encourages the reading, appreciation and further production of African-American literature. Awards scholarships to the disadvantaged, assists authors, prepares annotated bibliographies and other information on African-American literature.

Beatrice M. Murphy, Executive Director, 2737 Devonshire Place, NW, Ste. 222, Washington, DC 20008; (202) 387-6053.

Music Critics Association Works to improve standards and quality of music criticism in the US and Canada and to foster public interest in music. Members: 254.

Richard D. Freed, Executive Director, 6201 Tuckerman Lane, Rockville, MD 20852; (301) 530-9527.

National Alliance of Third World Journalists Works to increase quality and quantity of media coverage of the Third World. Acts as an informational bridge between minorities in the US and Third World. Helps US journalists travel to Third World; provides speakers; schedules forums and seminars. Members: 330.

Leila McDowell, Co-coordinator, PO Box 43208, Columbia Heights, Washington, DC 20010; (202) 387-1662.

National Association of Black Journalists To strengthen the ties between blacks in the black media and blacks in the white media, sensitize white media to institutionalized racism in its coverage, expand black coverage and promote professionalism among black journalists. Members: 1,200.

Carl E. Morris, Sr., Executive Director, 11600 Sunrise Valley Drive, Reston, VA 22091; (703) 648-1270. De Wayne Wickham, President.

National Association of Black Owned Broadcasters Represents the interests of existing and potential black radio and television stations. Members are black broadcast station owners, black formatted stations not owned by blacks and others. Members: 150.

James L. Winston, Executive Director, 1730 M Street, NW, Washington, DC 20036.

National Association of Government Communicators Works to make communication an essential government resource by: disseminating information; encouraging professional development, public awareness and exchange of ideas; and improving internal communications. Maintains placement service; sponsors awards. Members: 600.

Debbie Trocchi, Executive Director, 80 South Early Street, Alexandria, VA 22304; (703) 823-4821.

National Association of Hispanic Journalists To organize and support Hispanics involved in the media. Encourages Hispanics to enter the profession, including to increase career opportunities; seeks recognition for achievements of Hispanics in the field; promotes fair and accurate media treatment of Hispanics. Offers placement services; conducts census of Hispanics in media; offers award, scholarships, seminars and training workshops. Members: 700.

Frank Newton, Executive Director, 634 National Press Building, 529 14th Street, NW, Washington, DC 20045; (202) 783-6228.

National Black Media Coalition Media advocacy group working to increase media access for blacks and other minorities through employment, ownership and programming. Participates in FCC rulemaking, speaks before university and professional audiences, conducts training classes, and negotiates affirmative action plans with media corporations. Maintains resource center; job referral service.

Carmen Marshall, Executive Director, 38 New York Avenue, NE, Washington, DC 20002; (202) 387-8155.

National Conference of Editorial Writers Works to "stimulate the conscience and the quality of the editorial page." Sponsors professional seminars, two annual meetings, regional critique meetings and annual foreign tour for members. Also co-sponsors the Wells Award for exemplary leadership in offering minorities employment in journalism. Members: 575.

Cora Everett, Executive Secretary, 6223 Executive Boulevard, Rockville, MD 20852; (301) 984-3015.

National Federation of Hispanics in Communication Works to form a network that will increase public awareness of Hispanic media, improve media coverage of the Hispanic community, provide programs and materials and encourages Hispanics to enter media-related education and training programs. Disseminates materials and conducts seminars. Members: 100.

Idalie Munoz, Co-Chair, PO Box 5480, Washington, DC 20016; (202) 529-0250.

National League of American Pen Women Group of writers, composers, artists and professional women in the creative arts that sponsors art exhibits and contests in letters, music and art. Maintains biographical archives, library and research programs; offers scholarships; conducts seminars; sponsors competitions. Members: 6,000.

Juanita Carmack Howison, President, Pen Arts Building, 1300 17th Street, NW, Washington, DC 20036; (202) 785-1997.

National Newspaper Association Group of editors and publishers of small-town newspapers. Sponsors competitions and presents awards, compiles statistics and holds annual Government Affairs conference. Members: 5,000.

David C. Simonson, Executive Vice President, 1627 K Street, NW, Suite 400, Washington, DC 20006; (202) 466-7200.

National Newspaper Foundation   Educational arm of National Newspaper Association. Conducts Blue Ribbon Newspaper Evaluation Program, regional management seminars, and conferences. Presents awards and scholarships to journalism school students.

David C. Simonson, Executive VP, 1627 K Street, NW, Suite 400, Washington, DC 20006; (202) 466-7200.

National Press Club   Private professional organization for journalists. Sponsors sports, travel and cultural events, workshops and seminars, rap sessions with news figures and authors, press forums and newsmaker breakfasts and luncheons. Awards prizes for consumer journalism, diplomatic writing, Washington coverage and newsletters. Holds annual book sale and art exhibits; maintains computerized reference library. Members: 4,800.

Harry Bodaan, General Manager, National Press Building, 529 14th Street, NW, Washington, DC 20045; (202) 662-7500.

National Press Foundation   Provides grants, fellowships and seminars for journalists and journalism teachers to foster excellence in journalism. Offers awards. Commissions books, articles and research projects; supports organizations dedicated to freedom of the press; conducts labor-management conferences and seminars.

David Yount, President, 1282 National Press Building, 529 14th Street, NW, Washington, DC 20045; (202) 662-7350.

National Newspaper Publishers Association   Presents annual award to black leader for distinguished contribution to black advancement. Sponsors annual workshop; maintains hall of fame. Members: 148.

Steve G. Davis, Executive Director, 970 National Press Building, Rm. 948, Washington, DC 20045; (202) 662-7324.

National Writers Union (DC Chapter)   Represents the interests of book authors, freelance writers, poets, journalists and technical and public relations writers. Applies collective bargaining techniques to helping promote writers' rights and to improve contractual agreements with magazine and book publishers. Chapter publishes newsletter, *Rough Draft*. Members: 150.

National Writers Union, P.O Box 21235, Kalorama Station, Washington, DC 20009; (703) 532-4571.

Newsletter Association Members are newsletter publishers representing small and large companies. Conducts research and prepare reports; represents members before federal agencies and monitors legislation; compiles statistics; holds seminars and workshops; presents annual awards. Members: 883.

Frederick D. Goss, Executive Director, 1401 Wilson Boulevard, Suite 403, Arlington, VA 22209; (703) 527-2333.

The Newspaper Guild Sponsors International Pension Fund, which provides retirement benefits to persons employed in the news industry. Also bestows annual Heywood Broun Award for outstanding journalistic achievement. Members: 34,000.

Charles Dale Perlik, Jr., President, 8611 Second Avenue, Silver Spring, MD 20912; (301) 585-2990.

PEN Syndicated Fiction Project Editorial panel selects approximately 70 short stories from those submitted during open reading period each January. Chosen stories are then syndicated to newspapers nationwide, and read on weekly half-hour show on National Public Radio called "The Sound of Writing." Three of stories chosen from year's ten best read are by their authors at Library of Congress.

Caroline Marshall, Director, PO Box 15650, Washington, DC 20003; (202) 543-6322.

The Playwright's Unit A three-tiered organization for playlovers: the Unit, comprising experienced playwriting members; the Forum, a mid-level group with the aim of helping members write a play and possibly move into the Unit; and Associates, for people who have a strong interest in the theater.

Donna Gerdin, Director, 1733 Kilbourne Place, NW, Washington, DC 20010; (202) 667-3623.

Poetry Committee of Greater Washington, DC Promotes the appreciation and writing of poetry in the region. Confers annually The Poetry Committee Book Award on an area writer who has published a collection of poetry in the previous year. Also sponsors annual "Celebration of Washington Writers," held the first week in May.

Gigi Bradford, Folger Shakespeare Library, 201 East Capitol Street, SE, Washington, DC 20003; (202) 232-2158.

Producers Council Individuals and firms engaged in producing motion pictures, videotapes, slide shows and audio presentations for outside clients. Lobbies Congress, maintains Professional Training Institute and offers symposia. Members: 45.

Harry R. McGee, Executive VP, 3150 Spring Street, Fairfax, VA 22031; (703) 273-7200.

Recording Industry Association of America Establishes manufacturing and recording standards; certifies sales figures for recording awards in various categories; operates antipiracy intelligence bureau; presents award to individual or institution that has encouraged cultural activities in the US. Members: 41.

James D. Fishel, VP and Executive Director, 1020 19th Street, NW, Suite 200, Washington, DC 20036; (202) 775-0101.

Reporters Committee for Freedom of the Press Provides free legal advice to reporters whose First Amendment rights are infringed upon by subpoenas and other legal pressures. Offers legal defense and research services for journalists and media lawyers. Members: 2,500.

Jane E. Kirtley, Executive Director, 800 18th Street, NW, Ste. 300, Washington, DC 20006; (202) 466-6312.

Society for Scholarly Publishing Members include librarians, booksellers, publishers, printers, authors and editors interested in scholarly publication. Serves as educational forum; three seminars a year. Members: 1,200.

Alice O'Leary, Adm Officer, 200 Florida Avenue, NW, Ste. 305, Washington, DC 20009; (202) 328-3555.

Society for Technical Communications Group of individuals and organizations interested or involved in technical communications seeking to advance theory and practice of technical communication in all media. Presents awards, awards scholarships, sponsors high school writing contests. Members: 12,000.

William C. Stolgitis, Executive Director, 815 15th Street, NW, Washington, DC 20005; (202) 737-0035.

Society of American Travel Writers   Group of editors, writers, broadcasters, photographers and PR representatives that works to provide travelers with accurate reports on destinations, facilities and services. Encourages preservation of historic sites and conservation of nature, presents annual awards to honor efforts to conserve, preserve and beautify America. Provides referral service and job bank. Members: 850.

Ken Fischer, Administrative Coordinator, 1100 17th Street, NW, Suite 1000, Washington, DC 20036; (202) 785-5567.

Society of Professional Journalists (Sigma Delta Chi)   The oldest and largest organization for journalists in the country. Conducts development seminars, sponsors several awards and internships, holds annual contests, conducts forums on free press and publishes a monthly newsletter (*The Quill*). Members: 20,000 (National).

Washington Professional Chapter, P.O. Box 19555, Washington, DC 20036; (202) 393-0133.

Software Publishers Association   Principal association of the microcomputer software industry. Examines and researches topics raised by growth in industry. Represents members' interest before federal government, provides monthly sales data and works with US postal service to develop fourth-class mail rate for computer discs. Sponsors awards program; operates campaign to stop software theft and protect copyrights. Members: 250.

Ken Wasch, Executive Director, 1101 Connecticut Avenue, NW, Suite 901, Washington, DC 20036; (202) 452-1600.

Washington Area Writers   Purpose is to serve interests of writers and writing in the metropolitan area. Holds monthly meetings the second Saturday of each month at Palisades branch of D.C. Public Library (4901 V Street, NW), usually featuring a speaker. Publishes monthly newsletter. Members: 60.

Frank Sokolove, President, PO Box 2372, Falls Church, VA 22042; (703) 298-0800.

Washington Book Publishers   Informal alliance of those who work in book design, editing, production, marketing and other publishing activities. Group meets regularly to discuss topics suggested by members. Provides a job bank. Members: 275.

Rev. John B. Breslin, SJ, President, c/o Georgetown University Press, 111 Intercultural Center, Washington DC 20057; (202) 687-5641.

Washington EdPress   Provides professional development for those active in the education publications field. A majority of members work for associations or freelance. Conducts monthly luncheons as well as informal brown-bag sessions. Holds an annual workshop, publishes a monthly newsletter and maintains a Job Bank. Members: 250.

Debra Olcott-Taylor, President, 1710 Connecticut Avenue NW, Washington, DC 20009; (202) 369-1522.

Washington Independent Writers   Promotes the mutual interests of freelance writers and provides its members with a variety of services, including a newsletter (*The Independent Writer*), monthly workshops, a very active Job Bank, specialized publications about writing and publishing, regular social activities, a greivance committee, health insurance and legal and financial services plans. A number of WIW's "Small Group Evenings" are held around town during the week (usually in members' homes) to discuss aspects of the writing life. WIW's annual spring conference, held each spring, is a major literary event. Members: 2,000.

Isolde Chapin, Director, 220 Woodward Building, 733 15th Street, NW, Suite 220, Washington, DC 20005; (202) 347-4973.

Washington Journalism Center   Seeks new methods in journalism education and new approaches to public affairs reporting in order to increase potential for excellence. Sponsors conferences for journalists to discuss key issues.

Julius Duscha, Director, 2401 Virginia Avenue, NW, Washington, DC 20037; (202) 331-7977.

Washington Romance Writers   This local chapter of the Romance Writers of America holds monthly meetings where members can meet editors and agents, talk shop and trade information on educational resources and on the market. Critique groups meet regularly. Members receive monthly newsletter. Members: 75.

Mary Kilchenstein, President, PO Box 21311, Kalorama Station, Washington, DC 20009; (301) 494-8080.

White House Correspondents Association Members are newspaper, magazine and television-radio correspondents engaged exclusively in news work at the White House. Members: 600.

Edgar A. Poe, Executive Director, 1067 National Press Building, 529 14th Street, NW, Washington, DC 20045; (202) 737-2934.

Women in Communications Works towards providing equality for men and women in all professions and for First Amendment rights. Holds annual and regional conferences, publishes monthly magazine, monitors legislation and participates in coalitions with other media and national women's organizations. D.C. chapter publishes monthly newsletter (*Byline*), maintains job bank and sponsors regular ongoing programs. D.C. Members: 315.

Susan Lowell Butler, Executive Vice President, 2101 Wilson Boulevard, Suite 417, Arlington, VA 22201; (703) 528-4200 (National Office). Cindy Bissett, President—D.C. Chapter, PO Box 19795, Washington, DC 20036; (703) 525-2226 (D.C. Chapter).

Women in Film and Video (D.C. Chapter) A national organization of women active in the film and video fields. Produces a bi-monthly newsletter, sponsors public forums and educational programs and produces a biennial film festival, "Women Make Movies." Board member Liz Bjorkland coordinates a popular monthly workshop of aspiring screenwriters. Members: 500.

Elise Roader, President, P.O. Box 19272, Washington, DC 20036; (202) 463-6372. Lucinda Ebersole, Festival Director.

Women's Institute For Freedom Of the Press Women journalists and others concerned with the expansion of all women's roles in the major national and local news media. Conducts research and disseminates information.

Martha Leslie Allen, Director, 3306 Ross Place, NW, Washington, DC 20008; (202) 966-7783.

Women's Media Project Project of the NOW Legal Defense and Education fund whose aim is to eliminate sex role stereotyping in the media and to increase participation of women and minorities in broadcasting. Conducts public education and community action campaigns; monitors compliance with equal employment legislation; encourages development and distribution of radio and TV programming offering realistic images of women; conducts research in broadcast employment.

Alisa Shapiro, Director, 1333 H Street, NW, 11th Floor, Washington, DC 20005; (202) 682-0940.

Women's National Book Association (D.C. Chapter) Serves to bring authors together with readers while championing the role of women in book publishing. Supports and brings to public attention the contributions of women writers, booksellers, librarians, editors and publishers. Provides a stimulating forum for issues relating to the book world. The chapter's newsletter is regarded as one of the best sources of writing jobs in the D.C. area. Members: 275.

Kathleen Johnston, President, WNBA Washington Chapter, c/o 3508 Leland Street, Chevy Chase, MD 20815; (202) 326-6454.

World Press Freedom Committee Journalistic organizations united to oppose state control of the media, especially in Third World countries. The committee has sponsored more than 90 programs in Africa, Asia, Latin America and the Caribbean.

Dana R. Bullen, Executive Director, Newspaper Center, P.O. Box 17407, Washington, DC 20041; (703) 648-1000.

The Writers' Center The Center's main goal is to help the general public participate in the creation, distribution and enjoyment of literature and the graphic arts. Offers courses on every aspect of writing and graphic design, allows members access to typesetting and printing equipment and operates the Book Gallery, which sells magazines and books by local writers and small press publishers. Sponsors frequent readings by local and visiting writers and poets. Publishes monthly newsletter (*Carousel*). Members: 1,500.

Jane Fox, Executive Director, 7815 Old Georgetown Road, Bethesda, MD 20814; (301) 654-8664.

Readings & Resources

"Books have to be read (worse luck it takes so long a time). It is the only way of discovering what they contain. A few savage tribes eat them, but reading is the only method of assimilation revealed to the West."

—E.M. FORSTER

"The profession of book writing makes horse racing seem like a solid, stable business."

—JOHN STEINBECK

The reading and writing of books are intimate, private acts. A public reading gives authors and readers a chance to turn what is usually a solitary communion into a shared occasion. A reading class opens up new vistas of imagination for children and adults just learning to read. A writing class gives budding authors new confidence or helps established authors work out thorny problems. And book fairs bring out the literary passions and haggling skills in all of us.

LITERARY READINGS & PROGRAMS

Every week, in and around Washington, literary readings are taking place. They may occur in bookstores, public libraries, auditoriums, university lounges or a log cabin in Rock Creek Park. Writers also participate with critics and scholars in public discussions of particular works, literary trends or relevant issues. Most of these readings and discussions are free. In cases where fees are charged, the amounts are reasonable and serve to make possible the individual reading while helping to support awards programs or worthy causes.

A valuable resource to monitor the active literary scene in our area is the Literary Calendar of *The Washington Post Book World,* which appears the first weekend of every month. Virtually all of the following readings and programs have appeared in the Calendar at one time or another.

American University Visiting Writers Reading Series

Well-known visiting writers deliver readings from their works for faculty, students and the public. Past readings have featured Stanley Kunitz, Richard Yates, John Irving, Linda Pastan, Allen Ginsburg, William Stafford and Grace Paley. Readings are free.

Henry Taylor, Department of Creative Writing, Room 227, Gray Hall, American University, 4400 Massachusetts Avenue, NW, Washington, DC 20016; (202) 885-2977/8.

Ascension Poetry Reading Series

The focus in this series is on Black and Third World writers living in the United States, especially new writers. An average of six readings are held each year at various locations throughout the city. Recent readings have featured Alice Walker, June Jordan, Ishmael Reed and Lucille Clifton, as well as Chinese-American and Japanese-American poets.

E. Ethelbert Miller, Director, PO Box 441, Howard University, Washington, DC 20054; (202) 232-3066.

Capitol Writers Series

Readings by Washington area writers, moderated by Susan Stamberg and Alan Cheuse of National Public Radio. Each reading features at least two writers and is organized around a theme. Held in the Palm Court of National Museum of American History, the last Sunday of each month, at 7 pm.

Dwight Bowers, Director, Division of Museum Programs, NMAH, 12th Street & Constitution Avenue, NW, Washington, DC 20560; (202) 357-4181.

Chapters: A Literary Bookstore

Sponsors an average of two to four author signings, readings and other literary events each month. To keep up on times and days, ask to be put on Chapters' mailing list. You'll receive free copies of "Literary and Other To Do's" and "The Variable Foot," a selection of recently published books of poetry and announcements of upcoming literary events.

Robin Diener, Co-owner, Chapters, 1613 Eye Street, NW, Washington, DC 20036; (202) 861-1333.

Corcoran School of Art Readings

During the school year (roughly September through April), the Corcoran School offers an average of one author reading each month. Readings usually take place on Tuesdays in the Corcoran Gallery Auditorium.

Nan Fry, Chair of Academic Studies, Corcoran School of Art, 17th Street and New York Avenue, NW, Washington, DC; (202) 320-2690.

d.c. space readings This downtown nightclub holds an average of two or three poetry and short story readings each month, showcasing mostly local authors. For information about upcoming events, call (202) 347-4960.

Cynthia Connelly, dc space, 443 7th Street, NW, Washington, DC 20004; (202) 393-0255.

Folger Shakespeare Library Evening Poetry Series The oldest privately-run poetry series in the city (1988–89 marks its twentieth year), the Folger Series brings distinguished poets to Washington from all over the world. Past readings have featured Derek Wolcott, Octavio Paz, Marilyn Hacker, Yehuda Amic'hai and Peter Sacks. All readings begin at 8 pm, and are followed by a reception. Readings are open to the public, but a donation is requested at the door; reservations or tickets are not required.

Gigi Bradford, Poetry Coordinator, Folger Shakespeare Library, 201 E. Capitol Street, SE, Washington, DC 20003; (202) 544-7077.

George Mason University Readings GMU's English Department and the student-run Writers' Club (whose members are undergraduate and graduate creative writing students), co-sponsor as many as 10 major author readings during the school year. The emphasis is on (but not limited to) poetry and fiction. Poets Richard Wilbur and Sharon Olds and nonfiction writer Barry Lopez are among authors who have given recent readings. Readings are usually held in Student Union 2; free and open to the public.

Roger Lathbury, Director of the Writing Program, George Mason University, 4400 University Drive, Fairfax, VA 22030; (703) 323-2936.

International Poetry Forum Each year, IPF and the Smithsonian Resident Associate Program sponsor six readings by poets from around the world; occasionally programs combine poetry and music. The season runs from October to May, with readings usually held Sundays at 7:30 pm at the Hirschorn Museum and Sculpture Garden. Admission fee charged.

Smithsonian Resident Associate Program, 1100 Jefferson Drive, SW, Washington, DC 20560; (202) 357-3030.

Jenny Moore Fund for Writers With the George Washington University Department of English, offers an average of 3 to 4 readings each semester by writers from the area and around the country. Recent readings featured Sue Hubbel, N. V. Scot Momaday and U.S. Poet Laureate Howard Nemerov. Free and open to the public.

Department of English, GW University, 801 22nd Street, NW, Washington, DC 20052; (202) 994-6180.

Jewish Community Center Each year, the Center invites four to six local and national authors to read from their work. All authors featured have written books of Jewish interest. Hosts occasional readings and literature study sessions emphasizing Jewish heritage.

Ms. Tommy Feldman, Director—Literary Arts Development, 6125 Montrose Road, Rockville, MD 20850; (301) 881-0100.

Joaquin Miller Cabin Poetry Series Its organizers, Word Works, call this summer series "poetry under the stars." All the readings take place outdoors in Rock Creek Park, June through the first week of August.

The series chiefly focuses on local poets, with two poets reading each evening followed by a party. Past presenters have included Roland Flint, Ann Darr, Myra Sklarew and Pulitzer Prize-winner Henry Taylor. Readings are held every Tuesday at 7:30 pm at the Miller Cabin and are free.

Joaquin Miller Cabin, Beach & Military Drives, Rock Creek Park, Washington, DC. For information call Jacklyn Potter at (202) 726-0971.

Lammas Books & More Reading Series This bookstore has regular readings by feminist authors, generally held every other Sunday at 2 pm. Poetry readings are the most common, but you'll also hear fiction and essays. Wine and snacks served. A donation of $2 is requested for readings by out-of-town authors; otherwise programs are free. The store's free quarterly newsletter lists details of upcoming events.

Lammas-Dupont Circle, 1427 21st Street, NW, Washington, DC 20036; (202) 775-8218.

Library of Congress Literary Reading Series   From October to May, nationally known poets and authors are invited to read from their work (average of two readings each month). Past readings have featured Garrison Keillor, Herman Wouk, Tom Stoppard and poets Gwendolyn Brooks, Howard Nemerov and Ethelbert Miller. The free evening readings are usually introduced by the U.S. Poet Laureate, followed by a reception (tickets generally not required).

Nancy Galbraith, Director, Poetry & Literature Program, First & East Capitol Streets, SW, Washington, DC 20540; (202) 707-5394.

Lunchtime Author Series   The Literary Friends of the DC Public Library sponsor regular author discussions every Tuesday at noon in the main lobby of the library. Mostly local writers of fiction, nonfiction and poetry read from and talk about their work. Free to the public.

Jewel Ogonji, Library Services, Martin Luther King Memorial Library, 901 G Street, NW, Washington, DC 20001; (202) 727-1186. Alternate contact: Betty Parry, Lunchtime Authors Organizer, (301) 652-5665.

Montpelier Cultural Arts Center   From September through November, and sometimes in the spring, the Center sponsors free poetry and fiction readings (usually three a season). Programs are free, and generally take place Sunday afternoons or Friday evenings.

Montpelier Cultural Arts Center, 12826 Laurel-Bowie Road, Laurel, MD 20708; (301) 953-1993.

The National Archives Author Lecture Series   At least two lectures each month by authors who have published recent books focusing on American history or current events. Lectures take place midday at the Archives and are free to the public. For details on upcoming lectures, call the "Events Line" at (202) 523-3000, or get on the mailing list to receive a free monthly calendar of events.

The National Archives, Pennsylvania Avenue between 7th and 9th Streets, NW, Washington, DC 20408; (202) 523-3099.

PEN/Faulkner Reading Series   These readings, given by respected and popular authors, benefit the PEN/Faulkner Award. The season runs from October to May and averages eight readings. The Friday evening programs are followed by a short question and answer period, ending with a reception and book signing. One reading in the series generally features the winner of the previous year's PEN/Faulkner Award.

Recent authors reading from their work include novelists T. Coraghessan Boyle, William Styron, E. L. Doctorow and John Updike, playwright Arthur Miller and poet James Dickey. Admission is $10, with proceeds going to the PEN/ Faulkner Award.

Janice Delaney, Executive Director, PEN/Faulkner Award, The Folger Shakespeare Library, 201 E. Capitol Street, SE, Washington, DC 20003; (202) 544-7077.

Poetry Hotline   Dial (202) 291-POET for a listing of poetry events in the Washington, DC area. Updated weekly.

Poetry/PM   The International Monetary Fund sponsors regular lunchtime poetry readings (usually three a month), with a focus on international poets. All readings begin at 1 pm, and admission is free.

IMF Visitors Center, 700 19th Street, Washington, DC 20431; (202) 623-6869.

Politics & Prose Bookstore Readings   This neighborhood bookstore holds author readings at least five times each month. P & P also schedules regular Sunday brunches at 1 pm, where readers and writers can gather over coffee and doughnuts. The store's free quarterly newsletter and periodic updates provide details about upcoming events.

5010 Wisconsin Avenue, NW, Washington, DC 20008; (202) 364-1919.

Smithsonian Resident Associate Program   Among RAP's full annual schedule of lectures and events is nearly always something literary. In the spring of 1989, for example, writers as diverse as Neil Sheehan, Robert MacNeil and Nikki Giovanni gave talks. Times and locations vary. For details on upcoming events, join RAP or request a copy of the newsletter, *The Smithsonian Associate*.

Resident Associate Program, Smithsonian Institution, 1100 Jefferson Drive, SW, Washington, DC 20560; (202) 357-3030.

University of Maryland Readings Series The English Department sponsors "Writers Here and Now," twice-a-month readings by poets and novelists held in the Katherine Anne Porter Room of the main library. Recent author readings include poets Louise Gluck, Gerald Stern and Rita Dove and novelists Russell Banks and Marilynne Robinson.

Department of English, University of Maryland, College Park, MD 20740; (301) 454-2511.

Vintage Poets Monthly poetry readings, held from September to June, sponsored by Sarah's Circle, an organization providing housing and programs for low-income seniors. Each of the readings features a published poet from the Washington area, as well as seniors involved with Sarah's Circle. Readings are free and open to the public.

Sheila Carruth, Program Coordinator, Sarah's Circle, 2551 17th Street, NW, Washington, DC 20009; (202) 332-1400.

Visions International Poetry Reading Series The publisher of the poetry magazine *Visions* presents monthly readings by local and out-of-town poets at two locations: the Art Barn [2401 Tilden Street, NW, near Beach Drive in Rock Creek Park; (202) 426-6719] and the Reston Regional Library [11925 Bowman Towne Drive, Reston, VA; (703) 689-2700]. A small donation is requested.

Bradley Strahan, Director, Visions International, 4705 South 8th Road, Arlington, VA 22204; (703) 521-0142.

WPFW 89.3 FM Radio This progressive, multicultural radio station sponsors a weekly poetry show, "The Poet and Poem," every Sunday evening from 8 to 9 pm. Hosted by poet Grace Cavalieri, the program features readings by and discussions with local and internationally known guest poets. The program is also broadcast around the world on Voice of America.

Grace Cavalieri, c/o WPFW, 702 H Street, NW, Washington, DC 20001; (202) 783-3100.

The Writer's Center Local and visiting poets read from their work on Sundays at 2 pm, followed by a reception. Frequent open readings for local poets. Upcoming events listed in *Carousel*, the Center's free newsletter.

7815 Old Georgetown Road, Bethesda, MD 20814; (301) 654-8664.

LITERACY & READING PROGRAMS

To sustain an adult population of book readers and book buyers, children must be encouraged to read. The D.C. metropolitan area has a large number of literacy programs designed to raise reading proficiency in the young and nurture a love for books. These efforts are also making dramatic headway in improving reading skills for all ages, including adults in various adult education programs.

No single literacy program can claim greater successes in teaching all kids to read than *Reading Is Fundamental* (RIF), a national organization based here in Washington, D.C. RIF volunteers have taught thousands of children to love books while helping parents to encourage reading at home. There are now 3,500 RIF programs around the country, and a good number are spread throughout the metropolitan area. To find out more about RIF, or to get involved, contact: Reading Is Fundamental, 600 Maryland Avenue, SW, Washington, DC 20560; (202) 237-3220.

Another exciting national literacy project based here in Washington, D.C. is the *Barbara Bush Foundation for Family Literacy*, launched March, 1989. The foundation plans to support projects in schools and preschools that will teach reading skills to parents at the same time their children are learning to read. It will also support and promote local family literacy programs across the country, while encouraging literacy training for teachers and volunteers. For information, contact: The Barbara Bush Foundation For Family Literacy, 1002 Wisconsin Avenue, NW, Washington, DC 20007; (202) 338-2006.

Probably the two best places to go for up-to-date information about area literacy programs are:

The Metropolitan Washington Literacy Network A project of the Council of Governments and the D.C. Literacy Providers Network, MWLN is a clearinghouse for information on literacy programs in the region. Among its services, the Network has compiled a directory of all such programs (most recent edition, 1989) describing where they are, what they do and whether they charge a fee (very few do).

Jackie Flowers, Literacy Coordinator, Metropolitan Washington Literacy Network, Council of Governments, 1875 I Street, NW, Washington, DC 20006; (202) 223-6800.

D.C. Literacy Providers Network   Operated by the Adult Basic Education Office of the DC. Public Library, this active clearinghouse has compiled another directory (most recent edition, 1988) of all literacy programs in the District of Columbia. The directory, which is free, is cross-referenced based on cost, location and services.

Marcia Harrington, D.C. Literacy Providers Network, Martin Luther King Memorial Library, 901 G Street, NW, Rm 426, Washington, DC 20001; (202) 727-1616.

Most of the programs listed below, compiled from these two directories and other sources, help adults with limited or no reading skills (pre-K to 8th grade) learn how to read as well as offering other services. Some programs work with adults one-on-one; others use small groups or classes. Most depend heavily (some entirely) on volunteers. Many also have their own volunteer training programs, if you would like to get involved.

District of Columbia

Academy of Hope   1715 Columbia Road, NW, #301, Washington, DC 20009; (202) 387-2347.

Bruce Monroe Community School   3012 Georgia Avenue, NW, Washington, DC 20012; (202) 576-6215.

Cathedral Literacy Program   Washington Cathedral, Mt. Saint Albans, NW, Washington, DC 20016; (202) 537-6237/ 537-6240.

Center for Youth Services   921 Pennsylvania Avenue, SE, Washington, DC 20003; (202) 543-5707.

Community Based Instruction Services   P.O. Box 28537, Washington, DC 20038; (202) 332-4723.

D.C Office on Aging　1424 K Street, NW, Washington, DC 20005; (202) 724-5622.

D.C Tutors　735 8th Street, SE, Washington, DC 20003; (202) 543-7323.

Delta Adult Literacy Center　Delta Sigma Theta Sorority, Washington Alumnae Chapter, P.O. Box 4439, Washington, DC 20017; (202) 362-1700.

ENTRE/Community of Hope　1417 Belmont Street, NW, Washington, DC 20009; (202) 232-8415.

Franklin Adult Education Center　13th & K Streets, NW, Washington, DC 20005; (202) 724-4946.

Friendship Community School　4600 Livingston Road, SE, Washington, DC 20032; (202) 767-7184.

Friendship House Association　619 D Street, SE, Washington, DC 20003; (202) 675-9050/ 675-9068.

Gallaudet University Adult Basic Education Program　800 Florida Avenue, NE, Washington, DC 20002; (202) 651-5044.

Ideal Learning Center　4842 16th Street, NW, Washington, DC 20011; (202) 726-0313.

Kennedy Institute Continuing Education　801 Buchanan Street, NE, Washington, DC 20017; (202) 529-7600.

Language at Work　4115 Wisconsin Avenue, NW, Ste. 102, Washington, DC 20016; (202) 363-4521.

Literacy Volunteers of America　1325 W Street, NW, Washington, DC 20009; (202) 387-1772.

Maury Community School　13th Street & Constitution Avenue, NE, Washington, DC 20002; (202) 724-4481.

National Learning Center　800 3rd Street, NE, Washington, DC 20002; (202) 675-4156.

Phelps Career Development Center　26th Street & Benning Road, NE, Washington, DC 20002; (202) 724-4516.

PLAN (Push Literacy Action Now) 1332 G Street, SE, Washington, DC 20003; (202) 547-8903.

Project CALL (Armstrong Adult Education) 1st & P Streets, NW, Washington, DC 20001; (202) 673-7365.

Reading Center, George Washington University 2201 G Street, NW, Ste. 429, Washington, DC 20052; (202) 994-6286.

Sacred Heart Adult Education Center 1621 Park Road, NW, Washington, DC 20010; (202) 462-6499.

Samaritan Ministry St. Stephen's Church, 1525 Newton Street, NW, Washington, DC 20010; (202) 797-0360.

Southeast Neighborhood House 1225 Maple View Place, SE, Washington, DC 20020; (202) 889-8000.

Southeast Vicariate Cluster 1200 U Street, SE, Washington, DC 20020; (202) 889-5581.

Sursum Corda Adult Education Program P.O. Box 2255, Rm 316 Leavey, Georgetown University, Washington, DC 20057; (202) 687-3703.

Washington, D.C. Literacy Council 1825 Eye Street, NW, Ste. 975, Washington, DC 20006; (202) 331-9672.

Washington Urban League Basic Skills Center 728 8th Street, NE, Washington, DC 20002; (202) 544-8188/89.

Wider Opportunities for Women 1325 G Street, NW, Lower Level, Washington, DC 20005; (202) 638-3143.

Woodson Community School Adult Education 55th & Eades Streets, NE, Washington, DC 20019; (202) 727-5436.

Suburban Maryland

Telephone Reference, a member of the Montgomery/ Prince George's Coalition for Literacy Action, has compiled an excellent *Directory of Literacy Resources* (1987) in which many of the following programs are listed. The Coalition refers service providers and the public to appropriate literacy programs. The directory is available free from: Telephone Reference, Montgomery County Department of Public Libraries, 99 Maryland Avenue, Rockville, MD 20850; (301) 279-1637.

Extended Hand Adult Learning Center   Clifton Park Baptist Church, 8818 Piney Branch Road, Silver Spring, MD 20903; (301) 593-7239.

Literacy Council of Montgomery County   11701 Georgia Avenue, Lower Level, Wheaton, MD 20902; (301) 942-9292.

Literacy Council of Prince George's County   5012 Rhode Island Avenue, Hyattsville, MD 20781; (301) 864-6107.

Montgomery County Public Schools, Department of Adult Education   12518 Greenly Street, Silver Spring, MD 20906; (301) 942-8304.

Prince George's County Public Schools, Adult Continuing Education   14201 School Lane, Upper Marlboro, MD 20772; (301) 952-6088. Classes conducted at 16 locations throughout the county.

Suburban Virginia

Adult Learning Center   1501 Cameron Street, Alexandria, VA 22314; (703) 549-7755.

Alexandria Department of Human Services, Office of Employment Training   2525 Mount Vernon Avenue, Unit 7, Alexandria, VA 22301; (703) 838-0940. All instruction given at John Adams Site, 5651 Rayburn Avenue, Alexandria, VA 22312; (703) 931-6733.

Arlington County Adult Education   Drew Center, 3500 S. 24th Street, Arlington, VA 22206; (703) 521-3109 & Gunston School, 2700 South Lang Street, Arlington, VA 22206; (703) 684-9000.

Fairfax County, Adult & Community Education   7510 Lisle Avenue, Fairfax, VA; (703) 893-1090. Nine learning centers located throughout the county.

Falls Church Community Education, Adult Basic Education   7124 Leesburg Pike, Falls Church, VA 22043; (703) 241-7676.

Fauquier County Adult Learning Center   707 Waterloo Road, Warrenton, VA 22186; (703) 347-4372.

Literacy Council of Northern Virginia   2855 Annandale Road, Falls Church, VA 22042; (703) 237-0866.

Literacy Volunteers, Fauquier County   P.O. Box 3177, 65 Culpepper Street, Warrenton, VA 22186; (703) 349-8142.

Loudoun Literacy Council   P.O. Box 1555, Leesburg, VA 22075; (703) 777-2209.

Prince William County Schools, Adult Education Division   P.O. Box 389, Manassas, VA 22110; (703) 791-7356/57/58. Programs conducted at nine locations throughout the county.

Volunteer Learning Program   3976 Chain Bridge Road, Fairfax, VA 22030; (703) 691-2343. A joint program of Fairfax County Public Schools, the Fairfax Juvenile Court and the Fairfax Public Libraries.

WRITING COURSES & PROGRAMS

For those wanting to improve their writing (and who doesn't?), there are a number of local opportunities for taking writing classes. For those who write well and aspire to write professionally or tackle the creative forms, there are a number of outstanding writing programs in the area. These programs may be undertaken on a full-time basis or course-by-course, either through academic institutions or private organizations like The Writer's Center or Washington Independent Writers.

The American University

Creative Writing   An MFA degree in creative writing is offered through the university's Creative Writing Department within the Literature Department. Co-directors Henry Taylor and Richard McCann lead a staff of eight full and part-time writing instructors.

The program requires 48 semester hours, or approximately two-and-a-half years, to complete. The program allows people to audit creative writing classes. Additionally, the program sponsors three workshops per semester to which non-students may apply (but preference is given to enrolled writing students).

Henry Taylor/Richard McCann, Department of Creative Writing, The American University, Gray Hall (Rm 227), 4400 Massachusetts Avenue, NW, Washington, DC 20016; (202) 885-2977/8.

Journalism Bachelor's and master's degrees in communications, with focus in journalism and public affairs offered through School of Communications. Length of the undergraduate program is four years; for the MA program, 10 months (full-time students only).

Graduate Journalism Committee, School of Communication, The American University, 4400 Massachusetts Avenue, NW, Washington, DC 20016; (202) 885-2060/78.

Professional Development Workshops Offers on-site writing and editing programs for organizations, hosted by a corporation, government agency or individual organization. Courses, which can be credit or non-credit and last from several hours to fourteen weeks, are tailored to the needs and interests of the host organization and are, for the most part, taught by American University faculty.

Program Representative, Office of Contract Programs, The American University, Nebraska Hall, 1st Floor, 4400 Massachusetts Avenue, NW, Washington, DC 20016; (202) 885-3990.

Technical Writing Office of Continuing Programs offers undergraduate and graduate-level certificate programs in technical writing. Year-long program of mostly evening courses takes interdisciplinary approach. Credit can be applied toward degree.

University Programs Advisement Center, The American University, 4400 Massachusetts Avenue, NW, Washington, DC 20016; (202) 885-2500.

Editorial Experts

Workshops on Publication Skills This private editorial consulting & publishing firm offers basic through advanced workshops. One-to-three days long, the courses are taught by staff and area publication professionals.

Andrea Lentz, Manager, Training Division, Editorial Experts, 85 S. Bragg Street, Suite 400, Alexandria, VA 22312; (703) 642-3040.

Georgetown University

Certificate Program in Editing & Publications Georgetown's Professional Development Program offers evening courses (8 to 12 weeks) in the principles of writing and editing, graphic design and printing, advanced editing, copyediting, proofreading and developing resource skills.

Karan Powell, Director, Professional Development Program, 306 Intercultural Center, Georgetown University, Washington, DC 20057; (202) 687-6218.

George Mason University

Creative Writing Students can choose among three writing-related degrees: BA in English, with concentration in writing (minimum 12 hours in writing); MFA in writing, specializing in poetry or fiction (48 hours); and MA in English, with concentration on writing fiction or poetry (30 hours).

Program faculty members include: novelists Richard and Robert Bausch, Susan Richards Shreve, Alan Cheuse and Vassily Aksyonov; poets Carolyn Forche, C.K. Williams, Peter Klappert and Susan Tichy; and playwright Paul D'Andrea. The program also brings in distinguished visiting writers to teach each year, among them Carlos Fuentes, Edmund White and John Gardener.

Roger Lathbury, Director, Writing Program, English Department, George Mason University, 4400 University Drive, Fairfax, VA 22030; (703) 323-2936 (Geri Dolan, Program Secretary).

Extended Studies Adults who want to take any GMU writing course without enrolling in a degree program can do so by registering through Extended Studies. Credit given can be applied toward degree program in future.

George Mason University, School for Continued & Alternative Learning, 4400 University Drive, Fairfax, VA 22030; (703) 323-2436.

George Washington University

Creative Writing Program offers a BA in English, with emphasis in Creative Writing. Five creative writing instructors.

Faye Moskowitz, Department of English, George Washington University, Washington, DC 20052; (202) 994-6180.

Publication Specialist Program A year-long, graduate-level certificate program of mostly evening courses covering all aspects of brochure, newsletter, magazine and book publishing. Currently developing certificate program in desk-top publishing.

Kate McIntyre, Program Director, Publication Specialist Program, George Washington University, 801 22nd Street, NW, Ste. T409, Washington, DC 20052; (202) 994-7273.

Howard University Press

Book Publishing Institute Intensive, five-week certificate program covering the basics of book publishing. Key publishing executives conduct lectures and workshops on editing, design and production, marketing and financial management. Also covers specialty areas such as children's, university, textbook and direct-mail publishing. Enrollment limited and competitive.

Avis Taylor, Program Administrator, Book Publishing Institute, Howard University Press, 2900 Van Ness Street, NW, Washington, DC 20008; (202) 686-6498.

Smithsonian Institution

Smithsonian Resident Associates Program Sponsors extensive range of courses in the arts and humanities, taught by Smithsonian and other scholars and experts. Offerings vary year to year, but nearly always include something literary. In the spring of 1989, for example, the Resident Associates sponsored a course in collaboration with Washington Independent writers called "Six Evenings with Leading Washington Writers." Academic credit given by the University of Maryland for selected courses.

Resident Associates Program, Smithsonian Institution, 1100 Jefferson Drive, SW, Washington, DC 20560; (202) 357-3030.

University of the District of Columbia

National Capital Area Writers Project Offers courses and workshops designed to enhance the ability of teachers—from kindergarten to college level—to convey the importance of writing and to teach it well. Offers 5-week summer institute and shorter workshops throughout the year. Housed at UDC, but is a program of six area universities and colleges.

Dr. Virginia Newsome, University of the District of Columbia, 4200 Connecticut Avenue, Washington, DC 20008; (202) 282-7522.

Writing UDC is developing a masters degree program in writing, due to open in fall 1990. Program designed to be of use to scholars, teachers and practicing writers.

Renee Housman, Assistant Professor, Department of English Studies, UDC, 4200 Connecticut Avenue, NW, Washington, DC 20008; (202) 282-7522.

University of Maryland

Center for Professional Development Offers six-session evening course in "Effective Writing" in the fall and spring, as well as certificate program in marketing communication.

Center for Professional Development, Adult Education Building, University College, University of Maryland, College Park, MD 20742; (301) 985-7195.

College of Journalism Offers BA and MA in several journalistic specializations, both print and broadcast. Students can also pursue a PhD in public communications. A number of the college's 27 faculty members double as staff on the *Washington Journalism Review*, which is published by the college.

Greig Steward, Assistant Dean for Undergraduate Studies, College of Journalism, University of Maryland, College Park, MD 20742; (301) 454-1815.

Creative Writing Starting in fall 1989, the Department of English will offer a Masters of Fine Arts in

Creative Writing (two-year program). The Department offers an extensive selection of creative writing courses at the undergraduate level.

Among the eight full-time professors who teach creative writing are novelist Joyce Kornblatt, poets Stanley Plumly, Phillis Levin and Michael Collier, and novelist/translator Howard Norman.

Washington Independent Writers

Freelance Basics Course   Offers four-session evening course every February on the basics of being a freelance writer. Designed for established writers who want to freelance, the course covers practical issues from writing query letters to taxes to marketing.

The Freelance Basics course also includes seminars in which writers with various specialties (fiction, business, technical) can have their work critiqued. Participation open to non-WIW members.

WIW, 220 Woodward Building, 733 15th Street, NW, Washington, DC 20005; (202) 347-4973.

The Writer's Center

Writing Workshops   Offers a range of writing workshops in fiction, nonfiction, poetry, playwriting and screenwriting. Participants in writing workshops submit manuscripts for critical evaluation by peers. The Center also holds workshops in editing, phototypesetting and basic graphic design. Workshops last between four and eight weeks, and are offered four times a year.

Jane Fox, Director, The Writer's Center, 7815 Old Georgetown Road, Bethesda, MD 20814; (301) 654-8664.

WRITING CONTESTS, GRANTS & AWARDS

A surprising number of locally sponsored contests, grants and awards are available to area writers. These competitions and awards are designed to encourage emerging talent and give public recognition to distinguished writing in a number of genres and specialized fields.

American Historical Association Book Awards   Annual awards to honor books in the field of history, published in the year preceding the deadline. Deadline for most awards is June 15. Prize/Award Amounts: $1,000.

Committee Chairman, AHA, 400 A Street, SE, Washington, DC 20003; (202) 544-2422.

AMWA Medical Book Awards Competition   Annual awards presented by the American Medical Writers Association for books written in the previous calendar year, one in each of the following three categories: books for physicians, books for allied health professionals and trade books for the lay public. Deadline: April 1.

Book Awards Committee, AMWA, 9650 Rockville Pike, Bethesda, MD 20814; (301) 493-0003.

American Sociological Association Awards   Two of ASA's annual awards for outstanding contributions to the field are for written works. Entries for both awards should be sent to:

ASA, 1722 N Street, NW, Washington, DC 20036; (202) 833-3410.

Author's Recognition Day Reception & Special Awards Ceremony   Reception held each November by the Literary Friends of the D.C. Public Library, honoring all Washington writers. Special recognition given to three authors who have had a book published in the previous year, and also to three individuals who have made major contributions to the literary life in the nation's capital. Previous honorees have included Nien Cheng, author of *Life and Death in Shanghai*, Myra Sklarew, poet and president of Yaddo Writers' Colony, and Juan Williams, *Washington Post* reporter and author of *Eyes on the Prize*.

Molly Raphael, Executive Assistant to the Director, D.C. Public Library, 901 G Street, NW, Washington, DC 20001: (202) 727-1101. Mari Francis Hardison, President, Literary Friends of the D.C. Public Library.

Folio Fiction/Poetry Award   Two annual awards, co-sponsored by American University and *Folio Magazine* (AU's literary magazine), for short fiction and poetry. Work submitted must be unpublished. Manuscripts accepted from August to April. Deadline: March 1. Award, plus publication in spring issue of *Folio*.

Dept. of Literature, American University, 4400 Massachusetts Avenue, NW, Washington, DC 20016; (202) 885-2971.

Gallaudet Journalism Award   Annual awards for examples of print and broadcast journalism (previously published or aired) that "provide the public with a broad awareness and understanding of the achievements of deaf people, research in the field of deafness and the continuing documentation of deaf expression". Deadline: April 30.

Gallaudet Journalism Awards, Office of Public Relations, Gallaudet University, 800 Florida Avenue, NE, Washington, DC 20002; (202) 651-5505.

Jefferson Cup Award   Annual award for a work published in the fields of history, biography or historical fiction (1490 to present) written especially for young people. Deadline: December.

Debbie Tracci, Virginia Library Association, 80 S. Early Street, Alexandria, VA 22304; (703) 370-6020.

Robert F. Kennedy Awards   Given to honor the author or journalist whose work most faithfully and forcefully reflects Robert F. Kennedy's purposes and beliefs.

• *RFK Book Award*   For a work of fiction or nonfiction, published in the previous calendar year, "that shows compassion for the poor or powerlessness or those suffering from injustice." Deadline: late January.

Caroline Croft, Executive Director, RFK Book Awards, RFK Memorial, 1031 31st Street, NW, Washington, DC 20007; (202) 333-1880.

• *RFK Journalism Awards*   Given for accounts about the disadvantaged in the U.S. Entries must have been published or broadcast in the year prior to the award, and can be submitted by individuals or their appropriate organization. Deadline: late January.

Linda Semans, Staff Director, RFK Journalism Awards, RFK Memorial, 1031 31st Street, NW, Washington, DC 20007; (202) 333-1880.

Felix Morley Memorial Prizes   Annual prizes given to "discover and encourage college-aged writers who reflect an interest in the classical liberal traditions of private property and free exchange." Entries can be articles (editorials, columns, essays, criticism or investigative pieces) or short stories. Open to college-aged writers from the U.S. and abroad. Three submissions per person; judges consider entire body of work. Deadline: June 15.

Morley Prize Secretary, Institute for Humane Studies, GMU University, 4400 University Drive, Fairfax, VA 22030; (703) 323-1055.

National Awards for Educational Reporting Annual awards to honor the best in educational reporting in print, radio and television. Seventeen categories. Deadline: mid to late January.

Lisa J. Walker, Executive Director, Education Writers Association, 1001 Connecticut Avenue, NW, Ste. 310, Washington, DC 20036; (202) 429-9680.

The National Press Foundation Annual Awards Three annual awards for excellence in print and broadcast journalism. Winners often donate their checks to charity.

David Yount, President, National Press Foundation, 1282 National Press Building, Washington, DC 20045; (202) 662-7350.

Larry Neal Writing Contest Sponsored by the D.C. Commission on the Arts and Humanities, the contest helps to recognize and reward the talents of local writers. Candidates, who must have lived in the District of Columbia for at least one year, can submit entries in only one of five categories: poetry, fiction, criticism, essays or dramatic writing. Award: $500 in each category.

D.C. Commission on the Arts & Humanities, 1111 E Street, NW, Ste. B500, Washington, DC 20004; (202) 724-5613.

Alicia Patterson Foundation Fellowship Program for Journalists One-year grants awarded to working print journalists, reporters, editors or photojournalists with at least five years of professional experience, to pursue independent projects of significant interest. Between five and seven fellows selected each year. Deadline: October 1.

Margaret Engel, Director, Alicia Patterson Foundation, 1001 Pennsylvania Avenue, NW, Ste 1250, Washington, DC 20004; (202) 951-8512.

PEN/Faulkner Award for Fiction Annual award recognizing five American authors who have published works of distinction in the previous calendar year. Traditionally, winners are writers whose work has been widely overlooked. Recent award winners include T. Coraghessan Boyle (*World's End*), Richard Wiley (*Soldiers in Hiding*) and Peter Taylor (*The Old Forest & Other Stories*). Awards ceremony, held second Saturday in May, is open to public. Deadline: December 31.

Janice Delaney, Executive Director, PEN/Faulkner Award, Folger Shakespeare Library, 201 E. Capitol Street, SE, Washington, DC 20003; (202) 544-7077.

PEN/ Malamud Award Annual short story award for lifetime of achievement in writing short stories or for a collection of exceptional distinction published in previous year. Winner chosen by committee of PEN/Faulkner board members and literary executors of the Bernard Malamud Fund. First winner in 1988 was John Updike. Awards ceremony open to the public.

Janice Delaney, Executive Director, PEN/Faulkner Award, Folger Shakespeare Library, 201 E. Capitol Street, SE, Washington, DC 20003; (202) 544-7077.

Phi Beta Kappa Book Awards Awards given each year for notable books published in the United States. The *Ralph Waldo Emerson Award* is given for outstanding interpretive studies of the intellectual and cultural condition of man. The *Christian Gauss Award* is given for an outstanding work of literary criticism or scholarship. *The Science Award* is given for outstanding interpretations of the physical or biological sciences or mathematics. Deadlines: April 30. Awards: $2,500.

Kenneth M. Greene, Administrator, PBK Book Awards, 1811 Q Street, NW, Washington, DC 20009; (202) 265-3808.

Poet Lore Awards This quarterly poetry magazine, published by the Writer's Center, sponsors two annual awards: the John Andrews Narrative Poetry Award (Deadline: November 30/Award: $250) and the Ratner Feber Award for single poem by a poet who has not had a book published (Deadline: April 30/ Award: $1,000).

Poet Lore, Writer's Center, 7815 Old Georgetown Road, Bethesda, MD 20814; (202) 654-8664.

The Poetry Committee Book Award For published collection of poetry by a writer from the Washington metropolitan area. Deadline: April 1. Cash award given.

Poetry Committee, The Folger Shakespeare Library, 201 E. Capitol Street, SE, Washington, DC 20003 (Attn: Gigi Bradford): (202) 544-7077.

Regardie's Magazine's Annual Money/Power/Greed Fiction Writing Contest   Three annual prizes for "stories about money, power and greed, in the tradition of Fitzgerald's *The Great Gatsby*, Dreiser's *The Titan* and Dos Passos' *The Big Money*". Manuscripts should be from 2,000 to 10,000 words. The contest is co-sponsored and cojudged with the Sagalyn Literary Agency. Deadline: April. Prizes: $5,000 (first place); $3,000 (second place) and $2,000 (third place). The three winning stories will be published in the magazine.

Fiction Contest, *Regardie's Magazine*, 1010 Wisconsin Avenue, NW, Ste. 600, Washington, DC 20007; (202) 342-0410.

Mary Roberts Rinehart Fund   Annual grants for unpublished creative writers of fiction, poetry, drama, biography, autobiography or history with strong narrative quality. Writers must be nominated by a sponsoring writer or editor. Deadline: November 30. Award: Two awards of $2,500 given each year (fiction and poetry in even years; nonfiction and drama in odd years).

Roger Lathbury, Director, Mary Roberts Rinehart Fund, GMU, 4400 University Drive, Fairfax, VA 22030; (703) 323-2221.

Towson State University Prize for Literature   Annual prize for book or book-length manuscript of fiction, poetry, drama or imaginative nonfiction by a young (40 or younger) Maryland writer. Work must either have been published in the three years preceding the nomination year, or be scheduled for publication within the nomination year. Author must have been a Maryland resident for at least three years. Deadline: mid-May. Prize: $1,000.

Annette Chappell, Dean, College of Liberal Arts, Towson State University, Towson, MD 21204; (301) 321-2128.

Washington Independent Writers Awards   The nation's largest regional writers' organization, WIW gives out three awards during each calendar year:

• *President's Award* Established in 1989, award given each spring by the President of WIW to an individual, not necessarily a WIW member, who has contributed significantly to helping writers everywhere— whether by fighting for freedom of expression, providing assistance to writers or by exemplary writing. Names can be submitted for consideration during the first three months of the year.

• *Philip M. Stern Award* Annual award presented each spring to recognize the WIW member who, as judged by fellow members, has provided the greatest service to writers and the writing profession during the year. Previous winners include Paul Dickson (1986), Kitty Kelley (1987) and Joseph Foote & Barbara Raskin (1988).

• *Joan G. Sugarman Children's Book Award* Established in 1987 by WIW member Joan G. Sugarman in memory of her late husband, this annual award honors excellence in fiction or nonfiction writing for children (ages 1–15). Candidates must be residents of the District of Columbia, suburban Virginia or suburban Maryland. The two previous winners are Cynthia Voigt (*Tree by Leaf*, 1988) and Phyllis Naylor (*Beetles, Lightly Toasted*, 1987). Administered by WIW's Legal & Educational Fund.

Isolde Chapin, Executive Director, 200 Woodward Building, 733 15th Street, NW, Washington, DC 20005; (202) 347-4973.

Washington Journalism Review "Best in Business" Awards Every year in its October issue, WJR asks its readers—most of whom are people in the news business—to choose the people who have made the most significant contributions in print, radio and TV journalism. Results are announced in the March issue. The awards gala, a closely watched affair, is attended by a stellar media crowd.

Tim McDonough, Public Relations Director, Washington Journalism Review, 2233 Wisconsin Avenue, NW, Suite 442, Washington, DC 20007; (202) 333-6800.

The Washington Monthly Annual Political Book Award Annual award for a book of fiction or nonfiction, published in the previous calendar year, that "illuminates a major issue through rigorous reporting, trenchant analysis and literary grace." Previous winners include Taylor Branch, William Grieder, Tom Wolfe and Robert Kuttner. Deadline: January 30.

Nicholas Martin, Production Manager, *Washington Monthly*, 1611 Connecticut Avenue, NW, Ste. 7, Washington, DC 20009; (202) 462-0128.

The Washington Post/Children's Book Guild Award For Nonfiction   Annual award to recognize a body of nonfiction work aimed at young readers. Winner selected by jury of authorities in children's literature and honored at an awards luncheon sponsored by *The Washington Post*. Award: $1,000.

Patricia Markun, Society of Children's Book Writers, 4405 W Street, NW, Washington, DC 20007; (202) 965-0403.

The Washington Prize   Award for unpublished manuscript of poetry given each year. Open to any living American writer except those connected with sponsor, The Word Works. Submissions accepted between February 1 and March 1. Prize co-sponsored by the D.C. Commission on the Arts and Humanities. Deadline: March 1. Award: $1,000 and publication.

The Word Works, Box 42164, Washington, DC 20015; (301) 652-7638.

The Washingtonian Book Award   Annual award, given by *Washingtonian Magazine*, for the work of fiction or nonfiction that best portrays Washington, DC and the way it works. Recent winners include: Herman Wouk (*Inside, Outside*), Hedrick Smith (*The Power Game*), and Walter Isaacson and Evan Thomas (*The Wise Men*). Award: $1,000 donated in the author's name to the book fund of the Martin Luther King Memorial Library.

Mitchell Gerber, Senior Editor, *Washingtonian Magazine*, 1828 L Street, NW, Washington, DC 20036; (202) 296-3600.

Westinghouse Science Journalism Awards   Awards, given each year, sponsored by the American Association for the Advancement of Science, to "encourage and recognize outstanding reporting for a general audience on the sciences." Deadline: July 15.

Joan Wrather, Awards Administrator, AAAS Office of Communications, 1333 H Street, NW, Washington, DC 20005; (202) 326-6640.

Young Poets Competition Annual awards to recognize the talents of two area high school students. Deadline: mid-March. Award: honorarium and the opportunity to read with established poets at the Joaquin Miller Cabin Summer Poetry Series. A recent winner read with local poet Roland Flint.

The Word Works, Box 42164, Washington, DC 20015; (301) 652-7638.

LITERARY MAGAZINES, JOURNALS & TAPES

Small literary magazines and journals serve a vital need in any literary community: they become forums for views and expressions outside the mainstream. Often, here is where any city's most promising writers get their start.

Ariel Poetry magazine published once or twice each year (118 pp). Subscriptions are $12 for three issues. Enclose SASE with submissions.

Rod Smith, Editor, P.O. Box 25642, Washington, DC 20007.

Belles Lettres: A Review of Books by Women Quarterly tabloid featuring reviews of books published by trade, university and independent presses written by women. Both scholarly and popular works are reviewed in the genres of fiction, nonfiction, poetry, biography and criticism. Subscriptions for individuals are $15 p/year, $25 p/two years; for institutions, $30 p/year; for students, $12.50 p/year. Sample issues are $2 each.

Janet Mullaney, Editor, Belles Lettres, P.O. Box 987, Arlington, VA 22216; (301) 294-0278.

Delos Published four times a year by the Center for World Literature (in conjunction with the English Department of the University of Maryland), *Delos'* contents reflect the purpose of the Center, a nonprofit organization established in 1987 "to maintain and invigorate the world's literatures by making their best works widely available in other than their original languages."

Each issue contains nearly 150 pages of poetry (with translations) and other writing from around the world. Subscriptions for individuals are $20 p/year or $36 p/

two years; for institutions, $25 p/year or $45 p/two years and for students $15 p/year. Single issues are $5 each.

Reed Whittemore, Chair, English Department, University of Maryland, P.O. Box 2880, College Park, MD 20740; (301) 454-5746.

The Federal Poet   Poetry magazine published quarterly by the Federal Poets, the D.C. chapter of the National Federation of State Poetry Societies and the Academy of American Poets. Subscriptions are $8/year. The Federal Poets meet at 2 pm on the third Saturday of each month. Poets and guests are welcome.

Craig Reynolds, The Federal Poets, P.O. Box 65400, Washington, DC 20035; (301) 292-1053.

Folio: A Literary Journal   This journal of fiction, poetry, interviews, essays and artwork is published twice a year by the creative writing program of American University. Subscriptions are $9/year; back issues are available for $4.50 each. Manuscripts and subscriptions are welcome from writers from the U.S. and around the world.

Folio, Department of Literature, The American University, Washington, DC 20016; (202) 885-2971.

Gargoyle   This handsome and substantial 300-page magazine of poetry, fiction, photography, art, interviews, translations and reviews is published twice a year by Paycock Press. Contributors are paid with one copy of the magazine in which their work appears. The price for single issues varies; subscriptions for individuals are $15 p/two issues; for institutions, $20 p/two issues.

Richard Peabody, Editor, Paycock Press, P.O. Box 30906, Bethesda, MD 20814; (301) 656-5146.

GW Review   This literary magazine, published by George Washington University, accepts submissions in short fiction, poetry, essays and graphic arts. Subscriptions are $6 p/year; single issues are $1.50 p/year.

GW Review, P.O. Box 20, Marvin Center, George Washington University, 800 21st Street, NW, Washington, DC 20052.

Lip Service   Poetry magazine that "encourages submission of quality poetry from poets everywhere." Published twice a year by Lip Service, a nonprofit organization established in 1987. Subscriptions are $4 p/ issue.

Lip Service Magazine, P.O. Box 23231, Washington, DC 20026.

Phoebe The quarterly literary magazine of George Mason University accepts work in poetry, fiction and photography. A single issue is $3.25; double issue, $6.50; year subscription, $13.

Phoebe, GMU, 4400 University Drive, Fairfax, VA 22030; (703) 323-3730.

Poet Lore This magazine of poetry, translation and criticism celebrates its 100th anniversary in 1989. Now published by the Writer's Center, *Poet Lore* comes out four times a year. Subscriptions for individuals are $12 p/year; for institutions, $20 p/year; for Writer's Center members, $8 p/year. Single issues are $4.50; a sample issue costs $4. Submissions are welcome.

Poet Lore, Writer's Center, 7815 Old Georgetown Road, Bethesda, MD 20814; (301) 654-8664.

Tapes For Readers Engaging conversations by the publisher with well-known authors about their writing, lives, opinions and ideas—all on cassette tape. A sampling includes: Woody Allen, Maya Angelou, Isaac Asimov, Russell Baker, Saul Bellow, Art Buchwald, John Cheever, William Kennedy, Margaret Meade, James Michener, S.J. Perelman, Isaac Bashevis Singer, Tom Stoppard, John Updike, Tennessee Williams and Tom Wolfe (more than 100 in all). Free catalog available.

Stephen Banker, Publisher, 5078 Fulton Street, NW, Washington, DC 20016; (202) 362-4585.

Visions International Sponsors poetry readings and publishes two poetry magazines:

• *Black Buzzard Review* Poetry and illustrations. Exclusively English language poetry by mostly American poets. Published once a year ($4.50 an issue).

• *Visions International* Magazine of poetry, reviews and original artwork, now in its tenth year. Features many translations and poems from other countries. Published three times a year (subscriptions $11 p/year).

Bradley Strahan, Director, Visions International, 4705 S. 8th Road, Arlington, VA 22204; (703) 521-0142.

BOOK FAIRS & SALES

Writers and readers from every walk of life are drawn to several recurring book fairs and sales here in the Washington area, excited by the chance to pick up good books at bargain prices or to acquire rare or hard-to-find editions of valued works. Nearly always, proceeds from these sales and fairs go to support charitable causes, educational programs or organizations committed to improving literacy.

American Association of University Women McLean Branch, Annual Used Book Sale   Held the second weekend in November for the past twenty years, this book sale features thousands of books in more than 25 categories. Prices start at about $1. Proceeds benefit the Education Foundation of AAUW.

AAUW—McLean Branch, McLean, VA; (703) 938-4452 or (703) 356-5514. The Falls Church and Fairfax chapters of AAUW also hold annual used book sales; for details call (800) 821-4364.

Association of American Foreign Service Women Book Fair   Annual fall event, held usually the second or third week of October at the State Department Building. More than 100,000 books in every conceivable category are offered for sale at prices ranging from 60 cents on up. Everything categorized. Proceeds go to local charities and to sustain scholarships for children of State Department and foreign service employees.

Association of American Foreign Service Women, P.O. Box 70051, Washington, DC 20024; (202) 223-5796.

Brandeis National Women's Committee Used Book Sale   Annual sale sponsored by the Greater Washington Chapter of Brandeis University National Women's Committee, featuring up to 100,000 used books in all categories; some first editions and autographed books. Unsold books shipped to federal prisons for their libraries.

Estelle Jacobs, National President, Brandeis University National Women's Committee, 5909 Bradley Boulevard, Bethesda, MD 20814; (301) 320-3878.

Goodwill Industries Annual Book Sale   One of the biggest book sales in the area, held one week every year in the

Washington Convention Center. Offers more than 100,000 new and used books in more than 50 categories. Proceeds benefit Goodwill's many area programs.

Robin Allcut, Public Relations Associate, Goodwill Industries, 2200 South Dakota Avenue NE, Washington, DC 20018; (202) 636-4225.

Jewish Community Center   Two annual events, both free to public:

• *Annual Book Fair*   Now in its 20th year, this sale features mainly books of Jewish interest. The thousands of titles—new books, although some are discounted—include everything from scholarly works to popular fiction. Author appearances are scheduled regularly throughout the eight-day event, which takes place in November.

• *Annual Children's Book Fair*   A new event, this fair features books for children of all ages as well as a large selection of parenting books. Only new books are available for sale, and prominent children's writers (like Judith Viorst) are invited to talk and sign copies.

Mrs. Tommy Feldman, Director, Literary Arts Department, JCC, 6101 Montrose Avenue, Rockville, MD; (301) 881–0100.

National Press Club Book Fair and Authors' Night   Each year, around Thanksgiving, the Press Club sponsors a unique four-hour public fair for members, guests and the general public. A limited number of books is available—between 75 and 90 on average—but the authors appear with them (it's a prerequisite for having books sold at the fair). All books on sale are either written by club members or Washington area residents. Proceeds benefit the Resource Center of the National Press Club. Admission is free.

Paul D'Armiento, Chair, National Press Club Book Fair, c/o The National Press Club, 529 14th Street, NW, Washington, DC 20045; (202) 662-7523.

Stone Ridge Used Book Sale   Each year for the past 21 years, the Stone Ridge Country Day School has been assembling more than 100,000 used books—a third of them rare—for sale. On the final day of the three-day event, everything is half price; in the final few hours, $5 will get you all the books you can fit into a grocery bag.

Proceeds benefit the School's Scholarship Fund. Admission is free.

Development Office, Stone Ridge Country Day School, 9101 Rockville Pike (at Cedar Lane), Bethesda, MD 20814; (301) 657-4322.

Poetry Committee Sponsors annual "Celebration of Washington Writers", a combination book sale and reading festival lasting three hours at the International Monetary Fund the first week in May.

The Poetry Committee, Folger Shakespeare Library, 201 E. Capitol Street, SE, Washington, DC 20003; (202) 544-7077.

The Vassar Booksale The Vassar Club of Washington sponsors a week-long used book sale each spring. The public, admitted free, can choose among more than 100,000 general and rare used books. You'll also find art, collectibles, maps, photos and Washingtoniana. The last day of the sale, everything is half-price. Held each year in Departmental Auditorium, Constitution Avenue between 12th and 14th Streets, NW, Washington, DC.

Vassar Club of Washington Booksale, Washington, DC; (301) 299-4855.

Washington Antiquarian Book Fair For the past 14 years, antiquarian book dealers—about 70 of them—have come from around the country in March to sell their wares at this popular weekend fair, sponsored by the Concord Hill School and held in a local hotel. Some deal in general antiquarian books; many specialize. Proceeds from a silent auction benefit the school. Admission is $12 for the entire fair; $5 per day.

Concord Hill School, 6050 Wisconsin Avenue, Chevy Chase, MD 20815; (301) 654-2626.

WNBA Booksale, Author Autographing Party & Fundraiser Equal parts party and fundraiser, held by the local branch of the Women's National Book Association to benefit local literacy programs. This sale features author-signed books, along with other recent books in all genres and subjects, all at a discount. Most of the books are donated by local publishers, publishers with local offices, book services, local bookstores and bookstore chains. Proceeds are donated to metropolitan area literacy groups. Held every year in the first week of December.

Kit Johnson, WNBA/Washington Chapter, 3508 Leland Street, Chevy Chase, MD 20815; (202) 326-6454/ 656-5346.

Women In Communications Book Sale Features several thousand new (some autographed) and used books in many categories. Proceeds of this one-day spring event are divided equally among four metropolitan area literacy councils.

Kathy Correia, Vice President of Programs, WIC— Washington Chapter, c/o North American Network, 2316 18th Street, NW, Washington, DC 20009; (202) 265-3689.

Libraries, Archives & Special Collections

"Get your facts first—then you can distort 'em as much as you please."

—MARK TWAIN

For writers seeking information—*any* information—the Washington area is research heaven. Fully one-sixth of all U.S. library resources can be found here. From the amazing Library of Congress to the inexhaustible National Archives, from numerous special collections to an active public library system to numerous large campus libraries to dozens of U.S. government agency libraries, the nation's capital offers a wealth of information to industrious scribes.

Sometimes, though, taking in the surroundings of a library can be just as satisfying as browsing through the stacks. The main building of the Library of Congress, with its roccoco lobby and its spectacular Main Reading Room, was the most expensive building of its time and still commands attention. The palatial expanse of the Society of the Cincinnati is impressive. The lovingly attended formal gardens around Dumbarton Oaks lure to the point of dreamy distraction. Many other similar adventures await the sharp-eyed writer turned loose on fact-finding missions in the nation's capital.

In most cases, area libraries, archives and special collections are free and open to the public. Occasionally, as noted, permission must be sought ahead of time and fees are charged. Some small, highly specialized holdings have been omitted, as have those libraries that aren't open to the general public. Also left out, for space reasons, are hundreds of association libraries that are open to members (and usually the public) for specialized research.

What follows is only a portion of the vast research holdings that dot the Washington landscape. For a complete picture of the area's library resources, readers are encouraged to consult *Library & Reference Facilities in the Area of the District of Columbia, 12th Edition*

165

(American Society of Information Science/Knowledge Industry Publications, 1986). This is an excellent, invaluable resource on which these selected listings are based.

Here in Washington, we are punch drunk with information. If it's true, as Samuel Johnson once said, that an author "will turn over half a library to make one book," than we have a great deal of turning to go.

LIBRARY OF CONGRESS

The Library of Congress ranks alongside the Bibliotheque Nationale in Paris, the British Library in London and the Lenin Library in Moscow as one of the world's greatest libraries. Indisputably it is the largest, with over 90 million items stored in three buildings: the Thomas Jefferson Building, the John Adams Building and the James Madison Memorial Building.

Established by the United States Congress in 1800, today's Library is divided into 25 divisions. Chief among those open to the public are:

African and Middle Eastern Division

The African Section covers Africa south of the Sahara (all countries of that continent except Algeria, Egypt, Libya, Morocco and Tunisia). Its collections of Africana are among the best in the world, encompassing every major field of study except technical agriculture and clinical medicine (which are housed in the National Agricultural Library and the National Library of Medicine).

The Hebraic Section offers books in Hebrew (dominant at 118,00 volumes), Yiddish, Aramaic, Syriac, Ethiopic and cognate languages.

The Near East Section covers materials in Arabic (dominant holding), Turkish, Persian, Armenian and other languages of the area (from Afghanistan in the east to Morocco in the west, and from Turkey and Central Asia in the north to Sudan in the south, excluding only Israel). The Mansuri Collection contains over 5,000 volumes on all phases of Islam and Islamic culture. All sections open to the public.

Room 1015, John Adams Building, 2nd Street and Independence Avenue, SE, Washington, DC 20540. *African Section:* Room 1026A, (202) 707-7937 (ext 5528).

Hebraic Section: Room 1006, (202) 707-7937 (ext 5422).
Near East Section: Room 1005, (202) 707-7937 (ext 5421).

American Folklife Center

Created in 1976 with passage of the American Folklike Preservation Act, the Center has a mandate to "preserve and present American folklife." The AFC engages in a wide range of activities involving the many folk cultural traditions of the United States: research documentation, archival presentation, live presentation, exhibition, publication, dissemination and training.

AFC is active in lending field assistance for research and local presentations. The Archive of Folk Culture serves as the national repository for folk-related recordings, manuscripts and other raw materials. Holdings include 30,000 field recordings (cylinders, discs, wires and tapes) and over 100,000 sheets of manuscript material. Open to the public.

Thomas Jefferson Building, Ground Floor (Room G–104D), 1st Street and Independence Avenue, SE, Washington, DC 20540; (202) 707-6590/707-5510.

Asian Division

The Chinese Collection contains 525,000 volumes in the Chinese language. In addition, there are several thousands of volumes in Manchu, Mongol, Tibetan, and Moso (Nashi) languages. Collection is rich in Chinese local histories (4,000 volumes), works on traditional agriculture, botany and collected writings of individual authors.

The Korean Collection holds more than 82,000 volumes and 2,100 current serial titles. The Japanese Section contains over 691,000 volumes covering Japanese history, literature and institutions. Holdings are strong in the humanistic and social sciences on Japan, Formosa, Korea and Manchuria and in scientific and technological serials. Its 5,200 reels of microfilm contain the selected archives of the Japanese Foreign Office, Army, Navy and other government agencies from 1868 to 1945.

The Southern Asia Section contains over 500,000 volumes, of which 183,000 volumes are in the languages of the region. The scope of these holdings cover India,

Pakistan, Sri Lanka, Bangladesh, Nepal and Bhutan, Burma, Thailand, Laos, Cambodia, Vietnam, Singapore, Malaysia, Brunei, Indonesia and the Philippines. All sections open to the public.

John Adams Building, 2nd Street and Independence Avenue, SE, Washington, DC 20540; (202) 707-5420. *Chinese Collection:* Room 1008, (202) 707-5423/707-5425. *Korean Collection:* Room 1008, (202) 707-5424. *Japanese Section:* Room 1014, (202) 707-5430/707-5431. *Southern Asia Section:* Room 1018, (202) 707-5600/707-5428/707-9277.

Children's Literature Center

Mandated to serve "government officials, children's librarians, publishers, writers, and illustrators," the CLC publishes an annual annotated list of outstanding books as well as guides to children's books at the Library of Congress. Center also organizes symposia on children's books and related media. Open to the public.

Thomas Jefferson Building, Room 140H, 1st Street and Independence Avenue, SE, Washington, DC 20540; (202) 707-5535.

Copyright Office

The Office's Information & Reference Division gives advice and guidance on how to register a copyright claim (claims may be obtained by mail, telephone or in person at the Public Information Office). Also maintains records of all works registered in the U.S. since 1790—these records are available for public examination.

The Licensing Division receives fees and issues licensing certificates annually to operators of coin-operated jukeboxes in the U.S. Also receives and processes fees for cable television licenses semi-annually. Information on these licenses are a matter of public record, and may be obtained by correspondence, phone or personal visit.

James Madison Building, Rooms 401 & 454, 101 Independence Avenue, SE, Washington, DC 20540; (202) 479-0700 (Information Office)/(202) 707-8130 (Licensing Division).

European Division

Responsible for the Library's services and programs related to the social, economic, cultural and political life of Europe (excluding British Isles, Spain, and Portugal). Open to the public.

John Adams Building, Room 5244, 2nd Street and Independence Avenue, SE, Washington, DC 20540; (202) 707-8130.

Geography & Map Division

Collection is rich in historical material, particularly for the U.S. and other areas of the American continents. Includes about 4 million maps, 50,000 atlases, several hundred globes and a similar number of three-dimensional relief models. Open to the public.

James Madison Building, Room 454, 101 Independence Avenue, SE, Washington, DC 20540; (202) 707-8130.

Hispanic Division

Serves as a center for studies in Spanish, Portuguese, Brazilian and Spanish-American culture. This collection of Hispanic and Portuguese materials is among the finest in the world. Representing all major subject areas, holdings are strong in history, literature and social sciences.

Division also houses the Archive of Hispanic Literature on Tape, featuring more than 500 poets and prose writers from Latin America and the Iberian Peninsula reading from their own works. Open to the public.

Thomas Jefferson Building, Room 204, 1st Street and Independence Avenue, SE, Washington, DC 20540; (202) 707-5400/707-5397.

Law Library

Established in 1832, this collection now comprises the world's largest and most comprehensive collection of books on foreign, international and comparative law. Covers U.S. and international law throughout all historical periods, from ancient law to space law.

The Law Library's five divisions—American-British Law, European Law, Hispanic Law, Far Eastern Law, and Near Eastern and African Law—are all open to the public.

James Madison Building, Room 240, 101 Independence Avenue, SE, Washington, DC 20540; (202) 707-5065.

Manuscript Division

Provides a special reading room where manuscript collections may be consulted under supervision of attendants. These collections contain personal papers of eminent Americans (including those of 23 U.S. presidents), records of certain important national organizations, manuscripts concerning history of Latin America and more than 3 million pages of reproductions of manuscripts relating to America in foreign archives and libraries.

Manuscripts are open to inspection and copying (although not necessarily photocopying), except where restrictions on access are in effect (usually by request of recent donors).

James Madison Building, Room 102, 101 Independence Avenue, SE, Washington, DC 20540; (202) 707-5383.

Motion Picture, Broadcasting & Recorded Sound Division

Representative collection of contemporary motion pictures and television programs, dating from 1942 to the present. Division's holdings also include: the Mary Pickford, George Kleine and other collections of early motion pictures, dating from 1900 to 1925; the American Film Institute Collection, covering the 1920s, '30s and '40s; and German, Italian, and Japanese features, newsreels and documentary films dating from 1930 to 1945.

The Division houses around 300,000 film reels (about 80,000 titles) and more than 1.2 million recordings of music and the spoken word, dating from about 1890 to the present. Access to film, TV and sound recording materials is arranged through permission of the librarian. Use of the reference library is open to the public.

James Madison Building, Rooms 115 & 338, 101 Independence Avenue, SE, Washington, DC 20540. *Film & Television:* (202) 707-5840; *Sound Recordings:* (202) 707-7833.

Music Division

Houses the Library's music collection, including 6 million pieces of printed and manuscript music, 300,000 books, sound recordings and other print materials dating from pre-Colonial days to the present. Current mandate of Division is to collect and preserve American music and its documentation.

Holdings include the largest collection of operatic material in existence: full scores, piano-vocal scores, and librettos. Among original manuscripts are holographs of Bach, Handel, Haydn, Mozart, Beethoven, Schubert, Liszt, Brahms, Wagner and Debussy. Division sponsors chamber music programs performed for the public in Coolidge Auditorium.

James Madison Building, Performing Arts Reading Room, 101 Independence Avenue, SE, Washington, DC 20540; (202) 707-5504.

Prints & Photographs Division

Holds the Library's extensive collection of over 11 million items, including drawings, prints, posters, and related categories of applied graphic arts, photographs and photographic negatives. Notable among its collection: Historic American Buildings Survey/Historic American Engineering Record; Pictorial Archives of Early American Architecture; Carnegie Survey of the Architecture of the South; Civil War Photographs; and master photographs from daguerreotypes to the present with examples from different schools of photography.

Fine prints include the Hubbard and Pennell Collections, dating from 15th century to the present. Diverse graphic arts collections include political drawings, Art Noveau posters, World War I and II posters, advertising posters and performing arts posters. Copies of pictures may be purchased from the Library's Photoduplication Service subject to copyright and other restrictions. All holdings are open to the public.

Madison Building, 101 Independence Avenue, SE, Washington, DC 20540; (202) 707-6394.

Rare Book & Special Collections Division

Holds over 500,000 items, including books, pamphlets, periodicals, broadsides, playbills, title pages and a select number of prints, photographs, sheet music, manuscripts, ephemera and memorabilia associated with certain special collections. Greatest strengths of this collection are holdings in Americana and early imprints dating from pre–1501. Open to the public by permission.

Thomas Jefferson Building, Room 201, 1st Street and Independence Avenue, SE, Washington, DC 20540; (202) 707-5434.

Science & Technology Division

Library contains over 3 million volumes, nearly 60,000 journal titles and 3 million technical reports covering broad subject areas of science and technology.

Significant among technical data are the extensive reports issued by the Department of Energy (and its predecessor the Atomic Energy Commission), the National Aeronautics and Space Administration, the Department of Defense and other government agencies. Of particular note is the collection of World War II reports issued by the Office of Scientific Research and Development. Open to the public.

John Adams Building, Science Reading Room, 2nd Street and Independence Avenue, SE, Washington DC 20540; (202) 707-5639.

Serial & Government Publications Division

Holds more than 75,000 current periodical titles and other serials, plus a full depository set of U.S. government publications. Approximately 1,600 domestic and foreign newspapers are currently received (most are retained permanently on microfilm). The Division's Newspaper and Current Periodical Room is open to the public.

James Madison Building, Room 133, 101 Independence Avenue, SE, Washington, DC 20540; (202) 707-5690.

NATIONAL ARCHIVES

Popularly known as the museum housing many of our cherished national documents (including the Declaration of Independence, the Constitution and the Bill of Rights), the National Archives & Records Service also serves as the repository of official records created throughout the governance of our nation. Congress, the White House and executive departments, federal courts and all agencies have provided the Archives an ongoing historical record of our government from its inception. Today, the Archives houses more than 1.5 million cubic feet of materials in four sites.

The Archives' vast holdings extend beyond the strict accounting of Federal affairs. It's possible to trace the threads of any significant issue weaving through our nation's history. For instance, western expansion, immigration, agricultural developments, domestic and foreign trade growth, conservation, public health—all can be studied within the context of pertinent federal agencies. Most archival sources for the study of World War II are also held in the National Archives.

Among the Archives' holdings are: 350,000 books, 1.6 million maps, 54,000 motion picture reels, 69,000 sound recordings (including Nixon's famous White House tapes during Watergate) and 5 million still pictures (including about 6,000 Brady Civil War negatives). For visitors wanting to trace their family history, the Archive's pension and census records are exhaustively complete (as are those in the Library of Congress' Local History and Genealogy Room).

The National Archives are open to the public every day of the year except Christmas, but access to certain classified information may be restricted.

8th Street and Pennsylvania Avenue, NW, Washington, DC 20408; (202) 523-3218/523-3286. *Research Information:* (202) 523-3220.

PUBLIC LIBRARIES (MAIN & REGIONAL)

Alexandria Libraries   General public library system features a special collection of Virginiana/Southern history/local history comprising 12,000 books, as well as an archive of 7,000 miscellaneous manuscripts, papers, prints, photographs and maps. On-site Virginiana specialist available at Lloyd House Branch. Holdings include 345,000 volumes. (No regional libraries—3 branches).

717 Queen Street, Alexandria, VA 22307; (703) 838-4555/838-4557.

Arlington County Public Libraries General public library system has special collections on Virginiana, local history, continuing Oral History Project, college and career subjects and Illustrator's Collection on early children's books. Holdings include 542,000 volumes. (No regional libraries—6 branches).

1015 North Quincy Street, Arlington, VA 22201; (703) 284-8140/284-8160.

D.C. Public Library System General public library system has unique Washingtoniana Division, which collects history of the District of Columbia and contains *The Washington Star Collection* (including that now-defunct newspaper's working morgue and photo library). Special programs serve needs of children, young adults, the homebound, deaf, blind and physically handicapped. Holdings include 1.4 million volumes.

Main library and four regional branches:

• *Martin Luther King Public Library (Main)* 901 G Street, NW, Washington, DC 20001; (202) 727-1111/ 727-1126. *Washingtoniana Division:* (202) 727-1213.

• *Chevy Chase* Connecticut Avenue near McKinley Street, NW, Washington, DC 20015; (202) 727-1341.

• *Fort Davis* Alabama Avenue & 37th Street, SE, Washington, DC 20020; (202) 727-1349.

• *Georgetown* Wisconsin Avenue & R Street, NW, Washington, DC 20007; (202) 727-1353.

• *Woodridge* Rhode Island Avenue & 18th Street, NE, Washington, DC 20018; (202) 727-1401.

Falls Church/Mary Riley Styles Public Library In addition to general book collection, this small city library has an excellent record collection. Special collections include local history collection emphasizing history of Falls Church City. (No regional libraries).

120 North Virginia Avenue, Falls Church, VA 22046; (703) 241-5030/241-5035.

Fairfax County Public Libraries General public library system, with special collections on state and local history, business and technology, records, film and video materials, talking books and more.Holdings include 1.6 million volumes.

Five regional libraries:

- *Fairfax City* 3915 Chain Bridge Road, Fairfax, VA 22030; (703) 691-2281.

- *George Mason* 7001 Little River Turnpike, Annandale, VA 22003; (703) 256-3800.

- *Reston* 11925 Bowman Towne Drive, Reston, VA 22090; (703) 689-2700.

- *Sherwood* 2501 Sherwood Hall Lane, Alexandria, VA 22306; (703) 765-3645.

- *Tysons-Pimmit* 7584 Leesburg Pike, Falls Church, VA 22043; (703) 790-8088.

Montgomery County Dept. of Public Libraries General public library system, with Special Needs Library in Bethesda that provides braille books, talking books, large-type books and tapes. Circulating collection of videocassettes and 16mm films. Holdings include 1.1 million volumes; 31,000 phonograph records.

Four regional libraries:

- *Bethesda* 7400 Arlington Road, Bethesda, MD 20814; (301) 986-8450.

- *Gaithersburg* 18330 Montgomery Village Avenue, Gaithersburg, MD 20879; (301) 840-2515.

- *Rockville* 99 Maryland Avenue, Rockville, MD 20850; (301) 279-1953.

- *Wheaton* 11701 Georgia Avenue, Wheaton, MD 20902; (301) 949-7710.

Prince George's County Library System General public library system, with major special collections on horse breeding and racing (Bowie Branch), planned communities (Greenbelt Branch), children's books (Hyattsville Branch), local Maryland history (Hyattsville Branch) and African-Americans (Sojourner Truth Room, Oxon Hill Branch). Holdings include 1.1 million volumes. (No regional libraries—branches only).

Hyattsville Library, 6532 Adelphi Road, Hyattsville, MD 20782; (301) 729-9330.

SPECIAL COLLECTIONS & ARCHIVES

American Institute of Architects Library Emphasis on American architecture and practices. Additional holdings in urban planning and building technology. Small slide and film collection. Open to public for reference only. Contains 22,000 volumes.

1735 New York Avenue, NW, Washington, DC 20006; (202) 626-7493.

Army Corps of Engineers Technical Library Collection includes engineering monographs, technical reports, journals, and publications of scientific and technical institutions throughout the world. Primarily for use of Research Center staff, but may be used by technical personnel of other government agencies upon request. Contains 100,000 items; 500 journals.

Kingman Building, Fort Belvoir, VA 22060; (703) 355-2387/(703) 355-2388.

Assassination Archives & Research Center Created in 1984 for the study of political assassinations throughout American history, with special focus on post WW II era. Maintains biographical archives and 1,000 volume library, with bulk of holdings concerning the JFK and Martin Luther King slayings.

918 F Street, NW, Ste. 510, Washington, DC 20004; (202) 393-1917.

Bar Association of District of Columbia Library Includes among holdings records and briefs of the U.S. Court of Appeals for the District of Columbia; also National Reporter System. Restricted to members of the Bar Association of the District of Columbia; only the briefs and records of the U.S. District Court of Appeals are open to the public. Open 24 hours, 7 days a week. Contains 50,000 volumes.

U.S. Courthouse, Room 3518, Washington, DC 20001; (202) 426-7087.

Broadcast Pioneers Library Archive dedicated to the history and preservation of radio and television broadcasting. Holdings include books, scripts, oral histories, photographs and other resources from the beginnings of broadcasting to the present. Open by appointment only.

1771 N Street, NW, Washington, DC 20036; (202) 223-0088.

Brookings Institution Library Collection emphasizes information on politics and the social sciences. Primarily for use of the Brookings Institution staff. Contains 94,000 volumes; 800 periodicals.

1775 Massachusetts Avenue, NW, Washington, DC 20036; (202) 797-6240.

Children's Hospital National Medical Center Holdings pertaining to pediatrics, hospital administration, nursing, general medicine and dentistry. Open to public by appointment only; users must be college level or above. Contains 13,000 volumes; 480 journals.

111 Michigan Avenue, NW, Washington, DC 20010; (202) 745-3195/745-3196.

Clearinghouse on Child Abuse & Neglect Information Materials about child abuse and neglect. Also information about service programs, ongoing research and state laws. Audiovisual materials on computerized database. Open to the public, but please call first. Contains 8,000 volumes & journals.

Aspen Systems Corporation, 1600 Research Boulevard, Rockville, MD 20850; (301) 251-5157.

Columbia Historical Society Contains 20,000 volumes, 5,000 manuscripts and more than 80,000 prints pertaining to history and people of Washington, DC. Comprehensive holdings cover all aspects of the city. Open to the public ($2 admission charge for non-members of the Society).

1307 New Hampshire Avenue, NW, Washington, DC 20036; (202) 785-2068.

Congressional Quarterly/Editorial Research Reports Library Information on American political science, history, U.S. government and legislative process, current events and international relations. Contains 20,000 microforms covering all congressional hearings and voting records from 1973 to present. Open to subscribers by appointment. Contains 20,000 volumes.

1414 22nd Street, NW, 4th Floor, Washington, DC 20037; (202) 887-8569.

Conservation Foundation/World Wildlife Fund Library Holdings deal with conservation of natural resources, as well as titles on water conservation, environmental mediation, hazardous wastes, and wildlife. Holdings include 10,000 books, 10,000 technical reports and 300 periodicals and newsletters. Also have newspaper clipping service.

1255 23rd Street, NW, Washington DC 20037; (202) 293-4800.

Corcoran Archives & Library Reflects the Corcoran's longtime interest in American art and artists. Library holdings emphasize contemporary art in major media. Archive records are available for most time periods from 1869 to present. Open to the public by appointment only. Contains 10,000 books; 125 periodicals.

17th Street and New York Avenue, NW, Washington, DC 20006; (202) 638-3211.

Daughters of the American Revolution Library Materials on American family history and genealogy, plus U.S., state and local history. Also contains 80,000 research files of unpublished genealogical records drawn from various sources across the nation. Also, stores several thousand unpublished volumes written by DAR members. Open to researchers; non-DAR members pay daily entrance fee. Contains 75,000 volumes.

1776 D Street, NW, Washington, DC 20006; (202) 879-3229.

Dumbarton Oaks Research Libraries The Center For Byzantine Studies is the most extensive library of its kind in the nation, covering history and culture of the period and related periods (late classical, Hellenistic, Islamic, and medieval East European). Open to qualified researchers by application only. Holdings: 100,000 volumes; 800 periodicals.

The Center for Studies in Landscape Architecture covers history of garden design, landscape architecture, and horticulture. Open primarily to scholars. Contains 13,000 volumes.

1703 32nd Street, NW, Washington, DC 20007; (202) 342-3280.

Environmental Law Institute Library Contains 10,000 volumes and 300 periodicals on environmental law and policy, toxic substances, hazardous wastes and land use. Open to the public.

1616 P Street, NW, Washington, DC 20036; (202) 328-5150.

Fairfax Law Library Largest county law library in Virginia. Contains 30,000 volumes; additional materials on microforms, audio and videocassettes. Open to the public.

4110 Chain Bridge Road, Fairfax, VA 22030; (703) 691-2170.

Folger Shakespeare Library Houses the largest collection of Shakespeariana in the world, along with one of the best collections in the Western hemisphere of historical source materials for the study of English and Continental civilization from 1476 to 1700. Reading Room is open only to qualified scholars; Exhibition Hall is open to the public without charge.

201 East Capitol Street, SE, Washington, DC 20003; (202) 544-4600.

The Foundation Center Library Comprehensive collection of foundation materials: annual reports, IRS information returns for over 22,000 foundations and 5,000 books and pamphlets on private philanthropy. Open to the public; materials must be used in the library.

1001 Connecticut Avenue, NW, Ste. 938, Washington, DC 20036; (202) 331-1400.

James Carson Breckenridge Library & Amphibious Warfare Research Facility Contains 80,000 items, including books, manuscripts, maps, microforms, periodicals and other materials. Special subject fields include amphibious operations, the Marine Corps, military and naval art and science and military history. Open to the public for reference only.

Marine Corps Education Cener, MCDEC, Quantico, VA 22134; (703) 640-2248.

Medal of Honor Library Comprehensive collections are maintained in military science, management and investments. Contains 55,000 books and 2,200 pamphlets; books in foreign languages; records in 35 languages for familiarization. Open to the public.

Fort George Meade, Bldg 4418, Fort Meade, MD 20755; (301) 667-4509.

National Academy of Sciences Library Archival holdings comprising publications of National Academy of Sciences, National Academy of Engineering, National Research Council and Institute of Medicine. Also contains about 500 periodicals. Open to the public by appointment only for on-site use.

2101 Constitution Avenue, NW, Washington, DC 20418; (202) 334-2125.

National Center for Standards & Certification Information Reference collection of more than 240,000 standards, specifications, test methods, codes and recommended practices. Open to the public for reference and referral.

National Bureau of Standards, Administration Building (Rm A629), Gaithersburg, MD 20879; (301) 921-2587.

National Bureau of Standards Research Information Center Center provides standards of measurement, quality, performance and the standard physical constants needed in scientific and technical work. Contains 200,000 monographs, bound volumes of journals and publications of international scientific and technical institutions, plus 2,400 journals. Also has collection of rare books covering the development of the science of measurement.

NBS Administration Building (Rm E-106), Quince Orchard & Clopper Roads, Gaithersburg, MD 20899; (301) 921-3451.

National Civil Rights Library Materials devoted to civil and women's rights. Also material on minorities, age, handicapping conditions, economics, education, sociology, employment, housing and population. Contains 60,000 volumes.

1121 Vermont Avenue, NW, Room 709, Washington, DC 20425; (202) 376-8114.

National Clearinghouse for Alcohol Information Contains 50,000 items on a computerized database to educate on use and abuse of alcohol. Open to public.

1776 East Jefferson Street, 4th Floor, Rockville, MD 20852; (301) 468-2600.

National Genealogical Society Library Library specializes in American local history and genealogy, with source materials like bible records, cemetery inscriptions, probate records, vital records and pamphlets. Free to members; loans to members only; 35 vertical files 16,000 volumes containing unpublished genealogical compilations and source material. Open to the public for fee of $5 per day.

4527 17th Street North, Arlington, VA 22207-2363; (703) 525-0050.

National Geographic Society Library Holdings span a diversity of subjects supporing the Society's wide interests: guidebooks, histories, regional descriptions, reference, general science, geography, cartography, art, natural history, polar exploration, travel and voyages. Open to the public. Contains 76,000 volumes; 110,000 maps, 1,500 atlases, 1.5 million clippings and 750 periodical subscriptions.

16th and M Streets, NW, Washington, DC 20036; (202) 857-7783.

National Housing Center Library Collection concerned with all aspects of residential construction and home ownership. Open to the public. Contains 10,000 volumes, 20,000 pamphlets, catalogs and government publications (plus foreign material) and 350 journals.

National Association of Home Builders, 15th and M Streets, NW, Washington, DC 20005; (202) 822-0203.

National Trust for Historic Preservation Library Collection addresses subjects pertaining to historic preservation (archaeology, architecture, building industry, community development, museums). Open by appointment to members only. Contains 11,000 volumes, 13,000 vertical files, 500 periodicals, 35,000 slides & black-and-white prints, films & tapes and a special collection of microfiched newspaper clippings.

1785 Massachusetts Avenue, NW, Washington, DC 20036; (202) 673-4038.

Organization of American States/Columbus Memorial Library Collection examines all aspects of inter-American relations and the peoples and cultures of the Americas. Library houses a collection of more than 5,000 rare books. Open to the public. Contains 310,000 volumes, 4,500 periodicals, more than 200,000 documents and publications of the OAS and 100,000 documents issued by other international organizations and member governments.

17th Street and Constitution Avenue, NW, Washington, DC 20006; (202) 789-6038.

Pan American Health Organization/Bibliographic Information Office Emphasis on countries of the Americas; documents and publications of the World Health Organization included in holdings. Open to the public. Contains 50,000 volumes covering public health and related disciplines

525 23rd Street, NW, Washington, DC 20037; (202) 861-3200.

Saint Elizabeth's Hospital Health Sciences Library Main focus of holdings on psychiatry, psychology, psychoanalysis, neurology, nursing, social work and religion. Open to the public. Contains 35,000 volumes, 300 journals and files of bulletins, reports and catalogs.

2700 Martin Luther King Avenue, NW, Washington, DC 20032; (202) 574-7274.

Society of Cincinnati Library Magnificent building contains biographies, vertical files, maps, manuscripts, prints, and microfilms on history of the American Revolution. Open to the public. Contains 15,000 volumes.

2118 Massachusetts Avenue, NW, Washington, DC 20008; (202) 785-0540.

Textile Museum Library Contains resources and reference materials on textiles, tapestries and quilts from Asian, African, South American and Islamic cultures. Holdings include 10,000 books and about 500 periodicals.

2320 S Street, NW, Washington, DC 20008; (202) 667-0441.

U.S. GOVERNMENT AGENCY LIBRARIES

Bureau of the Census Library Contains 200,000 items on demography, economics, political science, business, education, public health, public administration, and data processing, along with 3,000 journals and periodicals. About 85% of the library's materials are government documents. An extensive historical collection about the U.S. Census dates from 1790 to the present and includes some 500 photographs. Open to qualified researchers.

Federal Bldg 3, Room 2451, Suitland, MD 20233; (301) 763-5042.

Commerce Department Libraries   The Main Library contains 50,000 volumes on economics and related subjects, along with 1,400 periodical titles (open to the public). The Law Library contains 90,000 volumes and 150 journals, including an extensive government document and legislative collection (open to the public).

• *Main Library*   Dept. of Commerce Building, 14th Street and Constitution Avenue, NW, Rm 7046, Washington, DC 20230; (202) 337-2167.

• *Law Library*   14th and E Streets, NW, Rm 1894, Washington, DC 20030; (202) 377-5517.

Comptroller of the Currency Library   Contains 40,000 volumes in the areas of banking, finance, economics and law. Open to the public.

Office of Comptroller of the Currency, 490 L'Enfant Plaza East, SW, Washington DC 20219; (202) 447-1843.

Congressional Budget Office Library   Federal budget, budget process and economics. Open to the public. Contains 10,000 volumes, 400 periodicals.

House Office Building (Annex 2), 2nd and D Streets, SW, Washington, DC 20515; (202) 226-2635.

Consumer Product Safety Commission Library   Contains 15,000 books, 12,000 indexed documents and 500 periodicals relating to safety of consumer products, law, business and economics, science and technology. Open to the public.

5401 Westbard Avenue, NW, Washington, DC 20207; (202) 492-6544.

Customs Service Library & Information Center   Contains some 50,000 volumes, 800 periodicals and microform collection on customs duties and tariffs dating from 1789 to present. Open to the public.

U.S. Customs Service, 1301 Constitution Avenue, NW, Rm 3340, Washington, DC 20229; (202) 566-5642.

Drug Enforcement Administration Library   Collection reflects history, study and control of narcotics and dangerous drugs, especially as related to law enforcement. Open to the public. Contains 10,000 volumes, 225 journals and 24 drawers of vertical file material.

1405 I Street, NW, Washington, DC 20537; (202) 633-1369.

Environmental Protection Agency   The Headquarters Library contains 12,000 volumes, 21,000 documents and reports from government and private sector, 300,000 documents on microfiche (including technical EPA reports) and 800 journals, abstracts, indexes, newsletters and newspapers (open to the public).

The Law Library contains 8,000 volumes and 70 periodicals concentrating on federal law, with special emphasis on administrative and environmental law. Open to the public by appointment; identification required to enter building.

401 M Street, SW, Rooms 2902/4, Washington, DC 20460; (202) 382-5919.

Federal Communications Commission Library   Contains 45,000 volumes relating to broadcasting, common carriers and telecommunications. Open to the public; does not provide reference assistance to the public.

1919 M Street, NW, Washington, DC 20554; (202) 632-7100.

Federal Deposit Insurance Corporation Library   Contains 65,000 volumes in fields of banking, finance, economics and law. Has current state codes and state bank commission annual reports. Open to researchers by appointment.

550 17th Street, NW, Washington, DC 20429; (202) 898-3631/898-7435.

Federal Emergency Management Agency Library   Subjects covered include disaster response plans, civil defense, natural and man-made disasters and nuclear preparedness. Contains 4,000 volumes, 7,500 state emergency plans, 50 periodicals; 500 still photographs, 400 films and 3,000 slides. Open to the public.

500 C Street, SW, Rm 123, Washington, DC 20472; (202) 646-3768.

Federal Energy Regulatory Commission Library   U.S. government documents, technical reports, and journals on electric power, natural gas, oil and gas pipelines, utility regulation and law. Open to the public. Contains 30,000 volumes.

825 North Capitol Street, Room 8502, Washington, DC 20426; (202) 357-5479.

Federal Maritime Commission Library Contains 10,000 volumes of legal materials relating to shipping industry and regulation of common carriers by water. Open to the public.

1100 L Street, NW, Washington, DC 20573; (202) 523-5762.

Federal Trade Commission Library Contains 105,000 volumes and 200,000 microforms on legal, business and economic subjects. Special emphasis on antitrust and consumer protection law and economics. Open to the public.

6th Street and Pennsylvania Avenue, NW, Rm 630, Washington, DC 20580; (202) 523-3871.

Foreign Service Institute Library Covers vital subjects pertinent to nations of the world—international relations, politics and government, economics and finance, history and culture, linguistics and communication and social conditions. Open to the public. Contains 35,000 volumes, 500 journals.

1400 Key Boulevard, Arlington, VA 22209; (703) 235-8717.

General Accounting Office Library Contains 75,000 volumes covering areas of program evaluation, policy analysis, energy, accounting, law and civilian and military regulation. The Law Library has a retrospective collection of legislative histories of all public laws. Open to the public.

441 G Street, NW, Washington, DC 20548; (202) 275-2180 (Technical Library); Law Library: (202) 275-2585; -5560.

General Services Administration Library Contains 135,000 volumes and 400 periodicals on legal, procedures and other matters pertaining to the General Services Administration and its predecessor agencies. Open to the public.

18th and F Streets, NW, Washington, DC 20405; (202) 535-7788.

Health & Human Services Department Library Houses one of the country's outstanding collections in social sciences, public welfare and health sciences. Contains 600,000 items and 2,500 periodicals. Open to the public.

330 Independence Avenue, SW, Rm G-600, Washington, DC 20201; (202) 245-6791.

International Trade Commission Libraries The Main Library contains 80,000 volumes and 2,500 periodicals covering tariffs, commercial policy, foreign trade, economic conditions in foreign countries, foreign and domestic statistics, technical and economic problems of industry and various commodities. Open to staff of government agencies and research workers.

The Law Library contains 10,000 volumes and 75 periodicals on legislative histories of trade and tariff acts. Open to staff of government agencies and research workers.

701 E Street, NW, Rm 301, Washington, DC 20436; (202) 523-0013.

Interstate Commerce Commission Library Contains 93,000 volumes examining administrative law, transportation law, economics and history. Holdings also comprise legislative histories pertaining to government regulation of transportation agencies. Open to the public.

12th and Constitution Avenue, NW, Rm 3392, Washington, DC 20423; (202) 275-7328.

Justice Department Library Contains 300,000 volumes and more than 1 million pieces of microfiche and microfilm on federal and state law, political science, public administration, American history, energy, the environment, business, taxation and history of the Justice Department.

The following library divisions are open to the public by appointment:

• *Main Library:* Justice Building, 10th Street and Pennsylvania Avenue, NW, Room 5400, Washington, DC 20530; (202) 633-3775.

• *Antitrust Library:* Justice Bldg, Rm 3310; (202) 633-2431.

• *Civil Library:* Justice Bldg, Rm 3344; (202) 633-3523.

• *Civil Rights Library:* Justice Bldg, Rm 7618; (202) 633-4098.

• *Criminal Library:* Justice Bldg, Rm 100; (202) 724-6934.

• *Land/Natural Resources Library:*   Justice Bldg, Rm 2333; (202) 633-2768.

• *Tax Library:*   Justice Bldg, Rm 4335; (202) 633-2819.

Labor Department Library   One of this country's most extensive collections on labor and economics, this library also carries congressional documents relating to the Department's areas of responsibility. Contains 535,000 books, bound periodicals and pamphlets and 3,000 periodicals. Open to the public.

200 Constitution Avenue, NW, Washington, DC 20210; (202) 523-6988.

Marine Corps Historical Center   Collection covers military and naval history in particular, with emphasis on the Marine Corps and amphibious warfare. Historians available for consultation on Corps history. Open to the public. Contains 30,000 books and documents, 50 journals and Marine Corps unit histories.

Washington Navy Yard, Bldg 58, Washington, DC; (202) 433-3447/433-4253.

National Air and Space Administration Libraries   The Headquarters Library contains a large book and journal collection devoted to aspects of the space program.

The Goddard Space Flight Center Library contains 70,000 volumes, 40,000 journals and an extensive microfiche collection concentrating on astronomy, physics, mathematics, space sciences, communications, computers, climatology and remote sensing.

Both libraries are open to the public for reference use, subject to security regulations.

Headquarters Library: 600 Independence Avenue, SW, Washington, DC 20546; (202) 453-8545. *Goddard Library:* P.O. Box 252, Greenbelt, MD 20771; (301) 344-6244/344-6930.

National Agricultural Library   Library has objective to acquire and retain at least one copy of all substantive publications in the field of agriculture, including botany, chemistry, entomology, forestry, food and nutrition, law, water resources, and economics. Open to the public. Contains 1.8 million volumes, 50,000 rare books,

60,000 photographs, 100,000 slides, 13,000 maps, 1,200 posters, 708,000 microfiche and 4,000 microfilm reels.

Rte 1, Beltsville, MD 20705; (301) 344-3755.

National Defense University Library 225,000 books, pamphlets, periodicals and government documents in open stacks; 100,000 classified documents in security vault. Emphasis on foreign affairs, political and social science, government, economics, management, industry, and resource management. Users must secure advance permission from library director.

Fort Lesley J. McNair, 4th and P Streets, SW, Washington, DC 20319; (202) 693-8437.

National Endowment for the Arts Library Covers all aspects of the arts in 20th-century America, including their development, financing, management, organization, perservation and promotion (most titles date from 1971). Open to the public by appointment only. Contains 6,000 volumes, 125 periodicals and 10 drawers of vertical file material.

Old Post Office Building, 12th Street and Pennsylvania Avenue, NW, Rm 213, Washington, DC 20506; (202) 682-5485.

National Endowment for the Humanities Library Provides resources to people applying for grants. Collection emphasizes major biographical and bibliographical tools in all areas of the humanities and social sciences, particularly political science. Open to the public by appointment only.

Old Post Office Building, 12th Street and Pennsylvania Avenue, NW, Rm 216, Washington, DC 20506; (202) 786-0245.

National Gallery of Art Library Emphasis on western European art (Middle Ages to present) and American art (post-Columbian to present). Special collections include: artist monographs, catalogs (exhibitions, auctions and private collections), Leonardo da Vinci, early source materials on history of art and photographic archives of European and American art and architecture. Open to visiting scholars, graduate students and advanced readers by permission. Contains 122,000 monographs and 888 periodicals.

4th Street and Constitution Avenue, NW, Washington, DC 20565; (202) 842-6511.

National Institutes of Health Libraries NIH Main Library contains 85,000 monographs, 183,000 bound periodical volumes, 3,600 current subscriptions, 2,700 monographic serials and 17,000 microforms on all aspects of health, illness, medical science, biology and experimental medicine. Open to the public.

The Division of Computer Research & Technical Library contains 6,000 monographs and reports and 200 periodicals covering computer science, mathematics, statistics, medical information systems, computer applications in biomedical sciences and information science. Open to the public.

Buildings 10 & 12A, Rms 1L25 & 3018, 9000 Rockville Pike, Bethesda, MD 20892; (301) 496-1658/496-2184.

National Labor Relations Board Library Covers fields of law, labor relations, labor history, economics and political science. Open to the public. Contains 45,000 volumes, including 3,000 bound volumes of NLRB briefs and records in closed cases before the Supreme Court and the U.S. Court of Appeals.

1717 Pennsylvania Avenue, NW, Rm 900, Washington, DC 20570; (202) 254-9055.

National Library of Medicine Library has been indexing and cataloguing world's biomedical literature for over a century; became part of National Institutes of Health in 1968. Contains 3.5 million books, journals, theses, microforms, audiovisual productions, manuscripts, prints and photographs. Open to the public.

8600 Rockville Pike, Bethesda MD 20894; (301) 496-6308/496-6095.

National Oceanic & Atmospheric Administration Libraries Library Service Division has information on meteorology, climatology, atmospheric physics, geodetic astronomy, nautical and aeronautical cartography, fisheries and fisheries science, ocean engineering, satellite meteorology, oceanography and marine biology. Also features rare book collection of 16th- and 17th-century scientific treatises. Contains 800,000 volumes, 9,000 serials, 300,000 reports, meterological data, synoptic weather maps and atlases. Open to the public. *Location:* 6009 Executive Boulevard, Rockville, MD 20852; (301) 443-8330.

National Science Foundation Library   Emphasis on history and philosophy of science, administration of science research and national and international science policy. Contains 15,000 volumes and 600 periodicals. Open to the public.

1800 G Street, NW, Washington, DC 20550; (202) 357-7811.

Natural Resources Library   Housed in the U.S. Department of the Interior, this is the lead library in the Department's Natural Resources Library and Information System, composed of over 400 libraries and information centers across the nation. Contains 1 million volumes, including 21,000 serial titles, 250,000 microfiche, 8,000 reels of microfilm and 20,000 doctoral dissertations. Open to the public.

18th and C Streets, NW, Washington, DC 20240; (202) 343-5815.

Naval Historical Center Archives   Holdings cover naval policy, strategy, operations, and tactics. Also included are histories of naval commands, documentation on German and Japanese naval operations during World War II and transcripts of oral histories by U.S. Navy personnel. Contains 10,000 feet of manuscript or processed material dating from 1939 to present. Most holdings are open to the public.

Washington Navy Yard, Bldg 108 (3rd Floor), 9th and M Streets, SE, Washington, DC 20374; (202) 433-4131.

Naval Observatory Library   Unique rotunda library contains 65,000 books and journals chiefly on astronomy, but also including fields of mathematics, physics and geophysics. Collection also contains periodicals in the field dating from 17th century, 800 rare books on astronomy published between 1500 and 1800 and a number of star charts and maps. Open to qualified scholars by permission of librarian.

34th Street and Massachusetts Avenue, NW, Washington, DC 20390; (202) 653-1499.

Nuclear Regulatory Commission Library   Holdings cover nuclear science and engineering, radiation biology, energy, environmental science and management. Contains 20,000 volumes, 1,100 periodicals and 450,000 technical reports on microfiche. Open to the public by prior appointment.

1717 H Street, NW, Washington, DC 20555; (202) 492-7748.

Office of Personnel Management (OPM) Library Collection covers personnel management and public administration. Contains 75,000 volumes, including 1,500 volumes comprising a special civil service history.

1900 E Street, NW, Washington, DC 20415; (202) 632-7640.

Patent and Trademark Office Scientific Library Contains 100,000 volumes and 12 million foreign patent documents. Copies of patents available through photoduplication service. Patent Library collects primarily in applied science and technology. Open to the public.

U.S. Patent and Trademark Office, 2021 Jefferson Davis Highway, Arlington, VA 20231; (703) 557-2957.

Pentagon Library Formerly known as The Army Library, contains 120,000 volumes, 1 million documents and 1,500 periodicals. Emphasis on military art and science, political and social science, foreign affairs, government, economics, administration, management, computer science, law and legislative materials, Army studies, military unit histories and theses prepared by Army personnel assigned to civilian universities and colleges. Members of the public who have access to the Pentagon may use library materials in the nonrestricted areas.

The Pentagon, Room 1A518, Arlington, VA 20310; (202) 697-4301.

Performing Arts Library A joint project of the Library of Congress and the John F. Kennedy Center for the Performing Arts, the library contains 5,000 volumes and 450 periodicals on all aspects of the performing arts. Users may make appointments to listen to any of the Library of Congress' 750,000 recordings; researchers may arrange to view films in audiovisual area. Open to the public.

John F. Kennedy Center For The Performing Arts, 2600 F Street, NW, Washington, DC 20566; (202) 254-9803/287-6245.

Postal Service Library Covers law, social sciences and technology. Also houses unique collection of postal materials, the congressional serial set, stamps, reports, clippings, photographs, general postal histories, periodicals of the national postal employee organizations and Universal Postal Union studies. Contains 100,000 items. Open to the public.

475 L'Enfant Plaza, SW, Washington, DC 20260; (202) 268-2904/268-2905.

Securities and Exchange Commission Library Covers fields of law, corporate and general finance, economics, accounting, public utilities and stock market activities and control. Also contains legislative histories of statutes administered by or affecting the Securities and Exchange Commission. Holdings comprise 60,000 volumes and 200 periodicals. Open to public (with prior permission).

450 5th Street, NW, Washington, DC 20549; (202) 272-2618.

Small Business Administration Libraries Reference Library contains 5,000 items and 180 journals covering business management, venture capital, entrepreneurship and research into problems of small business. Open to the public.

The Law Library focuses on legal issues related to small businesses. Open to the public.

1441 L Street, NW, Rooms 218 and 714, Washington, DC 20416; (202) 653-6914.

Smithsonian Institution Libraries & Archives Contain more than 1.5 million items in 36 branch and satellite locations. Holdings reflect the wide-ranging research interests of the Smithsonian: aeronautics & astronautics, space, American history and technology, natural history, museology, history of science and all aspects of culture and the arts. Following are the 11 major branches of this world-class museum and research complex housed in the nation's capital:

• *Archives of American Art* Contains 5,000 mirofilm rolls documenting visual arts in America, from 18th century to present. Open to qualified researchers (graduate students and scholars) for reference use only.

8th and F Streets, NW, Washington, DC 20560; (202) 357-4172.

• *Freer Gallery of Art Library* Library materials specialize in art and culture of the Far East, Near East and South Asia. Holdings also specialize in life and art of James McNeil Whistler and his contemporaries. All materials supplement gallery art and studies conducted by staff. Contains 30,000 volumes, about half of which are in Chinese and Japanese, and a large collection of slides. Open to the public.

12th and Jefferson Drive, SW, Washington, DC 20560; (202) 357-2091.

• *National Anthropological Archives*   Collection provides one of the world's greatest resources for the study of North American Indians, as well as other cultural groups of the world. Contains 3,500 cubic feet of manuscript material, 250,000 photographs, cartographic material and original art. Open to the public, but please call before visiting.

Natural History Building, Rm 60-A, 10th Street and Constitution Avenue, NW, Washington, DC 20560; (202) 381-5225.

• *National Museum of American Art & National Portrait Gallery Library*   Contains 50,000 volumes of monographs and journals on fine arts, with special emphasis on American painting and sculpture, American portraits and biography and art of the 20th century. Open to the public.

8th and F Streets, NW, Washington, DC 20560; (202) 357-1300.

• *Arthur M. Sackler Gallery Library*   Contains the Ernst Herzfeld Archive of Persian and Near Eastern Architecture and Archeological Sites, the Myron Bement Smith Archive (relating to the Islamic world) and the Carl Whiting Bishop Collection of Photographs on China. Open to the public.

1050 Independence Avenue, SW, Washington, DC 20560; (202) 357-2700.

• *National Air & Space Museum Library*   Contains information on aeronautics, space flight amd all other kinds of flight—ballooning, gliding, airplanes and jets, the stratosphere and earth studies. Contains 900,000 photographs of aviation events, 10,000 documentary files (including drawings), 661 reels of microfilm, 210,600 NASA microfiche and a special collection of rare publications in aerospace. Open to the public by appointment only.

7th Street and Independence Avenue, SW, Washington, DC 20560; (202) 357-3133.

• *National Museum of African Art Library*   Holdings comprise materials on the traditional and contemporary art of Africa, including sculptural and decorative arts. Of special note is the Eliot Elisofon Photography Archives. Open to the public.

950 Independence Avenue, SW, Washington, DC 20560; (202) 357-4600.

• *National Museum of American History Library* Contains 150,000 volumes on American history, history of science and technology, decorative and graphic arts, numismatics, philately, photography, electricity and the history of musical instruments. Also has 225,000 trade catalogs in special collection. Open to the public.

12th Street and Constitution Avenue, NW, Room 5016, Washington, DC 20560; (202) 357-2414.

• *National Museum of Natural History Library* Large collection of materials on systematic biology, anthropology, mineral sciences, zoology, paleobiology, ecology, environmental biology and botany. Open to the public.

10th Street and Constitution Avenue, NW, Washington, DC 20560; (202) 357-1496.

• *National Zoological Park Library* Collection of 5,000 books and journals on animals—care in captivity, nutrition, pathology and classification. Also contains a collection of zoo guidebooks from around the world. Open to the public.

National Zoological Park, Education/Administration Building, 3001 Connecticut Avenue, NW, Washington, DC 20008; (202) 673-4771.

• *Smithsonian Archives* Contains 12,000 cubic feet of manuscript materials with emphasis in history of American science (especially the 19th century). Collection also traces development of institutions with which Smithsonian continues to be associated. Open to the public. 900 Jefferson Drive, SW, Washington, DC 20560; (202) 357-1420.

Supreme Court of the United States Library Collection of primary American legal materials, with strong holdings in legislative history and materials about the Court and its justices. Contains 250,000 volumes. Only documents of record are open to the public.

1 First Street, NE, Washington, DC 20543; (202) 479-3000/479-3175.

Transportation Department Libraries The Main Library contains 425,000 volumes, 2,100 periodicals and 585,430 microforms. Holdings cover all aspects of transportation on land, underground and on sea, as well as related technical subjects. Open to the public. *Location:* 400 7th Street, SW, Washington, DC 20590; (202) 426-1792.

The Coast Guard Law Library contains items which pertain to laws of the sea and Coast Guard history. Open to the public. *Location:* 2100 2nd Street, SW, Rm 4407, Washington, DC 20593; (202) 755-7610.

Treasury Department Library Covers fields of economics and law, with emphasis on taxation and public finance, money and banking, international law, international economics and domestic economic conditions. Holdings contain congressional records, reports and documents dating from 1789 to present. Contains 74,000 volumes, 250,000 microfiche and 8,000 reels of microfilm. Open to the public; identification required to enter building.

U.S. Treasury Building, Rm 5030, 15th Street and Pennsylvania Avenue, NW, Washington, DC 20220; (202) 566-2777.

U.S. Geological Survey Libraries The Geological Survey Library has extensive holdings on geology, paleontology, mineralogy, petrology, mineral resources, water resources, surveying and cartography, chemistry and physics, oceanography, soil science, zoology, natural history, remote sensing, environmental science and geothermal energy. Contains 740,000 bound volumes, 270,000 pamphlets, 302,000 maps, 8,700 doctoral dissertations on microfilm and microfiche, 100,000 NTIS reports in microfiche, 5,000 Environmental Impact Statements on microfiche and 10,200 serial and periodical titles. Open to the public.

The National Cartographic Information Center contains 12 million aerial photographs, maps and charts. It serves as a clearinghouse for information about domestically produced maps and charts, mapping materials, aerial and space photographs, satellite imagery, mapping-related data in digital form and geodetic control data. Information provided on microfilm, microfiche, computer printouts and magnetic tape. Open to the public.

National Center, 12201 Sunrise Valley Drive, Reston, VA 22092; (703) 860-6604/860-6673.

U.S. Information Agency Library The agency that does public relations for America has a library that emphasizes Americana, international relations, area studies and political science. Contains 60,000 volumes, 850 current periodicals and an extensive 85-cabinet newspaper morgue. Open to the public by appointment only.

301 4th Street, SW, Rm 135, Washington, DC 20547; (202) 485-8947.

Veterans Administration Library The Central Office Library contains 13,000 monographs, 900 journal titles, 650 audiovisual titles and a great deal of microfilm and microfiche. It covers aging, health care planning and administration, herbicides, public administration and military and Veterans Administration history. Open to the public.

810 Vermont Avenue, NW, Rm 976, Washington, DC 20420; (202) 389-3085.

Walter Reed Army Medical Center Library The Main Medical Library contains 30,000 volumes and 725 periodical titles. Major subjects include clinical medicine, surgery, psychiatry, dentistry, military medicine, nursing and allied health. Open to the public.

Walter Reed Army Medical Center, Bldg 2 (Room 2-G), Washington, DC 20012; (202) 576-1238.

UNIVERSITY AND COLLEGE LIBRARIES

American University Libraries The Bender Library is the main campus library, containing 460,000 books, periodicals, theses, scores; 463,219 microforms; 10,646 nonprint media. Special collections include: Artemas Martin Mathematics Library (devoted chiefly to early works in the field of mathematics), Americana, early works on surveying, Charles Nelson Spinks Collection (rare Japanese materials) and the American Peace Society Library. Open to the public upon arrangement.

The Washington College of Law Library contains 121,000 volumes—special holdings include Richard Baxter Collection (international law). Open to the public upon arrangement.

The Wesley Theological Seminary Library contains materials on religion, philosophy, theology and related subjects. Special collection on Methodist church and history. Contains 112,000 volumes and 550 periodical titles. Open to the public.

4400 Massachusetts Avenue, NW, Washington, DC 20016. *Bender Library:* (202) 885-3238/*Law Library:* (202) 885-2626/*Theological Seminary Library:* (202) 885-2626.

Catholic University of America Libraries   The John K. Mullen Memorial Library (Main) contains 1 million volumes and 7,000 serials. Among its most important collections are holdings on anthropology, architecture, archives (papers of 19th- and 20th-century labor leaders), botany, canon law, Celtic philology, chemistry, medieval studies, music, social work, drama and theology. The Institute of Christian and Oriental Research also contains important collections. Open to the public (subject to library regulations).

The Robert J. White Law Library contains 140,000 items and 500 journal titles. Holdings cover wide range of legal subjects, including codes from all 50 states. Open to the public.

620 Michigan Avenue, NE, Washington, DC 20064. *Main Library:* (202) 635-5055/*Law Library:* (202) 635-5155.

Gallaudet University Library   Extensive holdings include archive of historical materials on deaf people and deafness. Special collection on deafness, including masters' theses and doctoral dissertations.

The Baker Collection has early books from 1526 to the Civil War period. General vertical files relating to deafness, and information specialists on deafness available for consultation. Contains 180,000 volumes and 1,500 periodicals concentrating in liberal arts. Open to the public upon permission.

800 Florida Avenue, NW, Washington, DC 20002; (202) 651-5585.

George Mason University Library   The main campus library is the Fenwick Library, whose special collections include: Federal Theatre Project Collection of the Library of Congress, the Mann Collection of Early Virginia Maps (dating from 1700), the American Symphony Orchestra League Archives and the Ollie Atkins Photograph Collection. Contains 265,000 volumes, 400,000 microforms and 3,200 current periodicals. Open to the public.

4400 University Drive, Fairfax, VA 22030; (703) 323-2393.

George Washington University Libraries The Melvin Gelman Library is the main library on campus, containing 1 million volumes, 9,000 current periodicals, 2,500 university publications and 18,000 theses and dissertations. Special collections include: 35,000 U.S. Geological Survey maps, 2,500 Defense Mapping Agency maps, microforms of English Literary Periodicals from the 17th and 18th centuries and American Periodicals Serials from the 18th and 19th centuries. Open to the public. *Location:* 2130 H Street, NW, Washington, DC 20052; (202) 676-6047.

The Jacob Burns Law Library is one of the very few depositories for records and briefs of the U.S. Court of Customs and Patent Appeals. Holdings also include much of the former library of the Carnegie Endowment for International Peace. Contains 60,000 volumes and microforms and 1,500 legal and scholarly periodicals. Not open to the public, but arrangements may be made with the reference librarian for special use of materials not available elsewhere. *Location:* 716 20th Street, NW, Washington, DC 20052; (202) 676-6648.

The Medical Center Library, named after Paul Himmelfarb, has sizable holdings in medicine and allied health, including 20,000 monographs, 1,400 serials and 1,220 audiovisual items. Open to the public. *Location:* 2300 Eye Street, NW, Washington, DC 20052; (202) 676-2850/676-2962.

Georgetown University Libraries The main campus library, named after Joseph Mark Lauinger, contains 983,000 volumes and 462,000 microtext items. There are 22 rare book collections totaling more than 33,000 volumes, including an outstanding Dickens collection, the Shea Collection (early Americana and American Indians), the Robert F. Wagner Papers, the McCarthy Historical Project Archive and 55,000 photographs in the photo morgue from Quigley Publications (publishers of "Motion Picture Herald" and "Motion Picture Daily"). General library area open to the public, rare book reading rooms open to qualified researchers. *Location:*

37th & O Streets, NW, Washington, DC 20057; (202) 625-3300/625-4173/625-4137.

The Fred O. Dennis Law Library contains 450,000 items, including microforms and audiovisuals, with an emphasis on administrative, comparative and international law. Open to law students, faculty and members of the Bar. *Location:* 600 New Jersey Avenue, NW, Washington, DC 20001; (202) 624-8061/624-8033.

The Medical Center Library, named after John Vinton Dahlgren, contains 110,000 volumes, 1,500 journal titles, 1,700 audiovisual programs and 2,000 historic and special collections on medicine, health and medical sciences. Open to the public. *Location:* 3900 Reservoir Road, NW, Washington, DC 20007; (202) 625-7673/625-7577.

The National Reference Center for Bioethics Literature is comprised of a unique collection in bioethics (the systematic study of the social and ethical implications of practices or developments in biology and medicine). Contains 10,000 volumes, 40,000 article-length documents and 220 periodicals. Open to the public. *Location:* Kennedy Institute of Ethics, Georgetown University, Washington, DC 20057; (202) 625-2383.

Howard University Libraries   There are two main libraries on campus: the Undergraduate Library and the Founder's Graduate Library. There are also a number of more specialized collections in various campus buildings.

• *Undergraduate Library*   General use library contains 100,000 volumes, 2,200 serials and 1 million microform items. The Media Center houses a phonograph collection, audiovisual software, support equipment and soundproof listening/viewing rooms. Open to the public.

500 Howard Place, NW, Washington, DC 20059; (202) 636-5060.

• *Founders Graduate Library*   Contains 500,000 volumes and 6,000 current periodicals. Special collections include an antislavery collection, English books dating from 1641 to 1700, urban documents and historic papers from the British Parliament. Open to the public.

500 Howard Place, NW, Washington, DC 20059; (202) 636-7252/636-7250.

• *Architecture & Planning Library* Contains 22,000 volumes, 25,000 slides and 375 current periodicals on architecture, landscape planning and other realted subjects. Special collection of stereophotogrammetric maps of Washington, DC. Open to the public.

2366 6th Street, NW, Washington, DC 20059; (202) 636-7773/636-7774.

• *Business & Public Administration Library* Contains 35,000 volumes and 2,100 current serials on business, management and public administration topics. Open to the public.

2600 6th Street, NW, Washington, DC 20059; (202) 636-5161.

• *Channing Pollock Theater Collection* Collection of books, manuscripts, pictures, playbills, posters, broadsides, and memorabilia of the performing arts. Emphasis on 19th- and 20th-century English and American drama and theater. Open to the public.

500 Howard Place, NW, Washington, DC 20059; (202) 636-7259.

• *Divinity Library* Focus of collection is on black church history, theology, religious education, biblical studies, and ministry. Contains 101,000 volumes and 356 current serials. Complete sets of numerous old journals, many acquired from New York's Auburn Seminary. Open to the public.

1240 Randolph Street, NE, Washington, DC 20017; (202) 636-7282.

• *Health Sciences Library* Extensive collections on medicine, dentistry, health and nursing, including many vertical files on prominent African-Americans in these fields. Contains 206,000 volumes, 4,000 serials and over 5,000 audio-visual materials. Open to the public.

600 W Street, NW, Washington, DC 20059; (202) 636-6433/636-6545.

• *Social Work Library* Contains 30,000 volumes and 746 current journals on intervention, direct services, community organization and development and social administration. Open to the public.

6th Street and Howard Place, NW, Washington, DC 20059; (202) 636-7316.

Johns Hopkins University Libraries The main campus of this prestigious academic institution is in the Baltimore area, but there are two satellite campuses in the Washington area of note.

• *The R. E. Gibson Library* The Applied Physics collection focuses on mathematics, physics, electronics, aeronautics, astronautics, computer sciences and biomedical engineering. Contains 50,000 volumes and 800 periodicals. Open to the public.

Johns Hopkins Road, Laurel, MD 20707; (301) 953-5151.

• *The School of Advanced International Studies Library* Named after Sydney and Elsa Mason, the library's holdings emphasize coverage of diplomacy, international relations, international law and organization, international economics, history, politics and the economics of world geographic areas. Contains 90,000 volumes, 900 periodicals and newspapers. Open to researchers by permission of the librarian.

1740 Massachusetts Avenue, NW, Washington, DC 20036; (202) 785-6805/785-6807.

Montgomery College Library Located on the college's Rockville campus, the library has extensive holdings in most subject areas. Especially strong in music and musical scores. Contains 108,000 volumes, 850 periodicals and 7,500 recordings. Open to the public.

51 Mannakee Street, Rockville, MD 20850; (301) 279-5066.

Mount Vernon College Library Smaller campus library, with especially strong holdings in women's studies, fine arts, interior design and the decorative arts. Contains 42,000 items in all formats. Open to the public.

2100 Foxhall Road, NW, Washington, DC 20007; (202) 331-3544.

Northern Virginia Community College Libraries Thousands of younger students and adults attend the five campuses of this outstanding community college program. Five libraries are available for use by students and the general public.

• *Alexandria* Contains 64,000 volumes and 400 periodicals. Open to the public. 3011 North Beauregard Street, Alexandria, VA 22311; (703) 845-6231.

• *Annandale* Contains 86,000 volumes and 525 periodicals. Open to the public. 8333 Little River Turnpike, Annandale, VA 22003; (703) 323-3128.

• *Loudoun* Contains 27,000 volumes and 300 periodicals. Open to the public. 1000 Harry Flood Byrd Highway, Sterling, VA 22170; (703) 450-2567.

• *Manassas* Contains 29,000 volumes covering automotive technology, aviation, business, welding, construction, secretarial science, administration of justice, liberal arts and science. Open to the public. 6901 Sudley Road, Manassas, VA 22110; (703) 368-0184.

• *Woodbridge* Contains 25,000 volumes, 240 periodicals and 1,800 audiovisual materials. Open to the public. 15200 Neabsco Mills Road, Woodbridge, VA 22191; (703) 670-2191.

Prince George's Community College Library General use library with many materials, including 75,000 volumes, 483 periodicals, microfilm backfiles and videocassettes, 12,000 slides, 3,000 audiotapes and 5,700 phonorecords. Also has special collections of books and periodicals on "The Film as Art" and on nursing. Listening and viewing facilities provided. Open to the public.
301 Largo Road, Largo, MD 20772; (301) 322-0462.

University of D.C.—Learning Resources Division Collection covers eight major subject areas: business, education, human ecology, life sciences, physical sciences, engineering, technology, and liberal and fine arts. Special collections include: Human Relations Area Files, Afro-Hispanic-American Media Collection, the Nichols Collection of American History and the Slave Narrative and Source Materials Collection. Open to the public.
Main Campus (Van Ness), 4200 Connecticut Avenue, NW, Washington, DC 20008; (202) 282-7109/282-7501.

University of Maryland Libraries The main library of the campus is the Theodore R. McKeldin Library, containing reference works, periodicals, circulating books and other materials in all fields. The McKeldin is open to graduates and undergraduates, and to the general public. Branches include: Hornbake Undergraduate Library, the Engineering & Physical Sciences Library, the Music Library, the Architecture Library, the Art Library and the Chemistry Library.
Total holdings comprise 1.7 million volumes, 2.4 million microform units, newspapers, and periodicals and a wealth of government documents, phonograph records, films and filmstrips. Open to the public.

University of Maryland, College Park, MD 20742; (301) 454-2853.

Virginia Theological Seminary Library Collection emphasizes Biblical studies, theology, Anglicanism, systematic theology, and church history. Contains 100,000 volumes. Open to the public.

3737 Seminary Road, Alexandria, VA 22304; (703) 370-6602.

Bookstores & Newsstands

"Where is human nature so weak as in a bookstore?"
—HENRY WARD BEECHER

"Lord! When you sell a man a book you don't sell just twelve ounces of paper and ink and glue—you sell him a whole new life. Love and friendship and humour and ships at sea by night—there's all heaven and earth in a book, a real book."

—CHRISTOPHER MORLEY

U pon entering a bookstore, lovers of books become seized with a passion that certain explorers, archaeologists and gold hunters know well—a keen expectation of discovering yet another treasure for the mind, yet another restorative for the soul. And each bookstore provides a unique excursion into the world of books, by emphasizing particular subjects and fostering an atmosphere that reflects its owner's habits, thinking and tastes.

In this section, you'll find a complete listing of bookstores and newsstands in the District of Columbia, suburban Maryland and suburban Virginia, along with information on private book dealers and specialized mail order book operations. From Winchester, VA to Annapolis, MD (west-east) and from just below Baltimore, MD to just above Charlottesville, VA (north-south), there are well over 450 places in the region to let one's bibliomania run wild.

One cautionary note: many of the private book dealers in the following listings serve the public by mail or by appointment only. Please be courteous, and write or call ahead during regular business hours. Don't just show up on a dealer's doorstep unannounced—after all, if your passion is books, you'll have to play by the rules.

Beyond that, there aren't many other rules to follow. Just let your enthusiasm be your guide.

DISTRICT OF COLUMBIA

General Bookstores

Independents

Bridge Street Books   Specializes in politics, literature, philosophy, Judaica, history and film. Mail, phone and special orders.

   2814 Pennsylvania Avenue, NW, W, DC 20007; (202) 965-5200. *Hours:* Mon-Thurs, 10 am to 7 pm; Fri & Sat, 10 am to 10 pm; Sun, 1 pm to 6 pm.

Calliope Bookshop   Strong in the humanities—literature, poetry, philosophy, mythology, history, criticism, music, fine art and photography. Also has good selections of travel books, children's titles, remainders, calendars and little-known fiction. Special orders.

   3424 Connecticut Avenue, NW, W, DC 20008; (202) 364-0111. *Hours:* Mon-Sat, 10 am to 11 pm; Sun, noon to 9 pm.

Chapters: A Literary Bookstore   A book lover's dream, this well-stocked store specializes in literature, poetry and criticism, small and university press titles. Free spring and fall calenders of "literary and other to-do's." Literary postcards. Regular author readings and book signings, Friday afternoon teas. Frequent buyer plan; mail, phone and special orders. Can reserve autographed books; gift wrapping at no extra charge.

   1613 I Street, NW, W, DC 20006; (202) 861-1333. *Hours:* Mon- Fri, 10 am to 6:30 pm; Sat, 11 am to 5 pm.

Francis Scott Key Bookshop   Emphasis on biography, art, travel, English literature, political science and gardening. Large stock of children's books. Special orders, local delivery.

   28th and O Streets, NW, W, DC 20007; (202) 337-4144. *Hours:* Mon-Sat, 9:30 am to 5 pm.

Kramerbooks & Afterwords   Bookstore that carries something for everyone; particularly strong in history, biography, literature, art, travel and non-North American fiction. Several shelves of remainders; also stocks magazines and some newspapers. Book signings, other customer services. Afterwords Cafe is a place to eat and sip espresso after feeding your mind.

1517 Connecticut Avenue, NW, W, DC 20036; (202) 387-1400. *Hours:* Sun-Thurs, 7:30 am to 1 am, Fri and Sat, 24 hours.

Olsson's Books & Records   Very large, full-service bookstores offering quality fiction and nonfiction in a broad range of categories. Books-on-tape, calendars and postcards; full line of records, tapes and CD's. Can join Penguin Book Club, through which discounts are available; also offers 25% discounts on *Washington Post* hardcover bestsellers. Regular book signings. Mail, phone and special orders; interstore transfers.

All five Olsson's stores carry much of the same stock, but each emphasizes certain lines, as reflected below:

• *Dupont Circle*   Strong in fiction, science fiction, mystery, travel literature, fiction, mythology and writer's reference books. 1307 19th Street, NW, W, DC 20036; (202) 785-1133. *Hours:* Mon-Sat, 10 am to 9 pm; Sun, noon to 6 pm.

• *Georgetown*   Emphasis on history, poetry, regional studies and university press titles. 1239 Wisconsin Avenue, NW, W, DC 20007; (202) 338-9544. *Hours:* Mon-Thurs, 10 am to 10:45 pm; Fri and Sat, 10 am to midnight; Sun, noon to 7 pm.

• *Metro Center/Downtown*   Opening late spring 1989. 1200 F Street, NW, W, DC 20004; (202) 347-3686.

• *Bethesda, MD*   See MD listings.

• *Old Town Alexandria, VA*   See VA listings.

Politics and Prose Bookstore   Full-service neighborhood bookstore, with large sections of fiction, biography, psychology, Penguin Classics, Vintage Contemporaries, health books, cookbooks and children's books. Also stocks greeting cards, bookmarks, wrapping paper and gifts. Author readings and book signings; free monthly calendar of literary events. Special orders.

5010 Connecticut Avenue, NW, W, DC 20008; (202) 364-1919. *Hours:* Mon-Sat, 10 am to 10 pm; Sun, 11 am to 6 pm.

Reprint Book Shop   Despite its name, this is a general interest bookstore which, except for a table of remainders, carries some 30,000 new books on every subject.

Also stocks books-on-tape, postcards and maps. Special phone and mail orders.

456 L'Enfant Plaza, SW, W, DC 20024; (202) 554-5070. *Hours:* Mon-Fri, 9 am to 6 pm; Sat, 10 am to 5 pm.

Simeon's Bookshop Full-service neighborhood bookstore, emphasizing classic fiction and children's books. Special and mail orders, local delivery.

3706 Macomb Street, NW, W, DC 20016; (202) 363-1112. *Hours:* Mon-Sat, 10:30 am to 6 pm; Sun, noon to 5 pm.

Trover Shop Each well-situated store offers large selections of hardcover bestsellers, travel guides, children's books and cookbooks. All stores carry Bibles, greeting cards, maps, magazines and newspapers. Capitol Hill store has large section of political books. Special orders. Three D.C. locations:

• *Capitol Hill* 227 Pennsylvania Avenue, SE, W, DC 20003; (202) 543-8006. *Hours:* Mon-Fri, 7 am to 9 pm; Sat, 7 am to 7 pm; Sun, 7 am to 3 pm.

• *Farragut Square* 1031 Connecticut Avenue, NW, W, DC 20032; (202) 659-8138. *Hours:* Mon-Fri, 8 am to 6:30 pm; Sat, 9 am to 6 pm.

• *McPherson Square* 800 15th Street, NW, W, DC 20056; (202) 347-2177. *Hours:* Mon-Fri, 8 am to 6 pm.

National Chain Stores

B. Dalton Bookseller Full selection of fiction and nonfiction titles in all categories, including large reference section, history, biography, psychology, mystery and romance. Special section for children's books (B. Dalton Junior).

All B. Dalton's stores carry computer books and magazines; a number have separate computer book and software stores within them (Software, Etc). Each store carries remainders, magazines and newspapers; offer 25% discounts on all hardcover bestsellers.

Three D.C. locations (for other area locations, see VA and MD listings):

• *Mazza Gallerie* 5310 Wisconsin Avenue, NW, W, DC 20015; (202) 362-7055. *Hours:* Mon-Fri, 10 am to 8 pm; Sat, 10 am to 6 pm; Sun, noon to 5 pm.

• *Shops at National Place* 1331 Pennsylvania Avenue, NW, W, DC 20004; (202) 393-1468. *Hours:* Mon-Fri, 10 am to 9 pm; Sat, 10 am to 7 pm; Sun, noon to 5 pm.

• *Union Station* 50 Massachusetts Avenue, NE, W, DC 20002; (202) 289-1724. *Hours:* Mon-Sat, 10 am to 9 pm; Sun, noon to 6 pm.

Crown Books Broad selection of best-selling fiction and nonfiction books—many deeply discounted—including reference, health, history, biography, mystery and detective, art and many other titles. Adult and children's books, magazines, newspapers, some videocassettes.

Discounts range from 25% to 35% off *New York Times* best-sellers; 20% to 50% off hardcover art, cook and reference books; 10% off paperbacks and magazines; and 25% off computer books, software and accessories. Most stores have large shelves of remainders, many for $2 or less.

Nine D.C. locations (for other area locations, see VA and MD listings):

• *Cleveland Park* 3335 Connecticut Avenue, NW, W, DC 20008; (202) 966-7232. *Hours:* Mon-Sat, 10 am to 9 pm; Sun, 11 am to 6 pm.

• *Downtown/K Street* 2020 K Street, NW, W, DC 20006; (202) 659-2030. *Hours:* Mon-Fri, 9 am to 8 pm; Sat and Sun, 10 am to 6 pm.

• *Farragut North* 1155 19th Street, NW, W, DC 20036; (202) 659-4172. *Hours:* Mon-Sat, 9 am to 9 pm; Sun, 11 am to 6 pm.

• *Franklin Square* 1275 K Street, NW, W, DC 20005; (202) 298-7170. *Hours:* Mon-Fri, 10 am to 7 pm; Sat, 10 am to 6 pm; Sun, 11 am to 5 pm.

• *Friendship Heights* Jenifer Mall, 4400 Jenifer Street, NW, W, DC 20015; (202) 966-8784. *Hours:* Mon-Sat, 10 am to 9 pm; Sun, 10 am to 6 pm.

• *Georgetown* 3131 M Street, NW, W, DC 20007; (202) 333-4493. *Hours:* Mon-Thurs, 11 am to 11 pm; Fri and Sat, 11 am to 12 pm; Sun, 11 am to 8 pm.

• *Lafayette Square* 1710 G Street, NW, W, DC 20006; (202) 789-2277. *Hours:* Mon-Fri, 9 am to 7 pm; Sat, 10 am to 6 pm.

• *Van Ness/UDC*   4301 Connecticut Avenue, NW, W, DC 20008; (202) 966-2576. *Hours:* Mon-Sat, 10 am to 9 pm; Sun, 11 am to 5 pm.

• *West End*   1200 New Hampshire Avenue, NW, W, DC 20036; (202) 822-8331. *Hours:* Mon-Sat, 9 am to 8 pm; Sun, 11 am to 5 pm.

Waldenbooks   Large variety of fiction and nonfiction titles in many categories, including reference, biography, history, mystery, health, New Age, literature and art. Adult and children's books, magazines, tapes, videocassettes, computer books and software.

Offer book clubs (kids, 60 +, mysteries, etc.) whose members receive special discounts. Also discounts hardcover bestsellers. The chain operates several separate computer stores in the metropolitan area (Waldensoftware.) Will handle special orders.

Four D.C. locations (for other area locations, see VA and MD listings):

• *Georgetown*   Georgetown Park, 3222 M Street, NW, W, DC 20007; (202) 333-8033. *Hours:* Mon-Fri, 10 am to 9 pm; Sat, 10 am to 7 pm; Sun, noon to 6 pm.

• *Spring Valley*   Spring Valley Shopping Center, 4845 Massachusetts Avenue, NW, W, DC 20016; (202) 362-6329. *Hours:* Mon- Fri, 9:30 am to 7 pm; Sat, 9:30 am to 6 pm; Sun, 10:30 am to 3:30 pm.

• *Presidential Mall*   409 12th Street, NW, W, DC 20004; 638-0225. Open Monday through Friday, 9:30 am to 5:30 pm.

• *Pennsylvania Avenue*   Formerly The Globe Bookstore, this store carries regular Waldenbooks stock and much of what Globe was best known for—language books, international tapes and periodicals, world travel and political affairs books. 1700 Pennsylvania Avenue, NW, W, DC 20006; (202) 333-1490. *Hours:* Mon- Fri, 9:30 am to 6 pm; Sat, 10 am to 6 pm.

Specialty Bookstores

African-American

Joy of Heritage   Used books on African-American topics, including history, biography, sports and literature.

1801 16th Street, NW, W, DC 20036; (202) 332-7435. Open by appointment only.

Pyramid Bookstore   Carries books by and about people of African descent, including titles on Islam, Black politics, the Caribbean, the arts, nutrition and meta-physics. Also carries children's books, video and audio cassettes, greeting cards, periodicals, posters, dolls and games. Two D.C. locations:

- *McMillan Park*   2849 Georgia Avenue, NW, W, DC 20001; (202) 328-0190. *Hours:* Mon-Sat, 11 am to 7 pm; Sun, noon to 5 pm.

- *Anacostia*   1421 Good Hope Road, SE, W, DC 20020; (202) 889-0002. *Hours:* Mon-Sat, 11 am to 7 pm; Sun, noon to 5 pm.

Arts & Architecture

American Institute of Architects Bookstore   Architectural city guides, children's books on architecture, posters, calendars, T-shirts, games, stationery, greeting cards and gifts. Mail order catalog, special and phone orders.
1735 New York Avenue, NW, W, DC 20006; (202) 626-7474. *Hours:* Mon-Fri, 8:30 am to 5 pm.

Backstage   Specializes in books on the performing arts: scripts, theater, acting, film/television, musicals, opera and dance. Also carries stage makeup, dance gear, cos-tumes (sale and rental), posters and gifts. Newsletter, special and mail orders.
2101 P Street, NW, W, DC 20037; (202) 775-1488. *Hours:* Mon-Sat, 10 am to 6 pm (except Thurs, 10 am to 8 pm).

Franz Bader Bookstore   Large selection of books on the visual arts: art and art history, architecture and design, graphic arts, photography and crafts. Carries German, French and Italian exhibition catalogs on architecture, art, and photography, plus many titles on German art history and fiction. Calendars and periodicals; mail, phone and special orders, world-wide shipping.
1911 I Street, NW, W, DC 20006; (202) 337-5440. *Hours:* Mon- Sat, 10 am to 6 pm.

Bird In Hand Bookstore & Gallery   Books on art and architecture. Also sells fine prints, small paintings and photography, mostly by local artists.

323 7th Street, SE, W, DC 20003; (202) 543-0744.
Hours: Tues-Sun, 11 am to 6 pm.

Bookworks   Carries books by and about local, national
and international artists, plus literature, art theory, children's and architecture titles. Also stocks cards, magazines, new music and rents videos. Bookstore of The
Washington Project for the Arts.

400 7th Street, NW, W, DC 20004; (202) 347-8393.
Hours: Mon-Fri, 11 am to 6 pm; Sat, 11 am to 5 pm.

Decatur House Bookshop   Carries many Preservation
Press titles, plus selection of books on Americana, antiques, architecture, arts and crafts and cooking. Also
sells fine gifts and jewelry. Owned and operated by
National Trust for Historic Preservation.

1600 H Street, NW, W, DC 20006; (202) 842-1856.
Hours: Mon-Fri, 10 am to 5:30 pm.

Children & Juvenile

A Happy Thought Children's Bookstore   Wide selection of
books for children and young teens, including large
selection of picture books. Book-related stuffed animals,
records, books-on-tape and music cassettes, greeting
cards, selected toys, videos and art supplies. Regular
workshops (frequently on art), puppet shows and con-
certs, author talks and signings, free newsletter (fall and
spring). Special and mail orders; school accounts.

4836 MacArthur Boulevard, NW, W, DC 20007; (202)
337-8300. *Hours:* Mon-Sat, 9:30 am to 5:30 pm.

Cheshire Cat Book Store   All kinds of books for and
about children (pre-K to early teens), including large
selection of picture books. Books-on-tape, music cassettes, posters and calendars for children. Events newsletter (5 times p/year), book signings and special events
(fall & spring). Gift wrapping and mailing; special and
phone orders.

5512 Connecticut Avenue, NW, W, DC 20015; (202)
244-3956. *Hours:* Mon-Sat, 9:30 am to 5:30 pm.

Fairy Godmother   Carries books for children under age
12 on all subjects, including large selection of picture
books. Also carries some books for young teens and
limited stock of books for adults (especially music and
architecture). Books-on-tape, music cassettes, toys,

cards and book-related stuffed animals. Gift wrapping and mailing; special orders, school accounts.

319 7th Street, SE, W, DC 20003; (202) 547-5474. *Hours:* Mon-Fri, 11 am to 6 pm; Sat, 10 am to 5 pm.

FAO Schwarz Book Dept.   Famous New York-based toy store stocks books for children and young teens on all subjects. Two D.C. locations (Mazza Gallerie store has larger quantity of books):

• *Georgetown Park*   3222 M Street, NW, W, DC 20007; (202) 342-2285. *Hours:* Mon-Fri, 10 am to 9 pm; Sat, 10 am to 7 pm; Sun, noon to 6 pm.

• *Mazza Gallerie*   Wisconsin & Western Avenues, NW, W, DC 20015; (202) 363-8455. *Hours:* Mon-Sat, 10 am to 9 pm; Sun, noon to 5 pm.

Tree Top Toys   Toy store that devotes about a quarter of its space to children's books for all ages in all categories, including lots of classics.

3301 New Mexico Avenue, NW, W, DC 20016; (202) 244-3500. *Hours:* Mon-Sat, 9:30 am to 5:30 pm.

Turtle Park Toys   Toy store with a room devoted to books for young children (pre-K to age six).

4115 Wisconsin Avenue, NW, W, DC 20016; (202) 362-8697. *Hours:* Mon-Fri, 8:30 am to 1 pm; Sat, 10 am to 5 pm; Sun, 1 to 4 pm.

Comics & Collectibles

Another World   New and old comic books and comic book paraphernalia (Batman hats, etc.). Comics for young children, baseball cards, T-shirts, posters, paraphernalia, toys, miniatures and role-playing adventure games. Also carries fantasy and science fiction paperbacks.

1504 Wisconsin Avenue, NW, W, DC 20007; (202) 333-8650. *Hours:* Mon-Thurs, 10 am to 9 pm; Fri and Sat, 10 am to 10 pm; Sun, 11 am to 7 pm.

Northwest Comics   Current, back issue and used comics. Also carries magazines about comics and role-playing adventure games. Discounts available through subscription service.

1728 Wisconsin Avenue, NW, W, DC 20007; (202)

333-0030. *Hours:* Tues-Thurs and Sat, 11 am to 7 pm; Fri, 10 am to 6 pm; Sun, noon to 6 pm.

Foreign Language

Chinese Culture & Arts Company   Books about China (in English and Chinese) and by Chinese authors. All subject areas—fiction and nonfiction. Also carries art and gifts.

736 7th Street, NW, W, DC 20002; (202) 783-1388. *Hours:* Daily, 10 am to 10 pm.

Hispania Books Distributors   Retail outlet and mail order distributor for fiction and nonfiction books about Latin America and by Latin Americans, in genres ranging from sociology to literary criticism. Also carries teaching aids, translation books and Latin American music and handicrafts.

2116 18th Street, NW, W, DC 20009; 265-2325. *Hours:* Mon-Sat, 11 am to 7 pm; Sun, 11 am to 5 pm.

International Learning Center   Specializes in foreign languages and international affairs. Materials in over 120 languages, dictionaries and grammar books, cassettes and video language courses for adults and children, children's books. Also carries foreign language newspapers and magazines, maps and travel books in English.

1715 Connecticut Avenue, NW, W, DC 20009; (202) 232-4111. *Hours:* Mon-Sat, 10 am to 7 pm.

Lado International Institute Bookshop   Instructional texts to help learn English. Foreign language materials, dictionaries, children's books and office supplies. Special and phone orders.

2233 Wisconsin Avenue, NW, W, DC 20007; (202) 338-3133. *Hours:* Mon-Fri, 9 am to 6:30 pm; Sat, 9 am to 2:30 pm.

Latin American Books   Warehouse with large selection of new, used, out-of-print and rare books on Latin America, the Caribbean, Spain and Portugal (and their former African and Asian colonies) and the Hispanic U.S. in all languages and disciplines. Will bring requested titles/subject matter to your home, office or hotel for inspection. Mail order.

P.O. Box 39090, W, DC 20016; 244-4173. *Hours:* Daily by appointment.

Modern Language Bookstore Specializes in French, German and Spanish imports, including bestsellers, classics, criticism and dictionaries. Also carries learning tapes, language study aids in all languages, children's books, books-on-tape, greeting cards, posters, travel guides and maps.

3160 O Street, NW, W, DC 20007; (202) 338-8963. *Hours:* Mon- Sat, 10 am to 7 pm; Sun, noon to 6 pm.

Gay & Lesbian

Lambda Rising Specializes in books for gay men and lesbians and their families and friends. Also carries greeting cards, videos, T-shirts, games, gifts, jewelry, calendars, newspapers and magazines.

1625 Connecticut Avenue, NW, W, DC 20009; (202) 462-6969. *Hours:* Daily, 10 am to midnight.

Hobbies & Diversions

A & A Fine Wines & Spirits Book Center Wine store that devotes a large corner to wine books from all the major wine-producing countries; cookbooks to complement wines carried in the store.

2201 Wisconsin Avenue, NW, W, DC 20007; (202) 337-3161. *Hours:* Mon-Sat, 10 am to 8:45 pm.

Mail Order & Private Dealers

Bickerstaff & Barclay Mail order only. Used, out-of-print and rare photography books.

P. O. Box 46259, W, D.C. 20050-6259; no phone listed.

Garden Variety Mail order only. Garden books, plus cards and gifts relating to gardening.

P.O. Box 40721, W, DC 20016; (202) 686-1229.

Mrs. Duff Gilfond Fugitive Books Intercepted Mail order only. Search service exclusively for out-of-print books on any subject.

1722 19th Street, NW, Ste. 811, W, DC 20009; (202) 387-1418.

Joshua Heller Rare Books Press and illustrated books; fine bindings. Private dealer; also handles mail order.

P.O. Box 39114, W, DC 20016; (202) 966-9411. *Hours:* By appointment only.

Oscar Schapiro Mail order only. Out-of-print, old and rare books on chess, music and the violin. Also autographs, manuscripts, lithographs and engravings on music. Catalog available.

3726 Connecticut Avenue, NW, W, DC 20008; no phone listed.

John Rather Mail order only. Out-of-print and some used books on chess, mountaineering and magic. Catalog available.

P.O. Box 273 Kensington, MD 20895; no phone listed.

Schweitzer Japanese Prints Books on Japan, China and Oriental art. Mail order; catalog available.

4309 Van Ness Street, NW, W, DC 20817; (202) 363-0308.

Voyages Books & Art Mail order only. Used, old and rare books of 20th-century literature. First editions, illustrated and limited editions, paperbacks, fine bindings.

4705 Buttersworth Place, NW, W, DC 20016 (Attn: William Claire); (202) 364-0378.

Military & Diplomatic

National Intelligence Book Center Specializes in nonfiction books on espionage, including how-to's of counterintelligence, wire tapping, surveillance and physical security, trade craft (cover identities, mail drops, letter opening and explosives), history of intelligence agencies, current and out-of-print case histories. Will import foreign books, in all languages, on these subjects. Mail order worldwide.

1700 K Street, NW, Ste. 607, W, DC 20006; (202) 797-1234. *Hours:* Mon, Wed & Fri, 10 am to 6 pm.

Rock Creek Bookshop   Used books, with emphasis on history, biography, military (especially the Civil War), philosophy and literature. One-person operation and moving soon, so call ahead.

3506 Connecticut Avenue, NW, W, DC 20008; (202) 966-2919. *Hours:* Mon-Sat, 1 to 7 pm.

Museums, Historic Sites & Art Galleries

The Corcoran Shop   Bookstore in Corcoran Gallery of Art, specializing in art and photography. Also carries greeting cards, games, jewelry, periodicals, art reproductions and toys.

17th Street and New York Avenue, NW, W, DC 20006; (202) 638-3211. *Hours:* Tues-Sun, 10 am to 4:30 pm (except Thurs, 10 am to 9:30 pm).

Folger Shakespeare Library Museum Shop   Books for all ages. Emphasis on the Renaissance, but also carries books on the late Medieval and post-Renaissance periods. Stock ranges from fun picture books to serious, scholarly works. Also carries books on English herbs, gardening and tea, plays-on-tape, posters, original etchings, jewelry, scarves, T-shirts and totes—all related to the Renaissance or Elizabethan periods.

201 East Capitol Street, SE, W, DC 20003; (202) 544-4600. *Hours:* Mon-Sat, 10 am to 4 pm.

Hillwood Museum Shop   Primarily Russian art books and literature (in English); children's books, gifts and reproductions. Museum specializes in Russian and French decorative arts.

4155 Linnean Avenue, NW, W, DC 20008; (202) 686-8505. *Hours:* Mon & Wed-Sat, 10:30 am to 4 pm.

National Archives Museum Store   Large book section specializes in American history. Also carries posters, crafts, jewelry, historic campaign buttons, postcards, calendars and gifts related to U.S. history.

Pennsylvania Avenue between 7th and 9th Streets, NW, W, DC 20408; (202) 523-1514. *Hours:* Daily, 10 am to 5:30 pm.

National Gallery of Art Museum Stores   Large selection of books on all the fine arts, from ancient Greece and Rome to contemporary. Subjects include: painting, sculpture and some decorative arts, art theory and criticism, photography and film, large section on architecture. Exhibits catalogs and books related to special exhibits and permanent collection. Also carries art reproductions (from cards to posters) of works in gallery.

West and East Wings each have a store. West Building store emphasizes ancient art up to 18th-century French salon painting; East Building store starts with French Impressionism and continues through contemporary art.

Constitution Avenue at 4-6th Streets, NW, W, DC 20565; (202) 842-6466. *Hours:* Mon-Sat, 10 am to 5 pm; Sun, noon to 9 pm.

National Museum of Women in the Arts Museum Shop   Carries books on art history, exhibition catalogs and literature by women artists. Also stocks video tapes about women artists, cards, posters and jewelry.

1250 New York Avenue, NW, W, DC 20005; (202) 783-5000. *Hours:* Tues-Sat, 10 am to 5 pm; Sun, noon to 5 pm.

Parks & History Association Bookshops   Shops in National Park Service monuments and memorials, with specialty books and materials (gifts, maps, posters, greeting cards, etc.) conforming to appropriate subjects for each location. PHAB operates seventeen shops in national parks throughout the metropolitan area. Call (202) 472-3083 for general information, as hours vary.

Eight D.C. locations (for other area locations, please see VA and MD listings):

• *Ford's Theatre & Lincoln Museum Bookshop*   Civil War books and Americana, Lincoln. Ford's Theatre, 511 10th Street, NW, W, DC 20004; (202) 426-6927.

• *Fort Washington Park Bookshop*   Civil War books, military history. Fort Washington Park, Natl Capital Parks East, 1900 Anacostia Drive, W, DC 20020; (202) 763-4600.

• *Frederick Douglass Home Bookshop*   Writings and biographies of Frederick Douglass, books on African-American history. Frederick Douglass Home, 1411 W Street, SE, W, DC 20020; (202) 426-5960.

• *Jefferson Memorial Bookshop*   Subjects covered include Revolutionary War, Jefferson history and biography. Jefferson Memorial, Natl Capital Parks—Central, W, DC 20242; (202) 426-2177.

• *Lincoln Memorial Bookshop* Civil War books and Americana, Lincoln. Lincoln Memorial, Natl Capital Parks—Central, 23rd and Lincoln Memorial Circle, W, DC 20242; (202) 653-9088.

• *Rock Creek Park Bookshop* Books on nature, gardening and the environment. Rock Creek Park, 1800 Beach Drive, W, DC 20015; (202) 426-6829.

• *Tower Bookshop* Historic Washington, general books on historic preservation. The Pavilion—Old Post Office Bldg, 12th Street and Pennsylvania Ave, NW, W, DC 20004; (202) 523-5695.

• *Washington Monument Bookshop* Writings and biographies of George Washington, books on the city of Washington, DC. Washington Monument, Natl Capital Parks—Central, 15th Street and Constitution Avenue, NW 20242; (202) 472-6419.

The Phillips Collection Museum Shop Books on the arts, including titles on architecture, art history, painting, sculpture, interior design and gardens. Museum publications and monographs on artists in the collection. Also carries large collection of posters, reproductions and postcards, plus journals, calendars, paper goods, jewelry, mobiles, windsocks and windchimes and art supplies. Books, puzzles and educational games for children. Special orders.

1600 21st Street, NW, W, DC 20009; (202) 387-2151. *Hours:* Tues-Sat, 10 am to 4:30 pm; Sun, 2 to 6:30 pm (closed Mon).

Smithsonian Institution Museum Shops Each of the major museums has its own shop, with books, posters, cards, jewelry and other gift items relating to the museum's holdings. All shops open Monday through Friday, 10 am to 5:30 pm; Saturday and Sunday, 10 am to 5 pm. For general information call (202) 287-3563.

• *Arts & Industries Building* Books on 19th-century America, crafts and customs; shop also carries cards, jewelry and extensive collection of Victoriana. 900 Jefferson Drive, SW, W, DC 20560; (202) 357–1368/9.

• *Freer Gallery of Art* Books on Oriental and early 20th-century American art, postcards, notecards, desk sets, slides, prints, ceramics, jewelry and needlepoint kits. 12th Street at Jefferson Drive, SW, W, DC 20560; (202) 357–2104.

• *Hirshhorn Museum & Sculpture Garden* Books on modern art and sculpture, postcards, posters and jewelry. Independence Avenue at 8th Street, SW, W, DC 20560; (202) 357–4405.

• *National Air & Space Museum* Books on aeronautics, astronautics and the history of human flight. Shop on lower level carries postcards, models, slides, posters and freeze-dried ice cream. Spacearium shop on upper level carries books, posters and first-day stamp covers. 6th and Independence Avenue, SW, W, DC 20560; (202) 357–1387.

• *National Museum of African Art* Books on African art, designs and crafts; shop also carries postcards, jewelry, textiles, baskets and carvings. 950 Independence Avenue, SW, W, DC 20560; (202) 786–2147.

• *National Museum of American Art* Books on art (especially by American artists), exhibition catalogs, slides, postcards and reproductions. 8th and G Streets, NW, W, DC 20560; (202) 357–1545.

• *National Museum of American History* Books on American history and related subjects, tape cassettes, posters, prints, toys, games, dolls, jewelry and other gift items. 14th Street and Constitution Avenue, NW, W, DC 20560; (202) 357–1527/8.

• *National Museum of Natural History* Books on natural history and anthropology; many dinosaur books and toys. Shop also carries postcards, posters, jewelry and original crafts. 10th Street and Constitution Avenue, NW, W, DC 20560; (202) 357–1535/6.

• *National Portrait Gallery* Books on history and art, exhibition catalogs, slides, postcards, posters, reproductions, jewelry, scarves, china and silver. 8th and F Streets, NW, W, DC 20560; (202) 357–2110.

• *Renwick Gallery* Books on crafts and design, and quality crafts on sale. Shop also sells jewelry and objects relating to the exhibitions. Pennsylvania Avenue at 17th Street, NW, W, DC 20560; (202) 357–1445.

• *Arthur M. Sackler Gallery of Art*   Books on Near and Far Eastern art; selection of books on American artists. Also carries gifts, cards, posters and reproductions. 1050 Independence Avenue, SW, W, DC 20560; (202) 357–1432.

Textile Museum Shop   Carries general books about textiles, including oriental carpets and how-to books on knitting, embroidering and lacemaking. Books, museum publications and other items relating to current exhibits. Sells jewelry (contemporary and ethnographic), baskets and textiles, including handpainted and imported ties and silk scarves.

2320 S Street, NW, W, DC 20008; (202) 667-0441. *Hours:* Tues-Sat, 10 am to 5; Sun, 1 to 5 pm.

Mystery/Science Fiction/Fantasy

Moonstone Bookcellars   Carries science fiction, mystery, fantasy, suspense and horror titles.

2145 Pennsylvania Avenue, NW, W, DC 20037; (202) 659-2600. *Hours:* Daily, 11 am to 6 pm.

Nature & The Outdoors

Audubon Naturalist Bookshop   Titles include botany, nature, natural history, the environment, ornithology, wildlife and children's nature books. Also carries gifts, posters, videos, records, stationery, binoculars and birdfeeders. Publishes newsletter (*Naturalist Review*); mail, phone and special orders. Owned by Audubon Naturalist Society (discounts to Audubon members). One D.C. location (see MD listings for other store):

1621 Wisconsin Avenue, NW, W, DC 20007; (202) 337-6062. *Hours:* Tues-Sat, 10 am to 5 pm, except Thurs, 10 am to 7 pm.

Friends of the National Zoo Bookstore   Books for children and young teens on the animal world, titles by and about Darwin, by women explorers and by naturalists. Also stocks books on wildlife, nature-related fiction for teens & adults and Audubon books. Nature films and videos (including National Geographic specials), bird feeders and birdseed, minerals, rocks, fossils, posters, gifts and cards.

3001 Connecticut Avenue, NW, W, DC 20008; (202)

673-4967. *Hours:* Mon-Fri, 10 am to 4:30 pm; Sat and Sun, 10 am to 5:30 pm.

Habitat   Owned and operated by the National Wildlife Federation, this book and gift shop carries titles on nature, wildlife and the environment and many reference books (including those published by the Federation). Books and other items for children, gifts, greeting cards, T-shirts and posters. One D.C. location (see VA listings for other location):

1412 16th Street, NW, W, DC 20036; (202) 797-6644. *Hours:* Mon-Fri, 10 am to 5:30 pm.

National Geographic Society   Books for children and adults published by the Society are sold here exclusively, along with Geographic Society postcards, atlases, maps and globes.

17th and M Streets, NW, W, DC 20036; (202) 921-1200. *Hours:* Mon-Sat, 9 am to 5 pm; Sun, noon to 5 pm.

The Nature Company   Chain of stores devoted to the "observation, appreciation and understanding of nature." Each store carries large selection of books on nature and the natural world. Subjects include plants and animals (including dinosaurs), science, the body and nature commentary. Children's book section. Two D.C. locations (for other area locations, see VA listings):

• *Georgetown*   Georgetown Park, 1323 Wisconsin Avenue, NW, W, DC 20007; (202) 333-4100. *Hours:* Mon-Fri, 10 am to 9 pm; Sat, 10 am to 8 pm; Sun, noon to 6 pm.

• *Union Station*   50 Massachusetts Avenue, NE, W, DC 20002; (202) 842-3700. *Hours:* Mon-Sat, 10 am to 9 pm; Sun, noon to 6.

New Age & Metaphysical

Blue Nile Trading Company   Metaphysical and health books on many subjects, including vegetarianism, vitamins and macrobiotics.

2826 Georgia Avenue, NW, W, DC 20001; (202) 232-3535. *Hours:* Mon-Sat, noon to 7 pm.

Divine Science Metaphysical Bookstore   Metaphysical books, Marian Heath cards, pamphlets and sermons-on-tape.

2025 35th Street, NW, W, DC 20007; (202) 333-7631.
Hours: Mon-Fri, 10 am to 3 pm; Sun, 9 am to 11 am,
closed 11 am to noon, then reopens noon to 2 pm.

Yes! Bookshop   Specializes in inner development, New
Age, travel and Asian studies. Titles in ancient history,
astrology, healing, body work, spirituality, meditation,
mythology, psychology, philosophy, religion and more.
Also stocks new age music (cassettes, records and CDs),
computer astrology charts and greeting cards. Special,
phone and mail orders; worldwide delivery.

1035 31st Street, NW, W, DC 20007; (202) 338-7874/
Video Department—1303 N. Fillmore Street, Arlington, Virginia; (703) 276-9522. *Hours:* Mon-Sat, 10 am
to 10 pm; Sun, noon to 6 pm.

Political Thought

The Brookings Institution Bookstore   Books and other
publications on governmental studies, economic studies
and foreign policy. Bookstore sells Brookings publications only.

1775 Massachusetts Avenue, NW, W, DC 20036; (202)
797-6258. *Hours:* Mon-Fri, 9 am to 4:30 pm.

Common Concerns   Books on contemporary political,
social and economic issues. Titles on African, Asian,
Latin American and Middle Eastern studies, Europe/
USSR, US/ Canada; African American studies; labor/
organizing; sexual politics; political economy and development. Fiction and remainders. Also carries calendars,
posters, note and postcards, records, T-shirts, buttons
and large selection of political periodicals. Domestic and
overseas mailing.

1347 Connecticut Avenue, NW, W, DC 20036; (202)
463-6500. *Hours:* Mon-Sat, 10 am to 8 pm; Sun, noon
to 6 pm.

Revolution Books   Mostly used books on economics,
history, science and technology, revolutionary interna-
tionalism, political theory, radical politics and current
events.

2438 18th Street, NW, W, DC 20009; (202) 265-1969.
Hours: Mon-Fri, noon to 7 pm; Sat, 11 am to 7 pm;
Sun, noon to 5 pm.

Professional/Academic/Business

Sidney Kramer Books Business and professional book center, with titles in political science, economics, business, management, computer sciences, foreign affairs, military history, science and technology and more. Phone, special and mail orders. Free catalog, worldwide shipping.

 1825 I Street, NW, W, DC 20006; (202) 293-2685/ (800) 423-2665. *Hours:* Mon-Fri, 9 am to 6:30 pm; Sat, 10 am to 5 pm.

Reiter's Scientific & Professional Books Subjects include business, computer science, architecture, economics, mathematics, engineering, math, physics, chemistry, business, biology, medicine, philosophy, psychology, military, physics and statistics. Special orders, worldwide shipping.

 2021 K Street, NW, W, DC 20006; (202) 223-3327. *Hours:* Mon-Fri, 9 am to 7:30 pm; Sat, 9:30 am to 6 pm; Sun, noon to 5 pm.

Washington Law Book Company Carries many law books and other textbooks (international trade, accounting, finance, etc.) for students of George Washington University Law School, but also carries non-textbooks on law and other subjects.

 1917 I Street, NW, W, DC 20006; (202) 371-6667. *Hours:* Mon- Fri, 9:30 am to 6 pm (subject to change).

Religious

Agape Bookstore Christian books, bibles, music tapes, comics, posters and greeting cards.

 1001 Connecticut Avenue, NW, W, DC 20036; (202) 223-3282. *Hours:* Mon-Fri, 10:30 am to 6:30 pm.

Battle's Religious Bookstore Religious books, sheet music, pulpit furniture and communion wear.

 4311 Sheriff Road, NE, W, DC 20019; (202) 399-2366. *Hours:* Mon-Sat, 9 am to 5 pm.

Buddhist Vihara Society Bookstore Books on Buddhism and meditation.

 5017 16th Street, NW, W, DC 20011; (202) 723-0773. *Hours:* Daily, 9 am to 9 pm.

Evangel Temple Bookstore   Religious books and bibles.
616 Rhode Island Avenue, NE, W, DC 20002; (202) 636-3615. *Hours:* Mon-Fri, 11 am to 7 pm; Sat, 11 am to 3:30 pm.

The National Presbyterian Church Books & Gifts
Religious books for adults and children, bibles, sermons-on-tape, gifts and greeting cards.
4101 Nebraska Avenue, NW, W, DC 20016; (202) 537-0800. *Hours:* Tues-Fri, 9 am to 5 pm; Sun, 9 am to 1 pm.

Newman Book Store of Washington   Religious books of interest to Catholics and mainstream Protestants, plus textbooks for the theology and religion departments of Catholic University and Howard University Divinity School. Owned by Paulist Press. Two D.C. locations:

• *Brookland*   3329 8th Street, NE, W, DC 20017; (202) 526-1036. *Hours:* Mon-Sat, 9:15 am to 5:30 pm.

• *Georgetown*   1300 36th Street, NW, W, DC 20007; (202) 337-0555. *Hours:* Tues-Wed, 10:30 am to 7 pm; Thurs-Sat, 10:30 am to 6:30 pm; Sun, 9:30 am to 2:30 pm.

Pursell's Church Supplies   Religious books and church supplies.
Waterside Mall, 401 M Street, SW, W, DC 20024; (202) 484-9563. *Hours:* Mon-Fri, 10 am to 6 pm; Sat, 10 am to 2 pm.

Rock Uniform and Christian Bookstore   Religious books, greeting cards, games, records and tapes and sheet music.
1104 H Street, NE, W, DC 20002; (202) 398-3333. *Hours:* Mon, Tues, Thurs-Sat, 10 am to 6 pm; Wed, 10 am to 5 pm.

The Way of the Cross Ministry   Religious books, bibles, cassettes, gifts, greeting cards and church supplies.
3466 14th Street, NW, W, DC 20001; (202) 265-0908. *Hours:* Mon-Sat, 10 am to 6 pm.

Washington Cathedral Museum and Bookshop   Carries many books on religion, theology, art and architecture. Also carries bibles, crafts, gifts, greeting cards, jewelry, posters, religious goods and stationery.

Wisconsin Avenue & Cathedral Street, Mount Saint Albans, W, DC 20016; (202) 537-6267. *Hours:* Daily, 9:30 am to 5 pm.

Wesley Seminary Bookstore Subjects include ethics, philosophy, theology, aging, dying, family, children's books. Also carries bibles, art supplies, crafts, gifts, greeting cards, jewelry and religious goods.

4500 Massachusetts Avenue, NW, W, DC 20016; (202) 885-8682. *Hours:* Mon-Fri, 10 am to 4 pm (call for evening hours).

Special Needs

Gallaudet University Bookstore See entry under "Universities & Colleges" below.

National Association of the Deaf Bookstore Carries books and other materials related to deafness. Books on sign language and hearing aid research, books for parents of deaf children, religious and children's books, fiction by deaf authors or with deaf charactears. Also carries videos and crafts. Open Monday through Friday, 9 am to 5 pm. 814 Thayer Avenue, Silver Spring; 587-1788 or 587-6282.

Travel & Tourism

Lloyd Books New, rare and unusal travel books of all kinds. Also carries practical guidebooks, ethnic cookbooks, maps, travel journals, language cassettes and dictionaries. Used book selections include first editions and voyages. Special and mail orders; worldwide delivery.

3145 Dumbarton Avenue, W, DC 20007; (202) 333-8989. *Hours:* Mon-Sat, 10 am to 6 pm; Sun, noon to 6 pm.

The Map Store Maps for the general buyer and the specialist, including nautical and aeronautical maps. Also carries atlases, globes, travel guidebooks, map pins and markers, geographic reference material, antique map reproductions and celestial charts. Map mounting and framing service; mail orders.

1636 I Street, NW, W, DC 20006; (202) 628-2608. *Hours:* Mon-Fri, 9 am to 5:30; Sat, 10 am to 4 pm.

Travel Merchandise Mart   Carries travel books, guides, language books and tapes, maps and electrical outlet converters.

1425 K Street, NW, W, DC 20005; (202) 371-6656. *Hours:* Mon-Fri, 9 am to 5:30 pm.

Universities & Colleges

American University Campus Store   General trade books, plus textbooks and remainders. Also carries gifts, cards, college supplies, posters, computer software and sundries.

American University, Massachusetts and Nebraska Avenues, NW, W, DC 20016; (202) 885-6300. *Hours:* Mon-Fri, 9 am to 6 pm; Sat, 11 am to 3 pm.

Catholic University Bookstore   General trade books, plus textbooks, school paraphernalia (sweat shirts, hats, etc.) and school supplies.

Catholic University of America, 620 Michigan Avenue, NE, W, DC 20064; (202) 635-5232. *Hours:* Mon-Tues, 9 am to 6:30 pm; Wed-Thurs, 9 am to 6 pm; Fri, 9 am to 5 pm; Sat, 11 am to 2 pm.

Galludet University Bookstore   Textbooks, with emphasis on liberal arts and deafness. Sign language books, books about deafness and by deaf authors. Also carries some trade books, as well as clothes, school supplies, gifts and devices for the deaf (wake-up devices, TV decoders, telephone devices).

Gallaudet University, 800 Florida Avenue, NE, W, DC 20002; (202) 651-5380/ (800) 672-6720. *Hours:* Mon-Fri, 9 am to 4:30 am.

Georgetown University Bookstore   General trade books, plus textbooks, school supplies and gifts.

Georgetown University, 37th & Prospect Streets, NW, Lauinger Bldg, W, DC 20057; (202) 687-7482. *Hours:* Mon-Fri, 8:30 am to 8 pm; Sat, 9 am to 5 pm; Sun, 11 am to 4 pm.

George Washington University Bookstore   Textbooks, technical books and general trade books (even some children's books). Also carries full line of art, school and technical supplies, as well as remainders, greeting cards, posters, reproductions, snacks, gifts and magazines (U.S. and foreign). Special orders.

George Washington University, 800 21st Street, NW, Marvin Center, NW, W, DC 20052; (202) 994-6870. *Hours:* Mon-Thurs, 8:45 am to 6:30 pm; Fri, 8:45 am to 5 pm; Sat, 11 am to 4 pm.

Howard University Bookstore New and used textbooks for Howard University classes, including the Dental-Medical School. Subject areas include African-American studies, health, dentistry, medicine and nursing. Also carries some trade, medical reference and African-American heritage books, college supplies.

Howard University, 2401 4th Street, NW, W, DC 20059; (202) 636-6657. *Hours:* Mon-Fri, 9 am to 4:45 pm.

Mt. Vernon College Bookstore New and used textbooks for Mt. Vernon college classes. Also carries some trade books, along with clothing, sundries and other items.

Mt. Vernon College, 2100 Foxhall Road, NW, W, DC 20007; (202) 331-3430. *Hours:* Mon-Fri, 9 am to 4 pm.

Trinity College Bookstore New and used textbooks for Trinity college classes. Also carries some trade books, along with clothing, sundries and other items.

Trinity College, 125 Michigan Avenue, NE, W, DC 20017; (202) 939-5117. *Hours:* Mon-Thurs, 9 am to 5 pm; Fri, 9 am to 6 pm; Sun, 10 am to 2 pm.

University of the District of Columbia Bookstore Textbooks, supplies and selection of trade books for students at the University of the District of Columbia. Also carries clothing, gifts, sundries and other items.

UDC Campus, 4200 Connecticut Avenue, NW, W, DC 20008; (202) 966-5947. *Hours:* Mon-Thurs, 9 am to 5 pm; Tues and Wed, 9 am to 7 pm; Fri, 9 am to 4 pm.

Used, Rare & Out-of-Print

Aberdeen Book Shop General interest used books, specializing in art, history, literature and philosophy. Also carries large selections of children's, science, reference and cookbooks. First editions.

3236 P Street, NW, W, DC 20007; (202) 338-2747. *Hours:* Mon-Fri, 11 am to 8 pm; Sat, 10 am to 8 pm; Sun, 10 am to 6 pm.

Booked Up   Carries delicious range of rare, out-of-print and antiquarian books. Many first editions. Co-owned by Pulizter Prize winner Larry McMurtry and partner Marcia McGhee Carter.

1209 31st Street, NW, W, DC 20007; (202) 965-3244. *Hours:* Mon-Fri, 11 am to 3 pm; other hours by appointment.

Book Market   Medium-sized general interest second-hand store, with emphasis on economics, political science, psychology, sociology, science fiction, mystery and general fiction.

2603 Connecticut Avenue, NW, W, DC 20008; (202) 332-2310. *Hours:* Sun-Thurs, 11 am to 6 pm; Fri and Sat, 11 am to 11 pm. Often open additional hours.

Books Plus   Used books of all kinds, fiction and nonfiction ($1 each hardcover, 50 cents each paperback). Also carries a few new titles—Washingtoniana, African-American history and others. Greeting cards, posters, mugs, jewelry and stationery. Owned and operated by Martin Luther King Public Library.

901 G Street, NW, W, DC 20001; (202) 727-6834. *Hours:* Mon-Sat, 11 am to 5 pm; Sun, 1:30 pm to 4:30 pm.

Estate Book Sales   General interest used books, emphasizing art, art history and literature. Also carries titles in biography, classics, military and diplomatic history, poetry, general fiction, literary criticism, philosophy and psychology.

2914 M Street, NW, W, DC 20007; (202) 965-4274. *Hours:* Mon-Sat, 11 am to 9 pm; Sun, 11 am to 7 pm.

Fullers & Saunders Books   Carries used, rare and out-of-print books on Americana and regional history.

3238 P Street, NW, W, DC 20007; (202) 337-3235. *Hours:* Thurs-Tues, 11 am to 7 pm (closed Wednesdays).

William F. Hale Books   General antiquarian, first editions, illustrated books, art books and scholarly literature.

1222 31st Street, NW, W, DC 20007; (202) 338-8272. *Hours:* Usually Mon-Sat, noon to 6 pm, but call ahead.

Idle Time Books   Current, used and out-of-print books on politics and current affairs. Also carries memoirs, literature and has large selection of current periodicals.

2410 18th Street, NW, W, DC 20009; (202) 232-4774.
Hours: Daily, 11 am to 9 pm or later.

The Lantern (Bryn Mawr Bookstore) Used books on a wide range of subjects, including fiction, travel, literature, children's, biography, Washingtoniana, literary criticism, history, psychology, African-American studies, poetry, classics and reference books. Section of 19th-century and rare books. Now carries antiques, including china, silver, oriental rugs and small furniture. Owned by Bryn Mawr College Scholarship Fund.

3222 O Street, NW, W, DC 20037; (202) 333-3222.
Hours: Tues-Thurs, 11 am to 3 pm; Fri & Sat, 11 am to 5 pm; Sun, noon to 4 pm.

Ptak Books Specialize in out-of-print, uncommon and rare science books. Subjects include history of science, math, medicine, logic, technical and electrical engineering. Also carries antiquarian maps, patent models and 19th-century technical drawings.

3236 P Street, NW, W, DC 20037; (202) 337-2878.
Hours: Daily, but call first.

The Rampant Lion Specializes in books about antique silver: new, old, rare, out-of-print, limited and first editions, remainders, foreign language books and more.

P.O. Box 5887, W, DC 20016; no phone listed.

Salvation Army Bookstore Low-cost used books acquired by donation to the Salvation Army—fiction, nonfiction, all genres and kinds. Although not always in great shape, these stacks of books sometimes yield valuable treasures (first editions and more). Patience has its rewards, and all proceeds go to a worthy cause.

512 First Street, NW, W, DC 20001; (202) 347-5878.
Hours: Mon-Sat, 10 am to 4:15 pm.

Second Story Books General interest bookstore, carrying used, rare and out-of-print books on all subjects. Facsimile editions, fine binding, first and limited editions. Also stocks remainders and some half-price new books. Services include book appraising, search service and more. Two other area stores (see MD listings).

2000 P Street, NW, W, DC 20036; (202) 659-8884.
Hours: Daily, 10 am to 10 pm.

Wayward Books Medium-sized general interest bookstore specializing in "choice, used, medium-rare and out-of-print books on Black literature and modern first editions." Good selections of books by or about women; unusual titles in literature and history. Owned by writer Doris Grumbach and librarian Sybil Pike. Search service.

325 Seventh Street, SE, W, DC 20003; (202) 546-2719. *Hours:* Mon-Fri, 10 am to 7 pm; Sat, 10 am to 5 pm; Sun, noon to 5 pm.

Yesterday's Books Used and rare books on all subjects, including history, religion, Americana, ecology, mysteries, children's literature, fiction, poetry, art, science fiction, travel and more. First editions and sections on literary criticism and belles-lettres. Search service.

4702 Wisconsin Avenue, NW, W, DC 20016; (202) 363-0581. *Hours:* Mon-Thurs, 11 am to 9 pm; Fri & Sat, 11 am to 10 pm; Sun, 1 pm to 7 pm.

U.S. Government

U.S. Government Printing Office Bookstores Carries hundreds of government publications on all subjects, including history, military history, outdoor activities, environment, foreign affairs, energy, environment, science and technology, transportation, aeronautics, space exploration, criminal justice, agriculture, employment, labor issues and business and finance.

Two D.C. locations:

• *Govt. Printing Office* 710 N. Capitol Street, NW, W, DC 20401; (202) 275-2091. *Hours:* Mon-Fri, 8 am to 4 pm.

• *Farragut West* 1510 H Street, NW, W, DC 20005; (202) 653-5075. *Hours:* Mon-Fri, 9 am to 5 pm.

Women's

Lammas Bookstore Feminist bookstore, specializing in women's literature, feminist theory and non-sexist child rearing books. Also carries small press publications, records and cassettes by women artists, videos, gifts, games, newspapers, magazines and cards. Community bulletin board. Ticket outlet for many community cultural events. Special orders.

Two D.C. locations:

• *Capitol Hill* 321 7th Street, SE, W, DC 20003; (202) 546-7292. *Hours:* Mon-Sat, 11 am to 7 pm; Sun, noon to 5 pm.

• *Dupont Circle* 1426 21st Street, NW, W, DC 20036; (202) 775-8218. *Hours:* Mon-Sat, 11 am to 9 pm; Sun, noon to 7 pm.

Newsstands

B & B News Stand Billing itself as "one of the world's largest newsstands," B & B carries a vast selection of U.S. and foreign newspapers and magazines. Stocks some paperback books, sundries and other items.

2621 Connecticut Avenue, NW, W, DC 20008; (202) 234-0494. *Hours:* Mon-Fri, 9 am to midnight; Sat & Sun, 7 am to midnight.

Hudson Country News In addition to a large selection of newspapers and magazines, carries souvenirs and candies.

The Shops at National Place, 1331 Pennsylvania Avenue, NW, W, DC 20004; (202) 783-1720. *Hours:* Mon-Fri, 8 am to 9 pm; Sat, 10 am to 7 pm; Sun, noon to 5 pm.

Key Bridge Newsstand Disguised as a convenience store, this small newsstand carries many U.S. and foreign newspapers and magazines, along with sundries and other items.

3326 M Street, NW, W, DC 20007; (202) 338-2626. *Hours:* Daily, 8 am to 8 pm.

The News Room Large assortment of newspapers, journals and U.S. and foreign magazines on every subject. Many collector's editions and significant back issues. Also carries sizeable selection of paperback books, literary and academic journals, computer books, cards, T-shirts, sundries and more. Two D.C. locations:

• *Dupont Circle* 1753 Connecticut Avenue, NW, W, DC 20009; (202) 332-1489. *Hours:* Mon-Fri, 7 am to 10 pm; Sat, 7 am to midnight; Sun, 7 am to 10 pm.

• *Vermont Avenue* 1110 Vermont Avenue, NW, W, DC 20005; (202) 331-8449. *Hours:* Mon-Fri, 8:30 am to 5 pm.

Periodicals Bursting with U.S. and foreign newspapers and magazines, this clean, well-organized store has a decent selection of paperback books and other publications. Sundries and gifts; some major back issues.

International Square, 1825 I Street, NW, W, DC 20006; (202) 223-2526. *Hours:* Mon-Fri, 7 am to 8 pm; Sat, 10 am to 5 pm.

SUBURBAN MARYLAND

General Bookstores

Independents

The Book Gallery A bookstore for writers and readers, this cozy place carries lots of local poetry, small press titles, books about writing and a large selection of literary magazines and other publications. Owned and operated by The Writer's Center.

7815 Old Georgetown Road, Bethesda, MD 20814; (301) 654-8664. *Hours:* Mon-Thurs, 10 am to 8 pm; Fri & Sat, 10 am to 5 pm; Sun, 1 pm to 5 pm.

Bookland of Greenbelt Inc. Large selection of books in all categories on sale all the time, with emphasis on bestsellers, children's books, business titles (taxes, career guides, computer books) and magazines.

Beltway Plaza Shopping Center, 6064 Greenbelt Road, Greenbelt, MD 20770; (301) 474-0033. *Hours:* Mon-Sat, 10 am to 9:30 pm; Sun, noon to 8 pm.

The Bookstall Emphasizes contemporary literature, poetry, travel (literature and guides) and children's books. Also carries large selection of books on the region, plus diaries, dictionaries in various languages and gardening books. Special orders. Moving spring, 1989.

Potomac Village Shopping Center, 9927-B Falls Road, Potomac, MD 20854; (301) 469-7800. *Hours:* Mon-Sat, 10 am to 6 pm, except Thurs until 7 pm.

Bowes Books Large selection of science fiction and romance books. Also carries some used books, office and art supplies, gifts, cake decorating supplies and does custom framing. Special orders.

718 Great Mills Road, Lexington Park, MD 20653; (301) 863-6200. *Hours:* Mon-Sat, 9 am to 6 pm.

Charing Cross Book & Cards Emphasizes regional books; 65% of store devoted to nonfiction, including many history and travel books. Large selection of mysteries, Penguins and books on music. Small but growing section of books in French; large-print books. Also carries cards and stationery. Special, mail and phone orders.

88 Maryland Avenue, Annapolis, MD 21401; (301) 268-1440. *Hours:* Mon-Sat, 10 am to 9 pm; Sun, 9 am to 4 pm (shorter hours in winter).

Corsica Bookshop Specializes in books on Maryland. Also carries cookbooks, children's books and some used books. Special orders, search service.

101 S. Commerce Street, Centerville, MD 21617; (301) 758-1453. *Hours:* Mon-Sat, 9 am to 5 pm.

Cover To Cover Bookstore and Cafe Emphasis on women's issues, spiritual and new age books, psychology, health, children's, health, parenting and science. Also carries new age music cassettes, books-on-tape, calendars and cards. Special orders on new and out-of-print books, mail orders. Cafe offers nourishment and elixir after a busy day of browsing (same hours as bookstore).

7284 Cradlerock Way, Columbia, MD 21045; (301) 381-9200. *Hours:* Mon-Thurs, 9 am to 10 pm; Fri & Sat, 9 am to midnight; Sun, 10 am to 8 pm.

The Cricket Bookshop Emphasis on children's books, cookbooks, mystery, fantasy and science fiction. Also large selections of gardening, outdoors and regional books. Discounts: 35% off hardcover bestsellers (*Washington Post* and *New York Times*). Carries cards, stationery and gifts. Special, mail and phone orders.

17800 New Hampshire Avenue, Ashton, MD 20861; (301) 774-4242. *Hours:* Mon-Fri, 10 am to 6 pm, Thurs until 8 pm; Sat, 10 am to 5:30 pm.

Landover Books Large selection of music reference books. Also sells comics and videos.

7441 Annapolis Road, Landover, MD 20784; (301) 459-9284. *Hours:* Mon-Thurs, 9 am to 11 pm; Fri & Sat, 9 am to 3 pm; Sun, noon to 10 pm.

Maryland Book Exchange Huge stock of general titles (80,000+) and technical and professional books (20,000+), plus full line of textbooks and school, office, art, engineering and business supplies for University of Maryland students.

General book section includes titles in every category, with largest selections in science, literature, fiction, science fiction and children's books. Professional/ Reference section emphasizes computer sciences, engineering, math, physics and industrial education.

4500 College Avenue, College Park, MD 20740; (301) 927-2510. *Hours:* Mon-Fri, 9 am to 6 pm; Sat, 9 am to 5 pm, Sun, noon to 5 pm (hours change in summer— call ahead).

Maxime's Books & Cards Emphasizes bestsellers, romances and mysteries. Also carries magazines and greeting cards.

Laurel Lakes Center, 14328 Baltimore Avenue, Laurel, MD 20707; (301) 776-1588. *Hours:* Mon-Thurs, 10 am to 9:30 pm; Fri & Sat, 10 am to 10 pm; Sun, 11 am to 5 pm.

Olsson's Books & Records Very large, full-service bookstore offering quality fiction and nonfiction in a broad range of categories. Books-on-tape, calendars and postcards; full line of records, tapes and CD's. Can join Penguin Book Club, through which discounts are available; also offers 25% discounts on *Washington Post* hardcover bestsellers. Regular book signings. Mail, phone and special orders; interstore transfers.

All five Olsson's stores carry much of the same stock, but Bethesda store strong in books about classical music, philosophy, science and remainders (for other area locations, see D.C. and VA listings):

• *Bethesda* Woodmont Center, 7647 Old Georgetown Road, Bethesda, MD 20814; (301) 652-3336. *Hours:* Mon-Sat, 10 am to 10 pm, Sun, 11 am to 7 pm.

National Chain Stores

B. Dalton Bookseller Full selection of fiction and nonfiction titles in all categories, including large reference section, history, biography, psychology, mystery and romance. Special section for children's books (B. Dalton Junior).

All B. Dalton's stores carry computer books and magazines; a number have separate computer book and software stores within them (Software, Etc). Each store carries remainders, magazines and newspapers; offer 25% discounts on all hardcover bestsellers.

Seven suburban MD locations (for other area locations, see D.C. and VA listings):

• *Annapolis* 147 Annapolis Mall, Annapolis, MD 21401; (301) 266-6370. *Hours:* Mon-Sat, 10 am to 9:30 pm; Sun, noon to 5 pm.

• *Bethesda* Montgomery Mall, 7101 Democracy Boulevard, Bethesda, MD 20817; (301) 469-8008. *Hours:* Mon-Sat, 10 am to 9:30 pm; Sun, noon to 5 pm.

• *Columbia* 1059 Columbia Mall, 10300 Little Patuxent Parkway, Columbia, MD (301) 997-7744. *Hours:* Mon-Sat, 10 am to 9:30 pm; Sun, noon to 6 pm.

• *Gaithersburg* Lake Forest Mall, 701 Russell Avenue, Gaithersburg, MD 20877; (301) 926-6443. *Hours:* Mon-Sat, 10 am to 9:30 pm; Sun, noon to 6 pm.

• *Glen Burnie* Marley Station, Glen Burnie, MD 21601; (301) 760-0177. *Hours:* Mon-Sat, 10 am to 9:30 pm; Sun, noon to 6 pm.

• *Kensington* White Flint Mall, 11301 Rockville Pike, Kensington, MD 20895; (301) 984-3730. *Hours:* Mon-Sat, 10 am to 9:30 pm; Sun, noon to 6 pm.

• *Laurel* Laurel Centre, 1139 Washington Boulevard, Laurel, MD 20707; (301) 490-7400. *Hours:* Mon-Sat, 10 am to 9:30 pm; Sun, noon to 5 pm.

Crown Books Broad selection of best-selling fiction and nonfiction books—many deeply discounted—including reference, health, history, biography, mystery and detective, art and many other titles. Adult and children's books, magazines, newspapers, some videocassettes.

Discounts range from 25% to 35% off *New York Times* best-sellers; 20% to 50% off hardcover art, cook and reference books; 10% off paperbacks and magazines; and 25% off computer books, software and accessories. Most stores have large shelves of remainders, many for $2 or less.

Twenty-three suburban MD locations (for other area locations, see D.C. and VA listings):

- *Annapolis I* 176 Main Street, Annapolis, MD 21401; (301) 261-1939. *Hours:* Mon-Sat, 10 am to 9 pm; Sun, 11 am to 5 pm.

- *Annapolis II* 150-Q Jennifer Road, Annapolis, MD 21401; (301) 266-3353. *Hours:* Mon-Sat, 11 am to 9 pm; Sun, 11 am to 5 pm.

- *Bethesda I* 4601A East-West Highway, Bethesda, MD 20814; (301) 656-5775. *Hours:* Mon-Sat, 10 am to 9:30 pm; Sun, 10 am to 6 pm.

- *Bethesda II* 5438 Westbard Avenue, Bethesda, MD 20816; (301) 986-0091. *Hours:* Mon-Sat, 10 am to 8 pm; Sun, 11 am to 5 pm.

- *Bowie* 3232 Superior Lane, Bowie. MD 20715; (301) 262-4101. *Hours:* Mon-Sat, 10 am to 9 pm; Sun, 11 am to 5 pm.

- *College Park* 7410 Baltimore Avenue, College Park, MD 20740; (301) 927-6511. *Hours:* Mon-Sat, 11 am to 9 pm; Sun, 11 am to 6 pm.

- *Columbia* 6435 Dobbin Road, Columbia, MD 21045; (301) 730-3099. *Hours:* Mon-Sat, 10 am to 9 pm; Sun, 11 am to 5 pm.

- *Gaithersburg I* 632 Quince Orchard Road, Gaithersburg, MD 20879; (301) 258-9330. *Hours:* Mon-Sat, 10 am to 9 pm; Sun, 11 am to 5 pm.

- *Gaithersburg II* 9643 Lost Knife Road, Gaithersburg, MD 20879; (301) 869-1636. *Hours:* Mon-Sat, 10 am to 9 pm; Sun, 11 am to 5 pm.

- *Germantown* 13004 Middlebrook Road, Germantown, MD 20874; (301) 540-8799. *Hours:* Mon-Sat, 11 am to 9 pm; Sun, 11 am to 5 pm.

- *Greenbelt* Greenway Shopping Center, 7495 Greenbelt Road, Greenbelt, MD 20770; (301) 441-8220. *Hours:* Mon-Sat, 10 am to 9 pm; Sun, 11 am to 5 pm.

- *Laurel* 352 Donner Avenue, Laurel, MD 20707; (301) 953-9663. *Hours:* Mon-Sat, 10 am to 9 pm; Sun, 11 am to 5 pm.

- *Olney* 18153-5 Village Mart Drive, Olney, MD 20833; (301) 774-3917. *Hours:* Mon-Sat, 10 am to 9 pm; Sun, 11 am to 5 pm.

- *Potomac* 7727 Tuckerman Lane, Potomac, MD 20854; (301) 299-4104. *Hours:* Mon-Sat, 10 am to 9 pm; Sun, 11 am to 5 pm.

- *Rockville I* White Flint Mall, 12111 Rockville Pike, Rockville, MD 20857; (301) 468-1006. *Hours:* Mon-Sat, 11 am to 9 pm; Sun, 11 am to 5 pm.

- *Rockville II* 15132 Frederick Road, Rockville, MD 20850; (301) 424-1676. *Hours:* Mon-Sat, 10 am to 9 pm; Sun, 11 am to 6 pm.

- *Rockville III* 1677 Rockville Pike, Rockville, MD 20850; (301) 468-2912. *Hours:* Mon-Sat, 10 am to 9 pm; Sun, 11 am to 5 pm.

- *Rockville IV* 5518 Norbeck Road, Rockville, MD 20853; (301) 871-2663. *Hours:* Mon-Sat, 10 am to 9 pm; Sun, 11 am to 5 pm.

- *Silver Spring I* 13826 Outlet Drive, Silver Spring, MD 20907; (301) 380-6177. *Hours:* Mon-Sat, 10 am to 9 pm; Sun, 11 am to 5 pm.

- *Silver Spring II* 13663 Georgia Avenue, Silver Spring, MD 20907; (301) 949-6636. *Hours:* Mon-Sat, 10 am to 9 pm; Sun, 11 am to 5 pm.

- *Upper Marlboro* 5775A Crain Highway, Upper Marlboro, MD 20772; (301) 627-8500. *Hours:* Mon-Sat, 10 am to 8 pm; Sun, 11 am to 5 pm.

- *Waldorf* Waldorf Shopper's World, Rt. 301, Waldorf, MD 20601; (301) 645-3922. *Hours:* Mon-Sat, 10 am to 9 pm; Sun, 11 am to 5 pm.

- *Wheaton* 11181 Viers Mill Road, Wheaton, MD 20902; (301) 942-7995. *Hours:* Mon-Sat, 10 am to 9:30 pm; Sun, 10 am to 6 pm.

Waldenbooks Large variety of fiction and nonfiction titles in many categories, including reference, biography, history, mystery, health, New Age, literature and art. Adult and children's books, magazines, tapes, videocassettes, computer books and software.

Offer book clubs (kids, 60+, mysteries, etc.) whose members receive special discounts. Also discounts hardcover bestsellers. The chain operates several separate computer stores in the metropolitan area (Waldensoftware.) Will handle special orders.

Fourteen suburban MD locations (for other area locations, see D.C. and VA listings):

• *Annapolis I*   136 Annapolis Mall, Annapolis, MD; (301) 266-6065. *Hours:* Mon-Sat, 10 am to 9:30 pm; Sun, noon to 5 pm.

• *Annapolis II*   641 Security Square, 6901 Security Blvd, Annapolis, MD 21207; (301) 944-7344. *Hours:* Mon-Sat, 10 am to 9:30 pm; Sun, noon to 5 pm.

• *Annapolis III*   7749 E Point Mall, Annapolis, MD 21224; (301) 282-1077. *Hours:* Mon-Sat, 10 am to 9:30 pm; Sun, noon to 5 pm.

• *Annapolis IV*   2132 White Marsh Mall, 8200 Perry Hall Blvd, Annapolis, MD 21236; (301) 256-4112. *Hours:* Mon-Sat, 10 am to 9:30 pm; Sun, noon to 5 pm.

• *Bethesda*   143 Montgomery Mall, 7101 Democracy Blvd, Bethesda, MD 20817; (301) 469-8810. *Hours:* Mon-Sat, 10 am to 9:30 pm; Sun, noon to 5 pm.

• *Columbia*   The Mall at Columbia, 10300 Little Patuxent Parkway, Columbia, MD 21044; (301) 730-6990. *Hours:* Mon-Sat, 10 am to 9:30 pm; Sun, noon to 5 pm.

• *Forestville*   Forest Village Park Mall, 3325 Donnell Drive, Forestville, MD 20746; (301) 568-6911. *Hours:* Mon-Sat, 10 am to 9:30 pm; Sun, noon to 5 pm.

• *Gaithersburg*   Lake Forest Shopping Center, 701 Russell Avenue, Gaithersburg, MD 20877; (301) 921-9248. *Hours:* Mon-Sat, 10 am to 9:30 pm; Sun, noon to 6 pm.

• *Glen Burnie I*   258 Harundale Center, 7700 Ritchie Highway, Glen Burnie, MD 21061; (301) 761-1976. *Hours:* Mon-Sat, 10 am to 9:30 pm; Sun, noon to 5 pm.

• *Glen Burnie II*   Glen Burnie Mall, 6711 Ritchie Highway, Glen Burnie, MD 21061; (301) 760-1233. *Hours:* Mon-Sat, 10 am to 9:30 pm; Sun, noon to 5 pm.

• *Glen Burnie III*   Marley Station, 7900 Ritchie Highway, Glen Burnie, MD 21061; (301) 760-5733. *Hours:* Mon-Sat, 10 am to 9:30 pm; Sun, noon to 5 pm.

• *Landover*   Landover Mall, 2223 Brightseat Road, Landover, MD 20785; (301) 322-9220. *Hours:* Mon-Sat, 10 am to 9:30 pm; Sun, noon to 5 pm.

• *Laurel* Laurel Center, 1139 Washington Blvd, Laurel, MD 20707; (301) 953-3807. *Hours:* Mon-Sat, 10 am to 9:30 pm; Sun, noon to 5 pm.

• *Wheaton* Wheaton Plaza, Wheaton, MD 20902; (301) 946-0202. *Hours:* Mon-Sat, 10 am to 9:30 pm; Sun, noon to 5 pm.

Specialty Bookstores

Children & Juvenile

Building Blocks, A Children's Bookshop Complete line of children's books for ages pre-K up to junior high, with classics for older teens. Also carries foreign language books for children, parent and teacher resource books, books-on-tape, music and videos for children and greeting cards. Special orders; school accounts.
    69 Maryland Avenue, Annapolis, MD 21401; (301) 268-6848. *Hours:* Mon-Sat, 10 am to 5 pm; Sun, 1 to 5 pm.

Junior Editions Books for infants through teens in all subjects: classic picture books, fiction for older children, nonfiction, poetry, biography and reference. Also carries children's music cassettes, videos, books-on-tape and plush animals, including Beatrix Potter collection. Book club and special orders.
    Columbia Mall, Columbia, MD 21044; (301) 730-2665. *Hours:* Mon-Sat, 10 am to 9:30 pm; Sun, noon to 5 pm.

Lowen's Book Department Toy store with substantial number of books for children of all ages, as well as a small section of classics and mysteries for adults. All categories represented, including fiction, picture books, poetry, Newberry winners and anthologies. Adult books on parenting.
    7201 Wisconsin Avenue, Bethesda, MD 20814; (301) 652-1289. *Hours:* Mon-Sat, 9:30 am to 6 pm, Thurs, 9:30 am to 9 pm.

Toys Etc. Toy store with entire wing devoted to children's books. Full range of ages and subjects, including classics and science, biography and history. Also some books for adults: bestsellers, classics in paperback and mysteries.

Cabin John Mall, 11325 Seven Locks Road, Potomac, MD 20854; (301) 299-8300. *Hours:* Mon-Fri, 10 am to 7:45 pm; Sat, 10 am to 5:45 pm; Sun, noon to 4:45 pm.

Comics & Collectibles

Anything Collectible   Comics, baseball cards, antique prints, paperbacks, many collectibles and rare books on various subjects.

969 Ritchie Highway, Severna Park, MD 21146; (301) 647-5222. *Hours:* Tues-Fri, 10 am to 7 pm; Sat, 10 am to 6 pm; Sun, noon to 5 pm.

Blue Beetle Comic & Baseball Cards   Large selection of comics and baseball cards, with other collectibles on display as well. Two MD locations:

• *Camp Springs* 6814 Allentown Way, Camp Springs, MD 20748; (301) 449-3307. *Hours:* Mon-Fri, noon to 7 pm, Sat, 10 am to 5 pm; Sun, noon to 5 pm.

• *Waldorf* Heritage Square, Rte 5, Waldorf, MD 20601; (301) 843-1434. *Hours:* Mon-Fri, noon to 7 pm; Sat, 10 am to 4 pm; Sun, noon to 4 pm.

Big Planet Comics   New comics from every comic book publisher, plus large selection of back issues, including collectors' items, posters and T-shirts. Free subscription service.

4865 Cordell Avenue, Bethesda, MD 20814; (301) 654-6856. *Hours:* Mon-Sat, 11 am to 6 pm, Fri, 11 am to 8 pm; Sun, noon to 5 pm.

Book and Comic Outlet   Comics from all publishers, plus paperbacks—romance, science fiction, horror, adventure and westerns. Also carries magazines, posters, T-shirts and toys.

Carrollton Mall, 7736 Riverdale Road, New Carrollton, MD 20784; (301) 731-5851. *Hours:* Mon-Thurs, 10 am to 9 pm; Fri & Sat, 10 am to 10 pm; Sun, noon to 6 pm.

The Closet of Comics   New and back issues of comics from all comic book publishers, including DC, Marvel and small publishers.

7319 Baltimore Avenue, College Park, MD 20740;

(301) 699-0498. Hours; Daily, 11 am to 6 pm (except Fri, noon to 7 pm).

Collector's Choice Comic books, sports cards and related memorabilia from the 1800's to the present. Also carries mystery and science fiction and related books.

Laurel Shopping Center, Laurel, MD 20707; (301) 725-0887. *Hours:* Mon-Fri, noon to 8 pm; Sat, 10 am to 7 pm.

Collector's World All kinds of gum and tobacco cards, from the 1800s to the present, plus comic books and records.

612 Quince Orchard Road, Gaithersburg, MD 20878; (301) 840-0520. *Hours:* Mon, 11 am to 6 pm; Tues, closed; Wed & Thurs, 2 to 8 pm; Fri, 11 am to 8 pm; Sat, 11 am to 6:30 pm; Sun, 11 am to 4 pm.

Comic Classics In addition to comics and baseball cards, sells used paperbacks: science fiction, horror, romance and mystery.

365 Main Street, Laurel, MD 20707; (301) 490-9811. *Hours:* Mon, closed; Tues, 11 am to 5 pm; Wed & Fri, noon to 8 pm; Sat, noon to 6 pm; Sun, noon to 4 pm.

Galactic Enterprises Focus is comic books, but also stocks some books, mostly science fiction and fantasy. Also carries role-playing games and posters.

16 Crain Highway N., Glen Burnie, MD 21061; (301) 760- 9538. *Hours:* Mon-Fri, 10 am to 9 pm; Sat, 10 am to 8 pm; Sun, 11 am to 5 pm.

Geppi's Comic World of Silver Spring Large selection of comic books, cards, posters and other collectibles. Have recorded "Comic Hotline," which describes latest titles over phone.

8317 Fenton Street, Silver Spring, MD 20910; (301) 588-2545/ 792-2754. *Hours:* Mon-Fri, 11 am to 7 pm; Sat, 10 am to 7 pm; Sun, noon to 6 pm.

Luce's Book Exchange Comics, sports cards, posters and used paperbacks.

Freestate Mall, 15528 Annapolis Road, Bowie, MD 20715; (301) 464-3570. *Hours:* Mon-Sat, 10 am to 9 pm; Sun, noon to 5 pm.

Foreign Language

Iran Books   Mail order only. Books in Persian.
8014 Old Georgetown Road, Bethesda, MD 20814; (301) 986-0079.

Victor Kamkin Bookstore   Russian language books on all subjects. Mail order and retail outlet.
12224 Parklawn Drive, Rockville, MD 20852; (301) 881-5973. *Hours:* Mon-Sat, 9 am to 5 pm.

Sakura Book & Foods   Japanese books, magazines, gifts and food. 15809 S. Frederick Road, Rockville, MD 20850; (301) 948-5112. *Hours:* Tues-Sun, 10 am to 6 pm.

Hobbies & Diversions

G Street Fabrics Bookstore   Specializes in books on fabric, fashion, costume, sewing, textiles, needle arts and quilting. Also carries greeting cards, calendars, magazines, posters, newsletter, notebooks and period costume patterns. Special orders, mail and phone orders. Search service.
11854 Rockville Pike, Rockville, MD 20852; (301) 231-8998. *Hours:* Mon-Fri, 10 am to 9 pm; Sat, 10 am to 6 pm; Sun, noon to 5 pm.

Mail Order & Private Dealers

Artistic Endeavors   First edition and out-of-print books on the fine arts, performing arts and music. Also autographs, manuscripts, original art, prints and ephemera.
3810 Chesterwood Drive, Silver Spring, MD 20906; no phone listing.

Ashe & Deane   Concentrates on rare and out-of-print 18th and 19th century literature. Some earlier works also available. Mail order and search service. Moving to new location soon.
4931 Cordell Avenue, Bethesda, MD 20814; (301) 652-6680. *Hours:* By appointment only.

Steven Bernard First Editions   Modern first editions, including science fiction and mysteries. Mail order only; catalog available.
15011 Plainfield Lane, Darnestown, MD 20874; no phone listed.

Books of Colonial America   Mail order only. Used, rare and out-of-print books on America, history, Marylandiana, New Yorkiana, Pennsylvaniana, meteorology and climatology. Search service.

3611 Janet Road, Wheaton, MD 20906; (301) 946-6490.

Culpepper, Hughes & Head   Mail order only. New, used, rare and out-of-print books on Africa, black studies and Caribbean history. Also remainders.

9770 Basket Ring Road, Columbia, MD 21045; (301) 730-1484.

Q. M. Dabney & Co   Mail order only. Specializes in books on military history, especially U.S. and British military history. Also sells books on the humanities, law, the social sciences and history. Used, rare, illustrated and out-of-print books. Also sells remainders, first, facsimile and limited editions. Catalog available.

11910 Parklawn Drive, Rockville, MD 20850; (301) 881-1470.

Dar-Danelles Books   Specializes in scarce, out-of-print and unusual children's books and books on American history. By appointment only.

9305 Ewing Drive, Bethesda, MD 20814; (301) 652-4591.

Dragoman Books   General interest, mostly out-of-print scholarly books, emphasizing archaeology, foreign languages and poetry. Mail order only. Search service; book list by subject available. 680 Americana Drive, Annapolis, MD 21403; (301) 263-2757.

Hours: By appointment only.

Jeff Dykes Western Bookscout   Hardcover and out-of-print books on western America, the range livestock industry and western illustrators. Mail order only. Search service.

P.O. Box 38, College Park, MD 20740; (301) 864-0666. *Hours:* By appointment only.

Firstborn Books   Rare, used and out-of-print books on modern literature, western America, and country western music.

1007 E. Benning Road, Galesville, MD 20765; (301) 867-7050. *Hours:* By appointment only.

Frazier's Americana   Orders and shows books on the Civil War, history, presidents and the presidency. New, used, old and rare books; first, limited and facsimile editions. Also sells maps, posters, sheet music, autographs and manuscripts. Search service.

   10509 Walter Point Way, Mitchellville, MD 20716; (301) 336-3616.

Doris Frohnsdorf   Illustrated and children's books. Mail order only.

   P.O. Box 2306, Gaithersburg, MD 20879; (301) 869-1256. *Hours:* By appointment only.

John Gach Books   Huge inventory (30,000) of second-hand, out-of-print and rare books on the history of ideas, philosophy, psychiatry, psychology and psychoanalysis. Also has large collection of modern books on these subjects. Mail order; free catalogs available (4-6 p/year).

   5620 Waterloo Road, Columbia, MD 21045; (301) 465-9023. *Hours:* By appointment only.

Hirschtritt's "1712" History of Books   Mail order only. Specializes in rare and out-of-print books on Americana, Orientalia. Also carries general stock of out-of-print books. First and limited editions, illustrated books. Search service.

   1712 Republic Road, Silver Spring, MD 20902; (301) 649-5393.

Peter Koffsky   Mail order only. Out-of-print books on history, plus maps and ephemera.

   1708 Glenkarney Place, Silver Spring, MD 20902; (301) 649-6105.

Hiram Larew Books   Mail order only. Out-of-print books on natural history and Southern literature. First editions, frequently signed.

   3312 Gumwood Drive, Hyattsville, MD 20783; (301) 422-2738.

O'Boyle Books   General interest rare, out-of-print and modern books. First editions. Exhibits at book fairs. Mail order only. 14605 Pebblestone Drive, Silver Spring, MD 20904; (301) 384-9346. *Hours:* By appointment only.

Old Hickory Bookshop Ltd.   Old, rare and out-of-print medical, dentistry, science and technology books.
20225 New Hampshire Avenue, Brinklow, MD 20862; (301) 924-2225.

Old World Mail Auctions   Rare books (accounts by Europeans of U.S. travel and books with plates of U.S. views), 19th-century atlases, maps, prints and old newspapers. Five mail auctions annually; catalog available. Mail order only.
5614 Northfield Road, Bethesda, MD 20817; (301) 657-9074. *Hours:* By appointment only.

Quill and Brush   Specializes in 19th- and 20th-century first editions of collectible authors, principally literature. Publishes *Author Price Guides,* looseleaf bibliographies of 20th century authors (85 available). Mail order only; catalog available.
P.O. Box 5365, Rockville, MD 20851; (301) 460-3700. *Hours:* by appointment only.

John C. Rather   Mail order only. Illustrated, rare and out-of-print books on chess, photography, magic and conjuring, art history and mountaineering.
P.O. Box 273, Kensington, MD 20895; (301) 942-0515.

Recorded Books   Unabridged books-on-tape in all categories, for sale or rent (30 day maximum). Bestsellers, mysteries, history and classics. Each book is studio recorded by expert narrators—all own product. Mail order only; free catalog available.
P.O. Box 4094, Charlotte Hall, MD 20622; (800) 638-1304.

Waverly Auctions   Book auctions of fine and rare books on all subjects. Also sells prints and autographs. Eight catalogs each year for $25 subscription fee. Mail order only.
4931 Cordell Avenue, Suite AA, Bethesda, MD 20814; 951-8883. *Hours:* By appointment only.

Yak and Yeti Books   Used and out-of-print books on the Himalayas, Central Asia and Tibet. Mail order only; free book list available.
P.O. Box 5736, Rockville, MD 20855; (301) 977-7285. *Hours:* By appointment only.

Military & Diplomatic

Ground Zero Books Used books on war, peace and politics; emphasis on military affairs and conflict resolution.

946 Sligo Avenue, Silver Spring, MD 20910; (301) 589-2223. *Hours:* Mon-Sat, 11:30 am to 6:30 pm; Sun, noon to 5 pm.

Old Soldier Books New, used, rare and out-of-print Civil War books, autographs, letters, photographs and documents. Also undertakes publishing of reprints.

18779-B N. Frederick Avenue, Gaithersburg, MD 20879; (301) 963-2929. *Hours:* Mon-Fri, 10 am to 4 pm; Sat, 10 am to 3 pm.

Ron Van Sickle Military Books Mail order and retail. New, used and out-of-print books on military history, emphasizing the American Civil War. Catalog available.

22 Montgomery Village Avenue, Gaithersburg, MD 20879; (301) 330-2400. *Hours:* Mon-Sat, 9:30 am to 5:30 pm.

Museums, Historic Sites & Art Galleries

Parks & History Association Bookshops Shops in National Park Service monuments and memorials, with specialty books and materials (gifts, maps, posters, greeting cards, etc.) conforming to appropriate subjects for each location. PHAB operates seventeen shops in national parks throughout the metropolitan area.

Two MD locations (for other area locations, please see D.C. and VA listings):

• *Clara Barton House Bookshop* 5801 Oxford Road, Glen Echo, MD 20812; (301) 492-6245. *Hours:* Tues-Sun, noon to 5 pm.

• *Glen Echo Gallery* Carousel books and memorabilia; consignment art; exhibits. Glen Echo Park, MacArthur Blvd, Glen Echo, MD 20812; (301) 492-6282. *Hours:* Tues-Sun, noon to 5 pm.

Mystery

Mystery Bookshop "Home of Masterpiece Murder and Collectible Crime." Mysteries, detective fiction, espionage, true crime, thrillers, suspense, reference and children's mysteries. Also carries large selection of used books in these categories, plus mystery audio and video cassettes for sale. Holds author signings, readings and writers' symposia. Sponsors and hosts local chapter of Mystery Readers International.

7700 Old Georgetown Road, Bethesda, MD 20814; (3010 657-2665. *Hours:* Tues-Sat, 10 am to 8 pm; Sun, noon to 6 pm; Mon, closed.

Rogues' Gallery   Carries many mystery titles, but also stocks espionage books. Bargain books, classic works of mystery and espionage, true crime, mysteries for children, reference books, puzzles and games. Features educational displays and bibliographies ("History in the Mystery," for example). Sponsors author readings and signings. Special orders.

4934 Elm Street, Bethesda, MD 20814; (301) 986-5511. *Hours:* Tues-Sat, 11 am to 7 pm; Sun, 1 to 5 pm.

Nature & The Outdoors

Audubon Naturalist Bookshop   Titles include botany, nature, natural history, the environment, ornithology, wildlife and children's nature books. Also carries gifts, posters, videos, records, stationery, binoculars and birdfeeders. Publishes newsletter (*Naturalist Review*); mail, phone and special orders. Owned by Audubon Naturalist Society (discounts to Audubon members). One MD location (see D.C. listings for other store):

8940 Jones Mill Road, Chevy Chase, MD 20815; (301) 652-3606. *Hours:* Mon-Fri, 10 am to 5 pm, Thurs, 10 am to 7 pm; Sat, 9 am to 3 pm; Sun, noon to 5 pm (call ahead first).

Wild Bird Center   Stocks books on birds, nature and the environment. Also carries bird feeders and houses, field guides, binoculars, scopes, clothing and gifts.

Three MD locations:

• *Cabin John*   7687 MacArthur Boulevard, Cabin John, MD 20818; (301) 229-3141. *Hours:* Daily, 10 am to 6 pm.

• *Gaithersburg*   420 E. Diamond Avenue, Gaithersburg, MD 20879; (301) 333-9453. *Hours:* Daily, 10 am to 6 pm.

• *Annapolis*   101 Annapolis Street, Annapolis, MD 21401; (301) 280-0033. *Hours:* Mon-Fri, 11 am to 6 pm; Sat, 10 am to 6 pm; Sun, noon to 5 pm.

Wild Bird Company   Books and other items focus on local backyard birdwatching, although also carries general books on birdwatching. Also stocks feeders, houses and seed for backyard birdwatchers, plus video (for sale and rent) and audio cassettes, CDs, T-shirts, binoculars and scopes (for sale and rent), gifts and cards. Free newsletter and catalog, both list new books. Special orders, mail and phone orders; worldwide shipping.
617 Hungerford Drive, Rockville, MD 20852; (301) 279-0079. *Hours:* Mon-Tues & Sat-Sun, 10 am to 6 pm; Wed-Fri, 10 am to 8 pm.

Nautical

Fawcett Boat Supplies Book Department   Large selection of nautical (sail and power) books—subjects include rigging, splicing and repairing. Also carries books about the Chesapeake Bay and Annapolis.
110 Compromise Street, Annapolis, MD 21401; (301) 267-8681. *Hours:* Mon-Sat, 8:30 am to 5 pm.

New Age & Metaphysical

Beautiful Day Bookstore   Books for adults and children on subjects including alternative life styles, natural childbirth and healing, nature and the environment, nutrition, health, and organic and natural cooking. Also carries literary magazines and fine stationery.
5010 Berwyn Road, College Park, MD 20740; (301) 345-2121. *Hours:* Mon-Fri, 9 am to 7:30 pm; Sat, 8 am to 7:30 pm; Sun, 10 am to 4 pm.

North Door Books   Specializes in metaphysics, feminist books and earth religions. Also carries books on spirituality, astrology and mythology, plus Celtic and New Age music (tapes, records and CDs), candles, jewelry and some clothing. Special orders.
4906 Berwyn Road, College Park, MD 20740; (301) 345-4222. *Hours:* Wed-Fri, 6:30 pm to 9:30 pm; Sat, 11 am to 6 pm; Sun, 1 pm to 6 pm.

Professional/ Academic/ Business

Bookmaster   Medical, dental, nursing, health, veterinary and physical education books and texts.

911 Schindler Dr., Silver Spring, MD 20904; (301) 439-1262.

Leonard S. Blondes Used Law Books Used and out-of-print law books, specializing in larger sets of law books for Federal, Washington, DC and Maryland law practices.

7100 Crail Drive, Bethesda, MD 20817; (301) 229-7102.

Religious

Catholic Book Store Catholic books and full line of church supplies.

11272 Georgia Avenue, Wheaton, MD; 942-4700. Open Monday through Saturday, 9 am to 5:45 pm.

Chesapeake Book & Health Food Center Religious books for children and adults, with emphasis on Adventism. Also carries books on health, music, nature and the environment, plus vitamins, health food, magazines, gifts, greeting cards, records, videos, art, greeting cards and college and church supplies.

6600 Martin Road, Columbia, MD 21044; (301) 995-1913. *Hours:* Mon-Wed, 8:30 am to 5:30 pm; Thur, 8:30 am to 8 pm; Fri, 8:30 am to 1 pm; Sun, 9 am to 3 pm.

Christian Bookshop Religious books, church supplies, recorded music, gifts and greeting cards.

Arundel Plaza, 108 Old Solomons Island Road, Annapolis, MD 21401; (301) 266-8360. *Hours:* Mon-Fri, 8:30 am to 8 pm; Sat, 9:30 am to 5:30 pm.

Christian Family Bookstore Christian books, bibles, gifts and cards.

4506 39th Place, North Brentwood, MD 20748; (301) 864-5530. *Hours:* Daily, 9 am to 9 pm.

Evangel Bookstore Christian books, bibles, gifts, cards, tapes, records, cassettes, songbooks and gifts.

5900 Old Branch Avenue, Camp Springs, MD 20748; (301) 899-5940. *Hours:* Mon-Fri, 9 am to 5 pm.

Glad Tidings Christian Supply Religious books, supplies, music, cards and gifts. Two area locations:

• *Damascus* 9888 Main Street, Damascus, MD 20872; (301) 253-5226. *Hours:* Mon-Fri, 9:30 am to 8 pm; Sat, 9:30 am to 5:30 pm.

• *Rockville* 144 Congressional Lane, Rockville, MD 20852; (301) 881-5946. *Hours:* Mon-Fri, 10 am to 6 pm; Sat, 10 am to 5:30 pm.

Gospel Bookstore Christian books for adults and children, bibles, reference books, music, church supplies, gifts, greeting cards, toys, reproductions and videocassettes.

337 Hospital Drive, Ste AZ, Glen Burnie, MD 21061; (301) 761-3845. *Hours:* Mon-Fri, 10 am to 9 pm; Sat, 10 am to 6 pm.

Hope & Hesed—A Celebrate New Life Store Christian books for adults and children, gifts, tapes and greeting cards.

9017 Gaithersburg Road, Gaithersburg, MD 20877; (301) 840-1540. *Hours:* Mon-Sat, 9:30 am to 6 pm.

Jacob's Well Christian Books Books, gifts, sermons-on-tape, music tapes, videos and jewelry.

26 Shangri-La Drive South, Lexington Park, MD 20653; (301) 863-6388. *Hours:* Mon-Fri, 10 am to 6 pm; Sat, 10 am to 4 pm.

Jesus' Bookstore Bibles, study aids, church supplies, paperbacks, gospel music records, tapes, cassettes and songbooks. Family video center.

8857 Woodyard Road, Clinton, MD 20735; (301) 856-1290. *Hours:* Wed & Sat, 9 am to 5 pm; all other weekdays, 9 am to 8 pm.

Jewish Bookstore of Greater Washington Full line of fiction and nonfiction books about Judaism and Judaica. Subjects include religion, philosophy, music, children, cooking, law, holidays, prayer and travel. Also carries gifts, records and tapes.

11250 Georgia Avenue, Wheaton, MD 20902; (301) 942-2237. *Hours:* Mon-Thurs, 10 am to 7 pm; Fri, 10 am to 2 pm; Sun, 10 am to 5 pm.

Lamplighter Christian Bookshop Religious books, bibles, records, tapes and videocassettes. Library and reading room.

1506 University Boulevard East, Langley Park, MD 20783; (202) 434-8780. *Hours:* Mon-Fri, 9:30 am to 9 pm; Sat, 9:30 am to 6 pm.

Libson's Hebrew Books & Gifts Full line of books about Judaism and Judaica. Gifts, line of 14-carat jewelry. Will also produce invitations for weddings, bar mitzvahs, etc.

2305 University Boulevard West, Wheaton, MD 20902; (301) 933-1800. *Hours:* Mon & Tues, 9:30 am to 6 pm; Wed, 9:30 am to 7 pm; Thurs, 9:30 am to 8 pm; Fri, 9:30 am to 2 pm; Sun, 9:30 am to 5 pm.

The Master's Vineyard Religious books for adults and children, gifts, music, tapes, videos, toys and jewelry.

19707 Frederick Road, Germantown, MD 20874; (301) 972-6900. *Hours:* Mon, Wed, Thurs & Sat, 9 am to 7 pm; Tues & Fri, 10 am to 9 pm.

The Olive Branch Bibles, books, records, tapes, music, gifts, cards and church supplies.

765 Rockville Pike, Rockville, MD 20852; (301) 340-1129. *Hours:* Mon & Wed, 9:30 am to 6 pm; Tues, Thurs and Fri, 9:30 am to 9 pm; Sat, 9 am to 4:30 pm.

Potomac Adventist Book & Health Food Center Religious books for children and adults, with emphasis on Adventism. Also carries books on health, music, nature and the environment, plus vitamins, health food, magazines, gifts, greeting cards, records, videos, art and college and church supplies.

8400 Carroll Avenue, Takoma Park, MD 20912; (301) 439-0700. *Hours:* Mon-Wed, 9 am to 5:30 pm; Thurs, 9 am to 9 pm; Fri, 9 am to 2:30 pm.

Rejoice Christian Store Books, bibles and church supplies. Mail order service for Christian materials.

8509 Walker Mill Road, Capital Heights, MD 20743; (301) 350-5222. *Hours:* Mon-Fri, 11 am to 6 pm; Sat, 10 am to 5 pm.

Shahar Christian Bookshoppe Bibles, books, tapes & CDs, some records, sheet music, children's books & toys, gifts, cards and church supplies.

15426 New Hampshire Avenue, Silver Spring, MD 20904; (301) 384-9303. *Hours:* Mon-Fri, 9:30 am to 6 pm, Tues & Fri, 9:30 am to 8 pm; Sat, 9:30 am to 4:30 pm.

This Is The Place Bookstore Mormon Church books and supplies. Also carries titles on biblical and women's studies.

10408 Montgomery Avenue, Kensington, MD 20895; (301) 933-1943. *Hours:* Mon, 10 am to 4 pm; Tues & Fri, 10 am to 9 pm; Wed, Thurs & Sat, 10 am to 6 pm.

Washington Bible College Bookstore Sells more to general public than to students of the college. Large selection of religious trade books. Sections on theology, bible commentaries, Christian living, biography, great Christian leaders, counseling, fiction, family, books on women, men and health and social and ethical issues— all by Christian authors. Also carries videos, tapes, CDs and choral music.

6511 Princess Gardens Parkway, Lanham, MD 20706; (301) 552-1400. *Hours:* Mon-Fri, 9 am to 7 pm; Sat, 10 am to 5 pm.

Whosoever Will Church of God Christian and Religious Books Books, tapes and records. Health department carries books on the body, healing herbs, diet products and skin lotions.

3847 34th Street, Mt. Ranier, MD; (301) 699-5008. *Hours:* Mon-Wed, 10 am to 6 pm; Thurs & Sat, 10 am to 7 pm.

Remainders

Daedalus Books National mail order service for new and remaindered books on wide range of subjects. Huge warehouse has thousands of titles on virtually every subject, but especially strong in quality fiction, history, philosophy, science and art titles. Special orders, free catalog available (6 times p/year).

4601 Decatur Street, Hyattsville, MD 20781; (301) 779-4044.

Science Fiction/Fantasy

Barbarian Books General interest used bookstore specializing in science fiction. Broad general stock includes comics, literature, children's books and bibliographies.

11254 Triangle Lane, Wheaton, MD 20902; (301) 946-4184. *Hours:* Tues-Sat, noon to 6 pm; Sun, 1 to 6 pm.

Dream Wizards   Mostly nonfiction books on mysticism, magic, folklore, tarot, conjuring and strange phenomena. Also carries games, greeting cards, posters, toys and computer software.

17 Rockville Pike (Rear), Rockville, MD 20852; (301) 881-3530. *Hours:* Mon & Tues, 11 am to 6 pm; Wed-Fri, 11 am to 8 pm; Sat, 10am to 6 pm; Sun, noon to 5 pm.

John W. Knott, Jr.   Used science fiction, fantasy and horror. Sells limited editions and British first editions, as well as new small press books. Mail order only; catalog available.

8453 Early Bud Way, Laurel, MD 20707; (301) 725-7537. *Hours:* By appointment only.

Robert A. Madle Books   New, used, rare and out-of-print science fiction/ fantasy and related material, including science fiction magazines and pulps. Mail order only. Search service; catalog available.

4406 Bestor Drive, Rockville, MD 20853; (301) 460-4712. *Hours:* By appointment only.

The Magic Page   General interest used bookstore specializing in science fiction. Owned by Barbarian Books (see above).

7416 Laurel-Bowie Road, Bowie, MD 20715; (301) 262-4735. *Hours:* Tues-Thurs, 3pm to 6 pm; Fri, 3 pm to 8 pm; Sat, noon to 6 pm.

Travel & Tourism

Travel Books Unlimited & Language Center   Comprehensive selection of foreign language materials and cassette courses in more than 90 languages. Also carries maps, travel guides and diaries, atlases, histories, dictionaries, grammars, travel videos, books-on-tape and phrase books. Special and mail orders; free catalog available.

4931 Cordell Avenue, Bethesda, MD 20814; (301) 951-8533. *Hours:* Mon-Sat, 10 am to 9 pm; Sun, noon to 5 pm.

Universities & Colleges

Capitol College Bookstore   Textbooks and trade books in areas of electronics, computers and engineering. Also carries clothing and school supplies.

11301 Springfield Road, Laurel, MD 20708; (301) 953-7561. *Hours:* Mon & Tues, 8 am to 6 pm; Wed & Thurs, 8 am to 5 pm; Fri, 8 am to 3 pm.

Columbia Union College Bookstore   Textbooks and some trade books, plus art and college supplies, greeting cards, reproductions, computer software, videocassettes, sporting goods and calculators.

7600 Flower Avenue, Takoma Park, MD 20912; (301) 891-4096. *Hours:* Mon-Thurs, 9 am to 7 pm; Fri, 9 am to 2 pm.

Howard Community College Bookstore   Mostly textbooks, and some trade books emphasizing self-help, paperback bestsellers, cookbooks, reference and children's books. Also carries greeting cards, gifts, magazines, school supplies, sportswear and sundries.

Little Patuxent Parkway, Columbia, MD 21044; (301) 992-4816. *Hours:* Mon-Fri, 8:30 am to 3:30 pm; Mon-Thurs evenings, 5 to 8 pm.

Montgomery College Bookstores   Textbooks, trade books (mostly study aids, computer and reference books), greeting cards, clothes, school and art supplies and sundries.

Three campus locations:

• *Germantown Campus*   20200 Observation Drive, Germantown, MD 20874; (301) 972-2388. *Hours:* Mon-Thurs, 8:30 am to 1:30 pm & 4 to 7 pm.

• *Rockville Campus*   Campus Center, North Campus Drive, Rockville, MD 20850; (301) 279-5302.

• *Takoma Park Campus*   New York & Takoma Avenues, Takoma Park, MD 20912; (301) 587- 6243. *Hours:* Mon-Thurs, 8:30 am to 1:30 pm & 4 to 7 pm.

Prince George's Community College Bookstore
Textbooks, small trade section (fiction, nonfiction, reference books and study aids) and large nursing and nursing review section. Also carries school, art, engineering and office supplies, gifts and clothing.

301 Largo Road, Largo, MD 20772; (301) 336-6844. *Hours:* Mon & Tues, 9 am to 8 pm; Wed & Thurs, 9 am to 5:30 pm; Fri, 9 am to 5 pm.

University Book Center Serves University of Maryland students and general public. In addition to textbooks and supplies for undergraduate and graduate schools, carries large selection of trade books in all categories: history, politics, religion, women's studies, new age, psychology, sports, study guides, computers and computer science, reference books, math, engineering, sciences, the humanities, travel, media and film. Out-of-print book search for technical and professional books; special orders.

Adele H. Stamp Union, University of Maryland, College Park, MD 20742; (301) 454-3222. *Hours:* Mon-Fri, 8:30 am to 7:30 pm; Sat, 9 am to 5 pm; Sun, noon to 5 pm.

Used, Rare & Out-of-Print

Attic Books General interest used books, everything from art to zoology. Large sections of science fiction, fantasy and history, as well as literature, drama, poetry and the sciences.

357 Main Street, Laurel, MD 20707; (301) 725-3725. *Hours:* Wed-Sat, 11 am to 7 pm; Tues, closed; Sun, 1 to 5 pm.

Bartleby's Bookshop General interest used bookstore, emphasizing humanities, fiction (especially European fiction), history, scholarly editions and classics in all fields. Also has large selections in women's studies, cooking, gardening, poetry and travel literature; literary remainders. Search service.

7704 Woodmont Avenue, Bethesda, MD 20814; (301) 654-4373. *Hours:* Mon-Sat, 10 am to 8 pm; Sun, noon to 6 pm.

Bonifant Books General interest used bookstore, carrying everything from classics to comics, with vintage paperbacks a specialty.

11240 Georgia Avenue, Wheaton, MD 20902; (301) 946-1526. *Hours:* Mon-Fri, 10:30 am to 8 pm; Sat, 10 am to 6 pm; Sun, 11 am to 6 pm.

Book Alcove General interest used books and remainders, including classics, fiction, mystery, gardening, ecology, crafts, history, self-help, home repair and anthropology. Antique, rare and out-of-print books. Assortment of Heritage Press and Folio Society books. Custom bookcases. Two MD locations:

• *Gaithersburg* Shady Grove Shopping Center (Rear), 15976 Shady Grove Road, Gaithersburg, MD 20877; (301) 977-9166. *Hours:* Mon-Fri, 10 am to 8 pm; Sat, 10 am to 6 pm; Sun, noon to 5 pm.

• *Rockville* Loehman's Plaza, 5210 Randolph Road, Rockville, MD 20852; (301) 770-5590. *Hours:* Mon-Fri, 10 am to 9 pm; Sat, 9:30 am to 9 pm; Sun, noon to 6 pm.

The Book Cellar Used and rare books on all subjects and in many languages. Literature, politics, business, economics, sociology, archaeaology, music, art history and more; section devoted to small books. First editions.

8227 Woodmont Avenue, Bethesda, MD 20814; (301) 654-1898. *Hours:* Mon-Fri, 11 am to 6 pm; Sat, 11 am to 5 pm; Sun, 11 am to 5 pm.

The Book Nook Used and old collectible books on all subjects. Large selection of children's books and comics. Puppets and toys available for children to use while parents browse. Two MD locations:

• *College Park* 8911 Rhode Island Avenue, College Park, MD 20740; (301) 474-4060. *Hours:* Mon-Sat, 10 am to 5 pm.

• *Glen Burnie* Book Nook II, 143 Delaware Ave., NE, Glen Burnie, MD 21061; (301) 766-5758. *Hours:* Mon-Sat, 10 am to 5 pm.

Ellie's Paperback Shack General interest used books sold and traded.

Acton Square, Route 301, Waldorf, MD 20601; (301) 843-3676. *Hours:* Mon-Fri, 10 am to 5 pm; Sat, 10 am to 4 pm.

Encore Book Store General interest used, rare and out-of-print books. Categories include mystery and detective, science fiction and fantasy, romance, political science and Victorian poetry. Foreign language, UK imports, children's books, remainders and first editions. Also carries new books in some cataegories.

7120 Temple Hills Road, Camp Springs, MD 20748; (301) 297-5040. *Hours:* Mon-Sat, 10 am to 9 pm; Sun, noon to 5 pm.

The Georgetown Book Shop   General second-hand shop, specializing in history, especially military and Soviet history. Also carries books on most other subjects, including literature, art, photography, cookbooks, illustrated children's books, architecture, poetry, science and philosophy.

7770 Woodmont Avenue, Bethesda, MD 20814; (301) 907-6923. *Hours:* Daily, 10 am to 6 pm.

Imagination Books   Arcade of six used book shops specializing in general interest, romance, works by and about African-Americans, science fiction, mysteries, war & peace, politics and more. First and limited editions, illustrated books, old and rare books, out-of-print. Search service, library appraisal service.

946 Sligo Avenue, Silver Spring, MD 20910; (301) 589-2223. *Hours:* Mon-Sat, 11:30 am to 6:30 pm; Sun, noon to 5 pm.

Frank & Laurese Katen   Specializes in books on numismatics (coins and currency). Modern, rare, out-of-print, old and imported books. Mail orders and auctions.

708 Cloverly Street, Silver Spring, MD 20904; (301) 384-9444. *Hours:* Mon-Fri, 9 am to 5 pm; Sat, 10 am to 4 pm.

Kensington Used Bookshop   General selection, with emphasis on Americana, classic children's books and genre fiction (romance, mysteries, fantasy and science fiction paperbacks).

10417 Armory Avenue, Kensington, MD 20895; (301) 949-9411. *Hours:* Daily, 11 am to 5 pm, except Mon (closed).

The Old Forest Bookshop   General interest used bookstore, with broad specialization in literature, history (concentrating on Americana) and art. Named after a Peter Taylor short story.

7921 Norfolk Avenue, Bethesda, MD 20814; (301) 656-2668. *Hours:* Mon-Sat, 11 am to 7 pm; Sun, noon to 6 pm.

R. Quick, Bookseller   General interest scarce and out-of-print books, mostly nonfiction, emphasizing history, standard classics, cookbooks and children's books.

Montgomery Farm Women's Cooperative Market, 7155 Wisconsin Avenue, Bethesda, MD 20814; (301)

652-2291. *Hours:* Wed-Sat, 9 am to 3 pm (additional hours by appointment).

Second Story Books   General interest bookstores, carrying used, rare and out-of-print books on all subjects. Facsimile editions, fine binding, first and limited editions. Also stocks remainders and some half-price new books. Services include book appraising, search service and more. (For other area location, see D.C. listings).

4836 Bethesda Avenue, Bethesda, MD 20814; (301) 656-0170. *Hours:* Open daily, 10 am to 10 pm.

Stewart's Stamp & Book Store   General interest used books, with emphasis on history, especially military history. Also carries stamps and supplies for collectors, plus postcards and military board games.

6504 Old Branch Avenue, Camp Springs, MD 20748; (301) 449-6766. *Hours:* Tues-Fri, 11 am to 6 pm; Sat, 10 am to 5 pm.

U.S. Government

U.S. Government Printing Office Bookstore   Carries hundreds of government publications on all subjects, including history, military history, outdoor activities, environment, foreign affairs, energy, science and technology, transportation, aeronautics, space exploration, criminal justice, agriculture, employment, labor issues and business and finance.

One MD location:

• *Laurel*   8660 Cherry Lane, Laurel, MD 20707; (301) 953-7974. *Hours:* Mon-Fri, 9 am to 5 pm.

Newsstands

Cadmus Books   Primarily a newsstand, carrying newspapers and magazines. Small selection of used books. Two MD locations:

• *Silver Spring*   7898 Georgia Avenue, Silver Spring, MD 20910; (301) 495-0750. *Hours:* Mon-Sat, 8 am to 7 pm; Sun, noon to 5 pm.

• *Wheaton*   11236 Georgia Avenue, Wheaton, MD 20902; (301) 942-4119. *Hours:* Mon-Sat, 8:30 am to 10 pm; Sun, 8:30 am to 9 pm.

SUBURBAN VIRGINIA

General Bookstores

Independents

Ampersand Books and Records   Large selection of travel books (literary and guides), cookbooks, books for children (pre-K to early teens) and mysteries. Also strong in architecture, design and decorating, how-to, gardening, art, history, and political books. Sections on Japan and Britain (mostly nonfiction), self-help and health, plus some inspirational religious books. Books-on-tape and full line of records, tapes and magazines. Special, phone and mail orders.

118 King Street, Alexandria, VA 22314; (703) 549-0840. *Hours:* Mon-Thurs, 10 am to 10 pm; Fri & Sat, 10 am to 11 pm; Sun, noon to 7 pm.

Benjamin Books   Better stocked and better run than many other airport shops, these two bookstores offer a wide array of bestsellers, mass market paperbacks, nonfiction, history, mystery, children's and business books to literary travellers. Also carry books-on-tape, greeting cards, maps and bookmarks.

Two VA airport locations:

• *Dulles International Airport*   Fairfax, VA; (703) 661-8941. *Hours:* Daily, 7 am to 11 pm.

• *Washington National Airport*   Alexandria, VA; (703) 549-1941. *Hours:* Mon-Sat, 7:30 am to 11:30 pm; Sun, 9 am to 11:30 pm.

Book 'N Card   Bookstore and newsstand, emphasizing literature, science fiction and history (especially the Civil War). Large selection of magazines and newspapers.

8110 Arlington Blvd, Falls Church, VA 22042; (703) 560-6999. *Hours:* Mon-Fri, 9 am to 10 pm; Sat, 9 am to 9 pm; Sun, 9 am to 6 pm.

Books Unlimited   Emphasizes literature, Judaica and children's and parenting books (40% of the store is devoted to children's books and there's a children's play area). Also has large selection of mysteries, science fiction, history and biography. Greeting cards and note paper. Free newsletter. Special orders.

2729 Wilson Boulevard, Arlington, VA 22201; (703) 525-0550. *Hours:* Mon, Wed & Fri, 10 am to 9 pm; Tues, Thurs & Sat, 10 am to 6 pm.

Brentano's   General interest bookstore, with emphasis on quality fiction, history, sociology, business, travel (literature and guides), cookbooks and art books. Also carries Mont Blanc pens, Crane stationery, desk calendars, magazines and newspapers. Special, mail and phone orders; book signings. (Two more stores opening at Landmark Mall, Alexandria and Pentagon City, Arlington by December 1989).

Tyson's Corner Center, McLean, VA (703) 760-8956. *Hours:* Mon-Sat, 10 am to 9:30 pm; Sun, noon to 5 pm.

Crest Books Towncenter   Large collection of books for juveniles. Art, cooking, fiction, reference, self-help, travel, computer science and music titles. Also rents and sells musical instruments and accessories, including sheet music and instructional materials for music teachers.

115 Harry Flood Byrd Highway, Sterling, VA 22170; (703) 450-4200. Open Monday through Saturday, 10 am to 9 pm; Sunday, noon to 5 pm.

Gilpin House Bookshop   Emphasizes politics, history and biography. Also carries large selection of gardening books, cookbooks and travel books. Stocks unusual gifts from around the world, and large selection of magazines and newspapers. Opens early on Sunday for neighborhood "coffee klatch." Invites locally prominent people to join other residents for good talk over doughnuts, coffee and *The New York Times.* Extensive special ordering (35% of book business), mail and phone orders.

208 King Street, Alexandria, VA 22314; (703) 549-1880. *Hours:* Mon-Thurs, 10 am to 10 pm; Fri, 10 am to 11 pm; Sat, 9 am to 11 pm; Sun, 8:30 am to 10 pm.

New Leaf Bookstore   Carries some of everything, including literature, philosophy, religion, psychology, reference, metaphysics, and books on cooking, diet and health. Also carries local authors' works, plus audio and video cassettes and globes. Search service.

285 Frost Avenue, Warrenton, VA 22116; (703) 347-7323. *Hours:* Mon, Wed & Fri, 10 am to 7 pm; Tues, Thurs and Sat, 10 am to 6 pm; Sun, 1 to 5 pm.

Olsson's Books & Records   Very large, full-service book-store offering quality fiction and nonfiction in a broad range of categories. Books-on-tape, calendars and post-cards; full line of records, tapes and CDs. Can join Penguin Book Club, through which discounts are available; also offers 25% discounts on *Washington Post* hardcover bestsellers. Regular book signings. Mail, phone and special orders; interstore transfers.

All five Olsson's stores carry much of the same stock, but Old Town store strong in books about travel, history, regional titles, small press books and remainders (for other area locations, see D.C. and MD listings).

• *Old Town Alexandria*   106 South Union Street, Old Town Alexandria, VA 22314; (703) 684-0077. *Hours:* Mon-Thurs, 10 am to 10 pm; Fri & Sat, 10 am to midnight; Sun, 11 am to 6 pm.

National Chain Stores

B. Dalton Bookseller   Full selection of fiction and non-fiction in all categories, including large reference sections, history, biography, psychology, mystery and romance. Special section for children's books (B. Dalton Junior).

All B. Dalton stores carry computer books and magazines; a number have separate computer stores within them (Software, Etc). Each store carries remainders, magazines and newspapers; offer 25% discounts on all hardcover bestsellers.

Seven suburban VA locations (for other area locations, see D.C. and MD listings):

• *Arlington I*   Ballston Common Mall, 4238 Wilson Boulevard, Arlington, VA 22203; (703) 522-8822. *Hours:* Mon-Sat, 10 am to 9:30 pm; Sun, noon to 5 pm.

• *Arlington II*   Crystal Undergroud, 1661 Crystal Square Arcade, Arlington, VA 22202; (703) 553-9558. *Hours:* Mon-Wed & Fri, 10 am to 7 pm, Thurs, 10 am to 9 pm; Sat, 10 am to 6 pm.

• *Arlington III*   2117 Crystal Plaza Shops, Arlington, VA 22202; (703) 685-0075. *Hours:* Mon-Sat, 10 am to 9 pm; Sun, noon to 5 pm.

• *Fairfax*   Fair Oaks Mall, 12005 Lee Jackson Highway, Fairfax, VA 22030; (703) 591-0036. *Hours:* Mon-Sat, 10 am to 9:30 pm; Sun, noon to 6 pm.

• *Falls Church I* Seven Corners Shopping Mall, 6201 Arlington Boulevard, Falls Church, VA 22044; (703) 241-7505. *Hours:* Mon-Sat, 10 am to 9 pm; Sun, noon to 5 pm.

• *Falls Church II* Skyline Plaza Mall, 5155 Leesburg Pike, Falls Church, VA 22041; (703) 820-4250. *Hours:* Mon-Sat, 10 am to 9 pm; Sun, noon to 5 pm.

• *Springfield* Springfield Mall, 6712 Franconia Road, Springfield, VA 22150; (703) 971-7010. *Hours:* Mon-Thurs, 10 am to 9:30 pm; Fri & Sat, 10 am to 10 pm; Sun, noon to 5 pm.

Crown Books Broad selection of best-selling fiction and nonfiction books—many deeply discounted—including reference, health, history, biography, mystery and detective, art and many other titles. Adult and children's books, magazines, newspapers, some videocassettes.

Discounts range from 25% to 35% off hardcover *New York Times* bestsellers; 20% to 50% off hardcover art, cook and reference books; 10% off paperbacks and magazines; and 25% off computer books, software and accessories. Most stores have large shelves of remainders, many for $2 or less.

Twenty-three suburban VA locations (for other area locations, see D.C. and MD listings):

• *Alexandria I* 6244K Little River Turnpike, Alexandria, Va 22312; (703) 750-3553. *Hours:* Mon-Sat, 10 am to 9:30 pm; Sun, 10 am to 6 pm.

• *Alexandria II* 1716 Duke Street, Alexandria, VA 22314; (703) 548-9548. *Hours:* Mon-Sat, 9 am to 7 pm; Sun, 11 am to 5 pm.

• *Alexandria III* 3676 King Street, Alexandria, VA 22302; (703) 379-0944. *Hours:* Mon-Sat, 10 am to 9 pm; Sun, 11 am to 5 pm.

• *Alexandria IV* 500 King Street, Alexandria, VA 22314; (703) 548-3432. *Hours:* Mon-Sat, 10 am to 10 pm; Sun, 10 am to 6 pm.

• *Alexandria V* 6140A Rose Hill Drive, Alexandria, VA 22310; (703) 922-4672. *Hours:* Mon-Sat, 11 am to 8 pm; Sun, 11 am to 5 pm.

• *Alexandria VI* 6244 North King's Highway, Alexandria, VA 22302; (703) 765-1858. *Hours:* Mon-Sat, 10 am to 9 pm; Sun, 11 am to 5 pm.

- *Annandale I* 7428 Little River Turnpike, Annandale, VA 22003; (703) 941-7318. *Hours:* Mon-Sat, 10 am to 9 pm; Sun, 11 am to 5 pm.

- *Annandale II* 6914 Braddock Road, Annandale, VA 22003; (703) 941-1458. *Hours:* Mon-Sat, 10 am to 9 pm; Sun, 11 am to 5 pm.

- *Burke* 9232 Old Keene Mill Road, Burke, VA 22015; (703) 451-0350. *Hours:* Mon-Sat, 10 am to 9 pm; Sun, 11 am to 5 pm.

- *Chantilly* 13936 Lee Jackson Memorial Highway, Chantilly, VA 22021; (703) 378-2052. *Hours:* Mon-Sat, 11 am to 9 pm; Sun, 11 am to 5 pm.

- *Fairfax I* 9644 Main Street, Fairfax, VA 22030; (703) 425-9188. *Hours:* Mon-Sat, 10 am to 9 pm; Sun, 10 am to 6 pm.

- *Fairfax II* 5620B Ox Road, Fairfax, VA 22039; (703) 425-2363. *Hours:* Mon-Sat, 10 am to 9 pm; Sun, 11 am to 5 pm.

- *Falls Church I* 6112 Arlington Boulevard, Falls Church, VA 22042; (703) 534-4830. *Hours:* Mon-Sat, 10 am to 9 pm; Sun, 11 am to 5 pm.

- *Falls Church II* Loehman's Plaza, 7271 Arlington Boulevard, Falls Church, VA 22042; (703) 573-3500. *Hours:* Mon-Sat, 10 am to 9:30 pm; Sun, 10 am to 6 pm.

- *Manassas* 8389 Sudley Road, Manassas, VA 22110; (703) 631-0409. *Hours:* Mon-Sat, 10 am to 9 pm; Sun, 11 am to 5 pm.

- *McLean I* 1711G Galleria at Tysons II, McLean, VA 22102; (703) 821-2041. *Hours:* Mon-Sat, 10 am to 9:30 pm; Sun, 11 am to 6 pm.

- *McLean II* 1449 Chain Bridge Road, McLean, VA 22101; (703) 893-7640. *Hours:* Mon-Fri, 10 am to 9:30 pm; Sat, 9 am to 9:30 pm; Sun, 10 am to 6 pm.

- *Oakton* 2924 Chain Bridge Road, Oakton, VA 22124; (703) 281-0820. *Hours:* Mon-Sat, 10 am to 9 pm; Sun, 11 am to 5 pm.

- *Reston* 11160H South Lake Drive, Reston, VA 22041; (703) 620-6569. *Hours:* Mon-Sat, 10 am to 9 pm; Sun, 11 am to 5 pm.

• *Springfield*   6435 Springfield Plaza, Springfield, VA 22150; (703) 569-6666. *Hours:* Mon-Sat, 10 am to 9:30 pm; Sun, 10 am to 6 pm.

• *Sterling*   121 Harry Flood Byrd Highway, Sterling, VA 22170; (703) 450-6889. *Hours:* Mon-Sat, 10 am to 9 pm; Sun, 11 am to 5 pm.

• *Vienna*   8365A Leesburg Pike, Vienna, VA 22180; (703) 442-0133. *Hours:* Mon-Sat, 10 am to 9 pm; Sun, 11 am to 5 pm.

• *Woodbridge*   14567A Jefferson Davis Highway, Woodbridge, VA 22191; (703) 491-2144. *Hours:* Mon-Sat, 10 am to 9 pm; Sun, 11 am to 5 pm.

Waldenbooks   Large variety of fiction and nonfiction titles in many categories, including reference, biography, history, mystery, health, New Age, literature and art. Adult and children's books, magazines, tapes, videocassettes, computer books and software.

Offer book clubs (kids, 60+, mysteries, etc.) whose members receive special discounts. Also discounts hardcover bestsellers. The chain operates several separate computer stores in the metropolitan area (Waldensoftware). Will handle special orders.

Five suburban VA locations (for other area locations, see D.C. and MD listings):

• *Arlington*   Ballston Commons Mall, 4238 Wilson Boulevard, Arlington, VA 22203; (703) 527-2442. *Hours:* Mon-Sat, 10 am to 9:30 pm; Sun, noon to 5 pm.

• *Fairfax*   Fair Oaks Shopping Center, Fairfax, VA 22030; (703) 591-8985. *Hours:* Mon-Sat, 10 am to 9:30 pm; Sun, noon to 5 pm.

• *Manassas*   181 Manassas Mall, 8300 Sudley Road, Manassas, VA 22110; (703) 368-8366. *Hours:* Mon-Sat, 10 am to 9:30 pm; Sun, noon to 6 pm.

• *McLean*   Tysons Corner Center, McLean, VA 22102; (703) 893-4208. *Hours:* Mon-Sat, 10 am to 9:30 pm; Sun, noon to 6 pm.

• *Springfield*   6725 Springfield Mall, Springfield, VA 22150; (703) 971-9443. *Hours:* Mon-Sat, 10 am to 9:30 pm; Sun, noon to 5 pm.

Specialty Bookstores

Children & Juvenile

John Davy Toys Toy store with substantial children's book section. Books in English, French, German and Spanish for all ages and in all genres—from classics and nursery rhymes to novels for teens.

301 Cameron Street, Alexandria, VA 22314; (703) 683-0079. *Hours:* Mon-Sat, 10 am to 5:30 pm; Sun, 11 am to 5 pm.

Imagination Station All ages represented, but focus on earliest years. Adventure books, classics, science fiction, religious books and novels for teens. Books for children in French, German and Spanish; also foreign language dictionaries. Extensive collection of books-on-tape and book/cassette combinations. Videos for sale and rent. Publishes free newsletter three times a year, featuring book reviews and upcoming events and programs. Sponsors author readings, story telling and other special events. Special orders.

4530 Lee Highway, Arlington, VA 22207; (703) 522-2047. *Hours:* Mon–Fri, 10 am to 7 pm; Sat, 11 am to 6 pm; Sun, 11 am to 4 pm.

A Likely Story Complete bookstore for kids and their parents. Lots of classics and how-to's for older kids with questions about growing up; adult books on parenting and other themes. Stocked from floor to ceiling with plush animals, cassettes, cards and gift wrapping. Children's play and reading area; occasional weekend readings for kids. Mail, phone and special orders; school accounts.

110 S. West Street, Alexandria, VA 22314; (703) 836-2498. *Hours:* Mon-Sat, 10 am to 5:30 pm.

Storybook Palace Books for children from pre-K through mid-teens. Large selection of first books, books on parenting and nonfiction. Also carries books-on-tape, music tapes and book-related stuffed animals and puppets. Parent workshops, author appearances and story times. Special and mail orders; school accounts. Free newsletter available.

Burke Town Plaza, 9538 Old Keene Mill Road, Burke, VA 22015; (703) 644-2300. *Hours:* Mon-Fri, 10 am to 7 pm; Sat, 10 am to 6 pm.

Stories Unlimited   Books and gifts for kids from pre-K through early teens, with emphasis on fiction. Large selection of poetry and problem-solving books. Also carries video and audio cassettes, stationery, book-related stuffed animals, posters and toys.

Market Station, Loudon Street, Ste 112D, Leesburg, VA 22075; (703) 777-6995. *Hours:* Mon-Sat, 10 am to 6 pm; Sun, noon to 5 pm.

The Travelling Talesmen   This "portable" children's bookstore allows you and your friends to shop for children's books at home. Operating on the same principle as Tupperware parties, The Travelling Talesman brings a broad selection of commercially published (and age-appropriate) children's books to your home. You simply bring a group of parents and children together and let the Talesman know the age level and subjects you're interested in. Catalog available.

JFA Enterprises, P.O. Box 12267, Arlington, VA 22209; (703) 528-2474.

Comics & Collectibles

Capital Comics Center & Book Niche   60% comics, 40% new and used books. Book subjects include biography, films and film-making, history, horticulture, mystery and detective, nature and the environment, science fiction and fantasy, comedy, metaphysics and the occult, art, music and the classics. Also carries trading cards, posters and novelties.

2008 Mount Vernon Avenue, Alexandria, VA 22301; (703) 548-3466. *Hours:* Mon-Thurs & Sat, 11 am to 7 pm; Fri, noon to 8 pm.

Fantasy Five & Dime   Specializes in comics and other collectibles.

1113 West Church Road, Sterling, VA 22170; (703) 444-9222. *Hours:* Mon-Fri, 11 am to 9 pm; Tues-Thurs, closed; Sat, 10 am to 8 pm; Sun, noon to 6 pm.

Foreign Language

Alfa Books (Interlingua Communications)   Foreign language books for adults and children. Also carries books-on-tape and videos (for sale and rent).

2615 Columbia Pike, Arlington, VA 22204; (703) 920-6644.

The He Bookstore   Vietnamese books in various categories, plus Vietnamese music on cassettes, records and CDs.

6763A Wilson Boulevard, Falls Church, VA 22034; (703) 532-7890. *Hours:* Daily, 10 am to 8 pm.

Media Bookstore   Korean books and music, including CDs.

3536 Carlin Spring Road, Bailey's Crossroads, VA 22041; (703) 931-1212. *Hours:* Mon-Sat, 11 am to 6 pm.

Saludos   Carries Spanish-language books in many categories, including fiction, children's, bestsellers, dictionaries and other reference works. Also carries music instruction books, videos, records, tapes and CDs, all in Spanish. Stocks greeting cards, magazines and newspapers.

3811I South George Mason Drive, Bailey's Crossroads, VA 22041; (703) 820-5550. *Hours:* Mon-Sat, 10:30 am to 9 pm; Sun, 10:30 am to 7 pm.

Universal Chinese Bookstore   Chinese books in various subject areas. Also carries Chinese records and tapes.

6763 Wilson Boulevard, Falls Church, VA 22034; (703) 241-7070. *Hours:* Daily, 11 am to 7 pm.

Mail Order & Private Dealers

AAHP Book Services   Mail order only. Used, old, rare and out-of-print books on hypnosis, hypnotherapy, and unusual or unorthodox forms of healing. Sometimes has new books (remainders and markdowns). Operated by American Association of Hypnotherapists.

P.O. Box 731, McLean, VA 22101; (703) 448-9623. *Hours:* By appointment only.

Agribookstore   Mail order only. Books from U.S. and imported from around the world on agriculture, forestry, natural resources and development. Also sells maps, computer software, slide sets. Operated by Winrock International, a nonprofit institute for agricultural development in the Third World.

1611 North Kent Street, Arlington, VA 22209; (703) 525-9455.

Antiquarian Tobacciana   Mail order only. Books on tobacco and smoking. Foreign language; facsimile, first and limited editions; used, imported, rare and out-of-print books; remainders.

11505 Turnbridge Lane, Reston, VA 22094; no phone listed.

Arlington Book Company   Mail order only. Books imported from England, France and Germany about clocks and watches.

P.O. Box 327, Arlington, VA 22210; (703) 280-2005.

Jennie's Book Nook   Mail order only. Old, rare and out-of-print biography, fiction, history, poetry and Virginiana; sells and publishes books on genealogy. Search service.

15 West Howell Avenue, Alexandria, VA 22301; (703) 683-0694.

William B. O'Neill   Books on modern Greece, Cyprus and the Middle East. Mail order only; catalog available.

P.O. Box 2275, Reston, VA 22090; (703) 860-0782.

Old Mill Books   Mail order only. Out-of-print books on the South Pacific, Southeast Asia and Antarctica. Search service and appraisal by mail. PO Box 21561, Alexandria, VA 22320.

Ross Book Service   Mail order only. Books for people in communications on many subjects, including advertising, public relations, public speaking, typography, the English language, reference, writing, editing, technical communications, graphic design, business and desktop publishing. Also sells new books, college textbooks, quality paperbacks and some remainders. Catalog available ($2 charge).

3718 Seminary Road, Seminary Post Office, Alexandria, VA 22304; (703) 823-1919.

Thistle & Shamrock Books   Mail order only. Books on Scottish and Irish history, literature and culture. Foreign language, imports, remainders and used books. Also carries children's books in these subjects.

P.O. Box 42, Alexandria, VA 22313; (703) 548-2207.

E. Wharton & Co.   Late 19th- and 20th-century literature (first editions). Also sells at book fairs. Mail order only; free catalog available.

3232 History Drive, Oakton, VA 22124; (703) 264-0129.

Military & Diplomatic

Bacon Race Books Specializes in new, used and rare books on the American Civil War. Mail order only.

3717 Pleasant Ridge Road, Annandale, VA 22003; (703) 560-7376.

Barcroft Books Specializes in military history worldwide, with emphasis on Queen Victoria's "little wars" and WWII. Also large sections on American Indians and the American West, travel (classic travel literature and picture books) and oversize military picture books. Mostly new books and imports, but some used and out-of-print books.

6349A Columbia Pike, Bailey's Crossroads, VA 22041; (703) 256-1865. *Hours:* Mon-Fri, 11 am to 7 pm; Sat, 10 am to 6 pm.

Museums, Historic Sites & Art Galleries

Parks & History Association Bookshops Shops in National Park Service sites, with specialty books and materials (gifts, maps, posters, greeting cards, etc.) conforming to appropriate subjects for each location. PHAB operates seventeen shops on National Park properties throughout the metropolitan area. Call (202) 472-3083 for general information, as hours vary.

Three suburban VA locations (for other area locations, please see D.C. and MD listings):

• *Arlington House, Robert E. Lee Memorial Bookstore* New and remaindered books for adults and juveniles on the Civil War, Robert E. Lee and southern culture (including cookbooks). Also stocks postcards, films and historic reproductions. Arlington National Cemetery, Arlington, VA 22101; (703) 557-3156. *Hours:* Open daily, 9:30 am to 4:30 pm (until 6 pm during daylight savings time).

• *Arlington Visitors Center Bookshop* Books on military history, including the Civil War, WWI and WWII and Vietnam. Also books about the Washington area, including guidebooks. Video of the Washington area. Arlington Cemetery, Arlington, VA 22101; (703)

557-1713. *Hours:* Daily, 9:30 am to 4:30 pm (until 6 pm during daylight savings time).

• *Great Falls Park Bookstore* Books on nature, the environment, geology and the outdoors, with a focus on the park. Books on history of the C & O Canal.

9200 Old Dominion Drive, Great Falls, VA 22066; (703) 235-1194. *Hours:* Daily, dawn to dusk.

• *Manassas National Battlefield Park Bookstore* Books on the Civil War and Manassas; also sells video-cassettes. Operated by Eastern National Park and Monument Association Bookstore in Philadelphia.

6511 Sudley Road, Manassas, Va 22110; (703) 754-7107. *Hours:* Daily, 8:30 am to (at least) 5 pm.

New Age & Metaphysical

Sun & Moon New age, metaphysical and holistic health books. Also carries meditation tapes, music tapes and gifts from 28 countries.

108 South Street, Leesburg, VA 22075; (703) 777-2466. *Hours:* Mon-Sat, 10 am to 6 pm; Sun, noon to 5 pm.

Nature & The Outdoors

Audubon Prints and Books New and used books by and about John James Audubon. Also carries original prints and reproductions. 9720 Spring Ridge Lane, Vienna, VA 22180; (703) 484-3334. *Hours:* By appointment only.

Habitat Owned and operated by the National Wildlife Federation, this book and gift shop carries titles on nature, wildlife, conservation, the environment and crafts (including those published by the Federation). Books and other items for children, gifts, T-shirts, posters and greeting cards. One suburban VA location (see D.C. listings for other location).

8925 Leesburg Pike, Vienna, VA 22184; (703) 790-4456. *Hours:* Mon-Fri, 8:30 am to 4 pm.

One Good Tern Specializes in nature books, including books published by the Sierra Club and Audubon Society, field guides by Roger Tory Peterson and other naturalists, travel guides and children's nature books. Also carries packs, binoculars, bird feeders and feed.

1710 Fern Street, Alexandria, VA 22302; (703) 820-

8376. *Hours:* Tues & Thurs, 10 am to 8 pm; Wed & Fri, 10 am to 6 pm; Sat, 9 am to 6 pm; Sun, noon to 5 pm.

The Nature Company Chain of stores devoted to "the observation, appreciation and understanding of nature." Each store carries large number of books on nature and the natural world. Subjects include plants and animals (including dinosaurs), science, the body and nature commentary. Children's book section. Two suburban VA locations (for other area locations, see D.C. listings).

• *McLean* Tyson's Corner Center, McLean, VA 22102; (703) 760-8930. *Hours:* Mon-Sat, 10 am to 9 pm; Sun, noon to 5 pm.

• *Pentagon City* Opening October 1989.

Professional/ Academic/ Business

Anderson Brothers Bookstores Carries full line of text-books for nearby George Mason University. Trade section features bestsellers, reference (general and nursing) and children's books. Also stocks clothing, office and school suppplies and novelty items.

10661 Braddock Road, Fairfax, VA 22032; (703) 352-8008. *Hours:* Mon-Sat, 10 am to 6 pm.

Hammett's Learning World Carries workbooks, reference books, teaching supplies and other materials for students, teachers and parents. Primarily for elementary school level.

Two suburban VA locations:

• *Oakton* 2914 Chain Bridge Road, Oakton, VA 22124; (703) 983-0047. *Hours:* Mon-Thurs, 10 am to 9 pm; Fri & Sat, 10 am to 5 pm.

• *Springfield* Springfield Tower Mall, 6420 Brandon Avenue, Springfield, VA 22150; (703) 569-2303. *Hours:* Mon-Fri, 10 am to 6 pm; Sat, 9 am to 5 pm.

Professional Book Center Specializes in books on science and technology imported from Germany and the UK. Also carries other foreign language books on these subjects.

80 Early Street, Alexandria, VA 22304; (703) 370-5160. *Hours:* Sat, 10 am to 6 pm; Sun, 1 to 6 pm.

Religious

The Almond Tree   Christian books for adults and children, gifts, videocassettes, greeting cards and tapes.
687 Warrenton Center, Warrenton, VA 22186; (703) 347-0303. *Hours:* Mon-Fri, 10 am to 7 pm; Sat, 10 am to 6 pm.

Ark & Dove   Christian books and supplies, bibles, candles, song and choral books, tapes, church supplies, cards and gifts.
6122 Rose Hill Drive, Alexandria, VA 22310; (703) 971-7000. *Hours:* Mon-Sat, 10 am to 6 pm, Tues & Thurs, 10 am to 8 pm.

Baptist Bookstore   Religious book and supply store for children and adults. Bibles, music.
7259 Commerce Street, Springfield, VA 22150; (703) 569-0067. *Hours:* Mon-Sat, 10 am to 6 pm, Tues & Thurs, 10 am to 8:30 pm.

Choice Books   Christian inspirational books, bibles and Bible studies.
11923 Lee Highway, Fairfax, VA 22030; (703) 830-2800. *Hours:* Mon-Fri, 8:30 am to 5:30 pm.

Evangelical Used Books   Used and out-of-print books on all religions, with emphasis on Protestant religions.
1815 N. Nelson Street, Arlington, VA 22207; (703) 522-0596. *Hours:* By appointment only.

Good Tidings Christian Book Store   Christian literature and gift items.
6401-A Shiplett Boulevard, Burke, VA 22015; (703) 455-6401. *Hours:* Mon-Fri, 10 am to 6 pm; Sat, 10 am to 5 pm.

Grace Christian Bookstore   Religious books, bibles, tapes and videos. Full-service print shop.
1102 West Church Road, Sterling, VA 22170; (703) 450-4121. *Hours:* Mon-Fri, 9 am to 6 pm; Sat, 9 am to 4 pm.

The Great Commission   Christian books, cards, prints, sheet music, tapes and gifts.
2107 North Pollard Street, Arlington, VA 22205; (703) 525-0222. *Hours:* Mon-Sat, 10 am to 7 pm.

His Presence   Religious books for adults and children, bibles, cassettes, CDs, gifts, cards and figurines.

3238 Old Pickett Road, Fairfax, VA 22030; (703) 273-6234. *Hours:* Mon-Sat, 10 am to 6 pm; later hours by appointment.

Jesus Bookstore   Religious books for children and adults, bibles, records, tapes, videocassettes, jewelry, gifts, cards and church supplies. Three suburban VA locations:

* *Alexandria*   7700 Richmond Highway, Alexandria, VA 22306; 780-3200. Open Monday, Wednesday and Friday, 10 am to 9 pm; Tuesday, Thursday and Saturday, 10 am to 6 pm.

* *Dale City*   14214 Smoketown Road, Dale City; 690-4777. Open Monday, Wednesday and Friday, 10 am to 9 pm; Tuesday, Thursday and Saturday, 10 am to 6 pm.

* *Woodbridge*   13426 Jeff Davis Highway, Woodbridge; 690-3161. Open Monday through Saturday, 10 am to 6 pm, Tuesday and Thursday until 8 pm.

Let There Be Praise   Religious books for adults and children. Bibles, church supplies, gifts, greeting cards, videos and tapes. 9 Catoctin Circle SE, Leesburg, VA 22075; (703) 777-6311. *Hours:* Mon-Wed, 9:30 am to 6 pm; Thur-Sat, 9:30 am to 8 pm.

Maranatha Christian Bookstore   Religious books, bibles, cards, gifts, music and jewelry.

1607 Commonwealth Avenue, Alexandria, VA 22301; (703) 548-2895. *Hours:* Mon-Fri, 10 am to 6 pm; Thurs, 10 am to 8 pm; Sat, 10 am to 5 pm.

Mustard Seed   Inspirational books, tapes and gifts. Greeting cards and gift wrap. Two suburban VA locations:

* *Arlington*   2401 Columbia Pike, Arlington, VA 22204; (703) 979-3549. *Hours:* Mon-Sat, 10 am to 6 pm; Thurs, 10 am to 8 pm.

* *Manassas*   7851 Sudley Road, Manassas, VA 22110; (703) 361-1125. *Hours:* Mon-Sat, 10 am to 9 pm.

* *New Creation*   Mail order only. Christian books and bibles.

8801 Quarry Road, Manassas, VA 22110; (703) 369-1345. *Hours:* By appointment only.

St. Paul Catholic Book & Media Center   Catholic books for all ages, family and religious instruction videos, cassettes and cards.

1025 King Street, Alexandria, VA 22314; (703) 549-3806. *Hours:* Mon-Fri, 9:30 am to 5:30 pm; Sat, 9:30 am to 5 pm.

Seminary Book Service   Mail order, retail and college store. Specializes in academic religious books: biblical titles, biblical commentaries, liturgical reference works, large sections on theology and the Episcopal church, spiritual classics. Also sells church supplies and gifts. Serves Virginia Theological Seminary.

900 Quaker Lane, Alexandria, VA 22304; (703) 370-6161/ (800) 368-3756. *Hours:* Mon-Sat, 10 am to 5 pm.

Truro Episcopal Bookstore   Religious books for children and adults, greeting cards, jewelry, videocassettes, tapes, records and CDs, songbooks.

10520 Main Street, Fairfax, VA 22030; (703) 273-8686. *Hours:* Mon-Fri, 9:30 am to 4:30 pm; Sat, 10 am to 2 pm; Sun, call ahead.

Words of Wisdom Books & Gifts   Christian books, bible monogramming, gifts, jewelry, greeting cards, religious goods, church supplies, tapes and CDs, videocassettes. Also carries books on current political and social issues from a Christian perspective.

4209 Annandale Center Drive, Annandale, VA 22003; (703) 256-3005. *Hours:* Mon-Sat, 9:30 am to 5:30 am, Thurs, 9:30 am-7 pm.

Zondervan Family Bookstores   Religious books, bibles, tapes, CDs, songbooks, gifts, cards and church supplies.

Fair Oaks Mall, Fairfax, VA 22033; (703) 352-1489. *Hours:* Mon-Sat, 10 am to 9:30 pm.

Science Fiction/ Fantasy

Hole In The Wall Books   Used bookstore specializing in science fiction and fantasy. Also carries horror, mystery and detective fiction and comics, plus new books and literary/historical fiction.

905 West Broad Street, Falls Church, VA 22046; (703)

536-2511. *Hours:* Mon-Fri, 10 am to 9 pm; Sat & Sun, 10 am to 6 pm.

Tomorrow Books   New, used and rare science fiction and fantasy books, plus new and back issue comics (independent and mainstream). Also carries autographs, library collections, literary magazines, cards, art, posters and reproductions. Search service. 1304 King Street, Alexandria, VA 22314; (703) 548-5030. *Hours:* Mon-Fri, 11 am to 7 pm; Sat, noon to 7 pm; Sun, noon to 6 pm.

Sports

Baseball Corner   Specializes in hard-to-find baseball books and publications: used, first editions and out-of-print. Also carries sports cards and paper sports collectibles.

 5224 Port Royal Road, Springfield, VA 22150; (703) 524-8640. *Hours:* Mon-Fri, 10 am to 8 pm; Sat, 10 am to 6 pm; Sun, noon to 5 pm.

Sports Books Etc.   Carries large selection of *new* books on all sports, plus extensive collection of sports videos, magazines, calendars, posters and trading cards. Special and mail orders. Shares space but not stock with *Baseball Corner.*

 5224 Port Royal Road, Springfield, VA 22150; (703) 321-8660. *Hours:* Mon-Fri, 10 am to 8 pm; Sat, 10 am to 6 pm; Sun, noon to 5 pm.

Universities & Colleges

George Mason University Bookstore   Textbooks and trade books in a full range of categories, from computers to literature. Also carries study aids, soft goods, clothes, school supplies, sundries, greeting cards and jewelry.

 Student Union, 4400 University Avenue, Fairfax, VA 22030; (703) 425-3991. *Hours:* Mon-Thurs, 8 am to 7:30 pm; Fri, 8 am to 4 pm; Sat, 10 am to 3 pm.

Marymount College Bookstore   Textbooks and trade books in many categories, including fiction and reference. Also carries clothing, art and college supplies, greeting cards, posters and gifts.

 2807 North Glebe Road, Arlington, VA 22207; (703) 284-1614. *Hours:* Mon, Tues & Thurs, 9 am to 4:30 pm; Wed, 9 am to 6 pm; Fri, 9 am to 2 pm.

Northern Virginia Community College Bookstores All stores carry college supplies, gifts and sundries. Four suburban VA campus locations:

• *Alexandria* New and used textbooks, with small supply of trade books. 3101 North Beauregard Street, Alexandria, VA 22311; (703) 671-0043. *Hours:* Mon & Tues, 9 am to 8 pm; Wed & Thurs, 9 am to 5 pm; Fri, 9 am to 1 pm.

• *Annandale* New and used textbooks, plus good selection of trade books. Strong in business and accounting. 8333 Little River Turnpike, Annandale, VA 22003; (703) 425-2558. *Hours:* Mon-Thur, 9 am to 7 pm; Fri, 9 am to 2 pm.

• *Loudon* New and used textbooks, specializing in horticulture, agriculture, art, interior design, veterinary medicine, computer science and data processing. Small selection of trade books. 1000 Harry F. Byrd Highway, Sterling, VA 22170; (703) 430-9639. *Hours:* Mon & Thurs, 9 am to 3 pm; Tues & Wed, 9 am to 7:30 pm; Fri, 9 am to noon.

• *Manassas* New and used textbooks, strongest in computers, computer science and business. Some trade books. 6900 Sudley Road, Manassas, VA 22110; (703) 368-8554. *Hours:* Mon-Fri, 9:30 am to 2:30 pm, Tues-Thurs evenings, 5 to 7 pm.

Universities Bookstore Serves University of Virginia and Virginia Tech extension campuses. Used, new and remaindered textbooks on business and management, computer science, economics, education, engineering, nursing, history, reference, public administration and planning. Carries some trade books, plus college supplies, gifts, greeting cards, videos, tapes and clothes.

2990 Telestar Court, Suite 400, Falls Church, VA 22124; (703) 698-6899. *Hours:* Mon-Thurs, 9:30 am to 8:30 pm; Fri, 9:30 am to 5 pm; Sat, 9 am to noon.

Used, Rare and Out-Of-Print

Air, Land & Sea Transportation books, models and collectibles. Some new, but mostly used and out-of-print books on subjects like aviation, surface and submarine navy, and modern armor and ships. Formerly called *The Nostalgic Aviator*.

1215 King Street, Alexandria, VA 22314; (703) 684-

5118. *Hours:* Mon-Fri, 10 am to 6 pm; Sat, 10 am to 5 pm; Sun, 1 to 5 pm.

Ben Franklin Booksellers Books on history, science and technology, art and music, plus classical literature and children's classics. Also sells prints, sheet music, toys and classic records. Special and mail orders.

27 South King Street, Leesburg, VA 22075; (703) 777-3661. *Hours:* Daily, 9 am to 5 pm.

Book Alcove General interest used bookstore, with large Civil War section and children's books. Also sells new books, most at below retail price (95 percent nonfiction, with large selections in history and the arts). Custom bookcases.

23373 Hunters Woods Plaza, Reston, VA 22091; (703) 620-6611. *Hours:* Mon-Sat, 10 am to 9 pm; Sun, noon to 5 pm.

Book Ends General interest used bookstore, specializing in American history and military, especially WW II.

2710 Washington Boulevard, Arlington, VA 22201; (703) 524-4976. *Hours:* Fri-Mon only, noon to 6 pm.

Bookhouse Literally one entire house filled with a full range of general interest used and rare books. Large selections of American and natural history. Search service.

805 North Emerson Street, Arlington, VA 22205; (703) 527-7797. *Hours:* Wed, Fri & Sat, 11 am to 5 pm; Tues & Thurs, 11 am to 7 pm; Sun, 1 to 5.

Book Rack Huge stock of "recent" used paperbacks in all categories. Carries a few new books and will order new books.

8727D Cooper Road, Alexandria, VA 22309; (703) 780-2325. *Hours:* Mon-Thurs, 11 am to 7 pm; Fri & Sat, 10 am to 6 pm; Sun, noon to 5 pm.

Book Stop Used books in all categories, with large sections on art and architecture, the Civil War, WW II, Virginia history, travel and railroading. First editions and rare books. Also carries sheet music and memorabilia. Search service.

Bradlee Shopping Center (Rear), 3640A King Street, Alexandria, VA 22314; (703) 578-3292. *Hours:* Mon-

Wed & Fri, noon to 6 pm; Thurs, closed; Sat, 11 am to 6 pm; Sun, 1 to 5 pm.

Burke Centre Used Books & Comics   One half general interest used books, one half comics. Books include science fiction, westerns, romance, biography, historical fiction, war, arts and crafts, cooking, children's, classics and science. New and back-issue comics. Also carries role-playing games and modules, posters.

5741 Burke Centre Parkway, Burke, VA 22015; (703) 250-5114. *Hours:* Mon-Fri, 11 am to 8 pm; Sat, 10 am to 6 pm; Sun, noon to 5 pm.

Colusa Books   General interest used books, with emphasis on military history, world history (especially Japan and China) and literature. Growing sections on the natural sciences and the arts; also carries university press titles. Search service.

Brookfield Plaza, 7008 Spring Garden Road, Springfield, VA 22150; (703) 644-1707. *Hours:* Mon-Fri, 10 am to 7 pm, Sat, 10 am to 6 pm; Sun, 10 am to 4 pm.

Flanagan's   General interest used and antique books.

Antique Emporium, 7120 Little River Turnpike, Annandale, VA 22030; (703) 256-4188. *Hours:* Wed-Sun, 11 am to 6 pm; Mon-Tues, closed.

Franklin Farm Used Books & Comics   General interest used books, with emphasis on science fiction, fantasy and romance. Also carries new and back issue comics.

13320I Franklin Farm Road, Herndon, VA 22070; (703) 437-9530. *Hours:* Mon-Fri, 11 am to 8 pm; Sat, 10 am to 6 pm; Sun, noon to 5 pm.

From Out Of The Past Books   General interest used, old and rare books in most categories, with large selections of Americana and military history and a lot of older fiction. Sections of regional material and African-American history. Large collection of back-issue magazines (up to the 1970s), plus decorative advertisements, posters and paper memorabilia, such as road maps.

6640 Richmond Highway, Alexandria, VA 22306; (703) 768-7827. *Hours:* Tues-Sat, 11 am to 6 pm.

Hearthstone Bookshop   Specializes in genealogy and related subjects, including Americana and local history. Also carries maps, genealogy software, preservation materials, family tree charts and forms, documents and photographs. Special orders for out-of-print books; handpainted coats of arms. Search service and restoration of old photographs; repair and preservation of old documents.

Potomac Square, 8405H Richmond Highway, Alexandria, VA 22309; (703) 360-6900. *Hours:* Mon-Sat, 9 am to 5 pm.

Richard McKay Used Books   General interest used bookstore, with large selections of children's books, reference, textbooks and fiction. Also carries books-on-tape.

Newgate Shopping Center, Lee Highway and Sully Road, Centerville, VA 22020; (703) 830-4048. *Hours:* Mon-Sat, 10 am to 9 pm; Sun, 11 am to 7 pm.

Novel Ideas of Fairfax City   General interest used bookshop, carrying "a little bit of everything" in the way of books, plus gifts and crafts.

3940 Old Lee Highway, Fairfax, VA 22030; (703) 385-5951. *Hours:* Mon-Sat, 10 am to 5 pm.

Jo Ann Reisler Ltd.   Sells only rare children's and illustrated books, principally from late 18th- through early 20th-century. Also sells original illustrative art (primarily from children's books). Mail order only.

360 Glyndon Street NE, Vienna, VA 22180; (703) 938-2237. *Hours:* By appointment only.

Reston's Used Book Shop   Used fiction and nonfiction books on all subjects.

Lake Anne Center, 1623 Washington Plaza, Reston, VA 22090; (703) 435-9772. *Hours:* Mon-Fri, 10 am to 7 pm; Sat, 10 am to 6 pm; Sun, noon to 5 pm.

U.S. Government

Pentagon Book Store   Specializes in military studies. Military reference, intelligence, technology. Also carries Washingtoniana, children's books, mass market fiction, psychology, health, family, sports and cooking. Not open to the general public, but will mail order. Phone for suggested reading lists: (703) 695-0868.

U.S. Pentagon, Arlington, VA 20301; no main phone listed.

Favorite Hangouts &
Watering Holes

"Many contemporary authors drink more than they write."

—MAXIM GORKY

A s surely as they need air, water or their daily bread, writers need to break away from their word processors after the last paragraph is done. You can find them taking refuge in places buzzing with straight talk, friendly banter and a good story or two. In a comfortable watering hole, the loneliness of writing eases and falls away. It's a great way, as Hemingway said, to "refill the well."

The following hangouts and watering holes are frequented—and highly recommended—by a number of authors who live and work here. As diverse as the writers they attract, these bars and restaurants represent a potpourri of atmospheres and personal styles. In some of these places, men wouldn't be caught dead wearing ties and women leave the fancy dresses and heels at home. In other establishments, proper attire is *de rigueur*.

The key word to remember in choosing any literary hangout is "character." Or maybe you'll just go to see some of the characters haunting the premises—writers and the subjects of writing.

DISTRICT OF COLUMBIA

Adams Morgan

Cafe Lautrec   French in motif and fare, this comfortable place is actually more bistro than cafe. It is, in any case, refreshingly free of snobbery.

You'll recognize the establishment's small namesake looming large on the outside facade. And, for entertainment, bar tapdancer John Forges keeps things hopping when he's in town. At the right moment—sipping a coffee-and-liqueur drink, feeling the ratta-tat-tat atop the bar, listening to the whoops and delighted laughter of nighttime patrons—at the right moment, one can imagine being transported back to Paris during the 1920s.

Cafe Lautrec, 2431 18th Street NW; (202) 265-6436.

Millie & Al's Think loud. You'll also have to talk loud. But as an antidote to the habits of silence, can there be any better cure for the working writer?

The neighborhood crowd gathers to drink down pitchers of beer, consume pizzas and get rowdy. Your fingers can trace the carved graffiti in the tables, your mind can imagine the stories behind all of them.

Millie & Al's, 2440 18th Street NW; (202) 387-8131.

Capitol Hill

The Dubliner Good times. And if you're not looking for good times, don't come here. The Dubliner's main password has always been fun. Decked out in Irish memorabilia throughout three drinking and eating rooms, this lively pub has native ales and stouts flowing freely on tap and the Jameson Whiskey is never out of reach. One room has a small stage for live music.

The Dubliner, 520 North Capitol Street; (202) 737-3773.

Duddington's One of the older, more relaxed haunts on Capitol Hill. There is a more timeless feeling here than in some of the trendier establishments closer to the Hill. Time to drink, think and chew on a burger.

Duddington's, 319 Pennsylvania Avenue, SE; (202) 544-3500.

Hawk And Dove An elbows-on-the table pub popular with the Hill press and congressional staffers. Here, you'll find a lively mix of ages and professions seeking to mingle and swap business cards.

Hawk and Dove, 329 Pennsylvania Avenue, SE; (202) 543-3300.

Jenkins Hill Saloon Scriveners of lean, contemporary, trendy copy feel at home in the glow of the overhead Tiffany shades. Perhaps for this reason, Hill staffers and journalists are drawn here. That smart clacking sound is produced by heels crossing the hardwood floors. Hot days are tempered by ceiling fans. When you order soda, say Perrier.

Jenkins Hill Saloon, 223 Pennsylvania Avenue, SE; (202) 544-6600.

Sherrill's Bakery   Recently immortalized in a local documentary film, Sherill's pulls a first-time patron into a sense of time warp—circa 1948. Except that, back then, the delightfully cranky waitresses were all younger than retirement age. You can't buy natural harassment like this any more. A faithful clientele, including writers and Congressmen, drops in for breakfast, a pastry or just a little coffee-shop theater from the hard-working crew.

Sherrill's Bakery, 233 Pennsylvania Avenue, SE; (202) 544-2480.

The Tune Inn   In a word: funky. The "eclectic" decor includes a plethora of stuffed animals and political memorabilia. There's another word for The Tune Inn: crowded. Choose the hour of your visit wisely. During lunch and happy hour, you'll discover harried waitresses wriggling through the throng of drinkers and eaters waiting for a spot to open in the rows of booths or along the bar. Stay happy, be cozy.

The Tune Inn, 331½ Pennsylvania Avenue, SE; (202) 543-2725.

Cleveland Park

Gallagher's Pub   This is an acoustical version of its charged-up competitor across the street (see next entry). Gallagher's is a place to mellow out or indulge in earnest conversation, while listening to folk, popular and bluegrassy jazz music. Live entertainment seven days a week.

Gallagher's Pub, 3319 Connecticut Avenue NW; (202) 686-9189.

Ireland's Four Provinces   Lively service, lively crowds and lively entertainment. Conversation gets exchanged in snatches. Guinness on tap, natch. A long bar and plenty of tables in the huge L-shaped room to allow writers to toast on high or quietly sink into their melancholy cups (sometimes both on the same night). Live entertainment seven days a week.

Ireland's Four Provinces, 3412 Connecticut Avenue, NW; (202) 244-0860.

Zebra Room Nothing fancy, and nothing to distract from an hour or two of simple relaxation. Surrounded by regulars along the bar, with the TV murmuring overhead, this is home with a bartender and company.

Zebra Room, 3238 Wisconsin Avenue, NW; (202) 362-8307.

Downtown/Pennsylvania Avenue

d.c. space A gathering place for the avant-garde. Poets, playwrights, actors, painters, poseurs and espousers of unique visions are drawn to this alternative forum. Poetry readings and performance art sessions crowd "the space's" busy schedule. Also presents eclectic, live music—from reggae to Mozart sonatas.

d.c. space, 443 7th St., NW; (202) 347-1445.

Hard Rock Cafe Watch this space. Soon to be the hippest addition to an often un-hip town. Decked out in the latest rock n'roll motif, Washington's version of this popular chain restaurant promises to be a smash hit. In fact, the Cafe's adjacent merchandise store was recently christened by a local DJ who smashed an electric guitar against the building's marble facade. Opening late 1989.

Hard Rock Cafe, 999 E Street, NW; (202) 737-2101 (Merchandise Store).

Hotel Washington's Sky Terrace The antithesis to dim smoky caves where other writers look to hide. Here, it's the outdoor view you'll be coming to see. In a city scaled scrupulously low, the Sky Terrace offers the unusual opportunity to sip iced drinks while gazing down on the bustle of Capital ambitions. For a spell, it's nice to feel above all that.

Hotel Washington, Pennsylvania Avenue and 15th Street, NW; (202) 638-5900.

Old Ebbitt Grill Blessed with a massive mahogany bar and wittily named drinks, the Old Ebbitt serves nouvelle cuisine, hearty fare and a swell Sunday brunch. The soft lights and potted plants serve to please, put patrons at ease and invite reverie. The only reminder of the "old"

Old Ebbitt are the hunting trophies still hanging on the walls.

Old Ebbitt Grill, 675 15th Street NW; (202) 347-4800.

National Press Club   Getting in can be tricky, if you're not with a card-carrying member of the National Press Club. Once inside, you'll find a colorful atmosphere of heavy wood furnishings filled with international news-hounds. Who knows: you might overhear the hottest tidbit since the rumored identity of Deep Throat.

National Press Club, 529 14th Street NW; (202) 662-7501.

Willard Hotel's Round Robin Bar   Festooned in green velvet around a setting of heavy wood tables, chairs and booths, this stylish, circular saloon is steeped in tradi-tion. Paintings of famous writers and American figures hang on the walls. Succeeding generations of journalists and lobbyists have hung out here since its creation. In fact, it was the loitering of men in the Willard's lobby seeking special favor from Lincoln and especially Grant that led to the invention of the term "lobbyist."

Round Robin Bar, Willard Hotel, 1401 Pennsylvania Avenue NW; (202) 637-7440.

Downtown/K Street

Duke Zeibert's   Wear your tie and come otherwise well-heeled to this one. This is no hangout for struggling writers. Here, well-known authors gather to bask in the glow of their success and exchange lamentations over lazy agents and irascible editors. Duke Zeibert's is that classy kind of dining establishment where literary types like to see each other and be seen.

Duke Zeibert's, 1050 Connecticut Avenue NW; (202) 466-3730.

Joe & Mo's   This popular steak and seafood restaurant is another fashionable place where Washington's literary and media elite hold court. A power breakfast gets the day going, and the table phone is ready at hand for those early morning wake up calls to one's sources. There isn't a Joe anymore, but owner Mo Sussman puts on a great show.

Joe & Mo's, 1211 Connecticut Avenue NW, (202) 659-1211.

The Post Pub A classic journalist's hangout, this small bar is a hop, skip and a dodged-libel from *The Washington Post's* digs at 15th and L Streets, NW. But don't look for ferns in the windows. The Post Pub is a "joint" and damned proud of it. It's the conditions that keep 'em coming back: reasonably priced libations, loud chatter, cigarette smoke, enthusiastic drink orders and plenty of inside scoops.

The Post Pub, 1422 L Street NW; (202) 628-2111.

Dupont Circle

Cafe Beaux Arts Slick, sleek and stylish. F. Scott Fitzgerald would have breezed into a spot like this, ordered a mixed drink and felt at home among the abstract art.

Cafe Beaux Arts, 2121 P Street NW; (202) 293-3100.

Brickskeller Forget that old ditty, "99 Bottles of Beer"—here, there's 500 varieties to sample from all corners of the globe. The basement alcoves are cozy and just right for long sessions of studious imbibing. A unique resource for any conscientious writer intent on absorbing the local flavor of far-flung locales.

Brickskeller, 1523 22nd Street NW; (202) 293-1885.

The Childe Harold Loud, happy, crowded place that takes its name from Lord Byron's famous epic hero. Lots of nooks and crannies to hide in, and the all-over-the-map jukebox pleases every musical taste. Just the kind of place for solitary word crafters hungry to mix.

Childe Harold, 1610 20th Street NW; (202) 483-6702.

Food for Thought A comfortable, reasonably priced place that evokes memories of the 1960s. Not long ago, the all-vegetarian menu finally made concessions to carnivores. On stage, local musicians ply their trade seven days a week: folk, contemporary, jazz and blues. Don't be surprised, either, to find the musician's hat passed your way, because that's how the performers get paid.

Writers and poets seem evenly divided between the smoking and nonsmoking sections. Check out the extensive bulletin board to get a glimpse of *all* that is happening in D.C.—underground, above ground and drifting somewhere through the mystical ether.

Food For Thought, 1738 Connecticut Avenue, NW; (202) 797-1095.

Herb's Owner Herb White has long been a friend and patron of local authors, and one of his walls is even covered with their book jackets. He's also set aside a large round table for a group of successful authors and media stars who meet every so often—call it The Algonquin Roundtable South. Theater, art and writers' groups often hold parties, benefits and celebrations here. Explore the garden seating in comfortable weather.

Herb's, 1615 Rhode Island Avenue, NW; (202) 333-4372.

Kramerbooks & Afterwords Combining a cafe with its bookstore, Kramerbooks' unique blend of food for thought and food for real has been a longstanding success. One may peruse the tables and shelves of hardbound and paperback books for a title or author that intrigues, then retire to a seat at the espresso bar or one of the cafe tables to savor the purchase. In temperate months, Afterwords serves patrons at sidewalk tables facing 19th Street.

Kramerbooks & Afterwords, 1517 Connecticut Avenue NW; (202) 387-1462.

Mr. Eagan's Darts, popcorn and cheap beer. Other fare is available, of course, but these three staples keep patrons coming back to this relaxed gathering place. A genuine neighborhood bar and restaurant, Mr. Eagan's has two fully-stocked bars amid the comfortable wood booths and casual decor.

Mr. Eagan's, 1343 Connecticut Avenue NW; (202) 331-9768.

Tabard Inn Romancing the writer's life: fresh flowers, intimate seating and a quiet garden patio. All amid a Victorian setting that today serves as a quiet Inn to overnight guests and was once the home of writer Edward Everett Hale. A late afternoon lunch at the Tabard serves up an opportunity for dreamy contemplation. Where better to hide out from the spectre of imminent deadlines, the scowl of a worried editor?

Tabard Inn, 1739 N Street, NW; (202) 785-1277.

Timberlake's On-the-level food and drink, with a fare that includes hearty burgers, chicken and fish. If, on a scale of one to ten, "funky" is a one and "hoity-toity" is a ten, give Timberlake's a solid five. A taste of just what frazzled writers are known to hanker for—balance.

Timberlake's, 1726 Connecticut Avenue, NW; (202) 483-2266.

Foggy Bottom

One Step Down The most genuine jazz bar in town. Which is to say: 1) it's affordable, 2) it's unpretentious and 3) it's honestly committed to jazz music—right down to the beloved jukebox proffering moods and standards worthy of any jazz aficionado. Comfy during the afternoons as well. Cover charge for evening live music.

One Step Down, 2517 Pennsylvania Avenue, NW; (202) 331-8863.

21st Amendment Dim, moody and delightfully scruffy. The kind of drinking joint in which James Jones might have kicked back and spun yarns. All wood, no ferns.

21st Amendment, 2131 Pennsylvania Avenue NW; (202) 223-2077.

Georgetown

Au Pied de Cochon One of the few 24-hour bistros in town, the "foot of the pig" (as it translates from French) is a good place to rev up, wind down, grab a bite or continue on a developing short story. This is the home of "the original Yurchenko Shooter," so named because Soviet spy Vitaly Yurchenko re-defected to the Soviet Union here, leaving his young CIA escort waiting for his return. There's even a copper plaque on the north wall describing the incident.

The best place to read or write is the sidebar seating along Dumbarton Street. Gets crazy after the bars close, and popular for weekend brunch.

Au Pied de Cochon, 1335 Wisconsin Avenue, NW; (202) 333-5440.

Chadwick's A comfortable pub off the beaten path in busy Georgetown, Chadwick's is located under the Whitehurst Freeway in the historic Dodge Warehouse Building. Offering mainstream American fare, this is a relaxed kind of place to eat, drink and socialize.

Chadwick's, 3205 K Street NW; (202) 333-2565.

Georgetown Cafe Don't look for atmosphere, but you can drop in any time you feel like it—24 hours a day, 7 days a week. This is the Georgetown Cafe's chief charm—it's always there. And it's the kind of laid-back place where a writer can comfortably work for hours on end without fear of annoying the management. A real hangout kind of place.

Georgetown Cafe, 1623 Wisconsin Avenue NW; (202) 333-0215.

La Ruche French Cafe Here's a charming hideaway where the desserts are heavenly and the atmosphere is down-to-earth. Taking its name from the French word for "beehive," La Ruche gives literary patrons hours of rich, satisfying pleasure away from the grind of a whirring disk drive or the complicated demands of character development, plotting and style.

La Ruche French Cafe, 1039 31st Street, NW; (202) 965-2684.

SUBURBAN MARYLAND

Hank Dietle's F. Scott Fitzgerald and his wife Zelda may be buried just down the road at St. Mary's Church Cemetery, but life is kicking in this saloon. Pinball bells can be heard over the country music on the juke, there's cheap beer in the glass and the nine-ball just hit the side pocket—here's the kind of place designed for enspiriting relaxation.

Hank Dietle's, 11010 Rockville Pike, Rockville, MD; (301) 881-5656.

Tastee Diner Ah, the clink of the formica and the smell of the grease. This old-fashioned, sleek diner is open 24 hours and day and draws a no-nonsense clientele interested in basic food, a low check and low-key ambiance. Got an impulse to compose a poem over a cup of coffee at 1 a.m.? This is an eatery designed for spur-of-the-moment, unfettered sensibilities.

Tastee Diner, 8516 Georgia Avenue, Silver Spring, MD; (301) 589-8171.

SUBURBAN VIRGINIA

Birchmere About as casual and laid-back as you're going to find. Here, beer tends to be ordered by the pitcher and folks come to relax to the pleasing sounds of live musicians (often of national stature). A great place to hear the finest in acoustic folk, blues or bluegrass.

Birchmere, 3901 Mt. Vernon Avenue, Alexandria, VA; (703) 549-5919.

Murphy's Delightfully raucous, this Irish bar can, after a sufficient round of pints, make friends of total strangers. Small, it nevertheless presents nightly music. An Irish music jukebox fills out the daytime lulls.

Murphy's, 713 King Street, Alexandria, VA; (703) 548-1717.

New York, New York Lights, glitz, loud music, mirrors—all combine to produce a bar for fast-movers, high rollers and dance-floor shakers. Popular with the print and broadcast crowd who drop in after a day's journalizing upstairs at USA Today.

New York, New York, 1100 Wilson Boulevard, Rosslyn, VA; (703) 243-4600.

The Red Derby A most unlikely saloon to also become a literary salon, this "mall bar" (with its ersatz stained glass windows) has become a popular gathering place for George Mason University's literati. Here faculty writers get together to drink and talk shop with each other and their students. Look and listen, and you might find poets Peter Klappert and C.K. Williams, or dramatist Paul D'Andrea or twin-brother novelists Richard and Robert Bausch. The literary life is alive and well in the 'burbs.

The Red Derby, 9984 Main Street, Fairfax, VA; (703) 591-9008.

Tastee 29 Diner It's always there. Even if you're surprised to find something like this is still around, a vision right out of the 1940s. Open 24 hours a day and serving up good, basic American grub, this is the sort of place that invites a body to linger and the imagination to wander. Bring change for the down-home, break-your-heart jukebox.

Tastee Diner, 10536 Lee Highway, Fairfax, VA; (703) 591-6720.

Vienna Inn   If there's a better beer joint in the area, you'll have to let us know. We're talking trophy cases, pinball, bowling machine, formica tables on cement floors and cheap, cheap beer. The ideal kind of place to unwind writer's cramp and loosen keyboard shoulder strain. If this place were any more laid back, patrons would fall over. Wine also served, but not mixed drinks.

Vienna Inn, 120 Maple Avenue East (Route 123), Vienna, VA; (703) 938-9548.

Whitey's   Writing is an exacting, interior process. Sometimes a body needs to just bust loose. Here's a terrific place to do that. Kick back, dance, shout—howl if the mood strikes. Your boisterous behavior will blend right in.

Whitey's, 2761 North Washington Blvd, Arlington, VA; (703) 527-2163.

About the Author

David Cutler is a writer, editor and literary agent. Formerly vice president of Washington Independent Writers, he is a founding partner of FeatureMedia Films & Books.

From 1984 to the present, he's been president of David Cutler & Associates, a literary agency representing authors to trade publishers in the U.S. and overseas.

He is also chairman and principal shareholder of Futurebooks, Inc., a company formed to package and develop new kinds of publishing technologies (including CD-ROM, hypermedia, lasercard and CD-Interactive reading systems).

Before starting his own companies, Mr. Cutler was communications manager at the Washington Convention & Visitors Association, where he wrote and produced seventeen tourism publications a year.

He holds a bachelors degree (magna cum laude) in English from Carleton College and a masters degree in English Literature from the University of Virginia. He lives in Oakton, VA with his wife Laurie and daughter Leah, to whom this book is dedicated.

Literary & Tour Maps

Washington's rich literary heritage, much of it now lost, can still be traced through these downtown and regional tour maps. Also included in the numbered key below are listings for major area libraries, favorite downtown tourist attractions and watering holes to slip into when the sightseeing is done.

For specific address information, please check back to the original chapter in which the corresponding listing appears. Map coordinates (such as E5, M14, etc.) indicate approximate locations, and are the only means of identifying places on the regional map.

DOWNTOWN WASHINGTON, D.C.

Historic Authors

Henry Adams
  1. Site of his former home, now Hay-Adams Hotel Q5
Louisa May Alcott
  2. Site of former Union Hotel, now gas station P2
Stephen Vincent Benet
  3. Site of early family home, now office bldg Q4
Frances Hodgson Burnett
  4. Site of her first home, now office bldg Q7
  5. Site of her second home, now office bldg Q5
  6. Her third and final home P6
Frederick Douglass
  7. His first home, now private offices S11
Edward Everett Hale
  8. Original home now part of Tabard Inn P6
Bret Harte
  9. Site of Old Riggs House, now office bldg Q5
Francis Scott Key
  10. Site of his first home, now Key Bridge Q1
  11. The Maples, now Friendship House U11
Walter Lippman
  12. His first home P6
  13. His second home P1
Henry Cabot Lodge
  14. His home for more than twenty years P6
John Howard Payne
  15. Buried in Oak Hill Cemetery P3
Drew Pearson
  16. His in-town home P3
Theodore Roosevelt
  17. Site of his former home, now office bldg Q5
Anne Royall
  18. Site of former Brick Capitol Building, now the Library of Congress T10
  19. Site of former Bank House, now U.S. Supreme Court T10
  20. Site of her third home T10
  21. Site of her fourth home S11
  22. Site of her fifth home, now the Library of Congress—Madison Building ... T10
E.D.E.N. Southworth
  23. Site of Prospect Cottage, now townhouses P1
  24. Buried in Oak Hill Cemetery P3
James Thurber
  25. Site of family's winter home, now office bldg Q4
Daniel Webster
  26. Site of former home, now U.S. Chamber of Commerce Q5
  27. Statue of Webster at Scott Circle P6
Walt Whitman
  28. Site of former boarding house, now office bldg P8
  29. Site of old Armory Square Hospital T11
  30. Site of old Patent Office, now National Portrait Gallery R8
Woodrow Wilson
  31. Woodrow Wilson House P4

continued